The Neutron Bomb

- by -

Michael A. Aquino, Ph.D.

ISBN-13:
978-1523318148

ISBN-10:
1523318147

Books by Michael A. Aquino

[all available in both printed and Kindle ebook editions]

Non-Fiction

The Church of Satan (2 Volumes)
Extreme Prejudice:
    The Presidio "Satanic Abuse" Scam
IlluminAnX: Rosicrucianism Reawakened
The MindWar Trilogy
    MindWar
    MindStar
    FindFar
The Neutron Bomb
The Temple of Set (2 Volumes)

Fiction

FireForce: A Star Wars *Parody*
    Including: Secret of the Lost Ark
Morlindalë: Song of Illuminate Darkness
    - by "The One Ring"
Ode to Esmé: Memoirs of Captain Nemo
We Break the Sword: The Nazi Peace of 1940

Autobiographical

Ghost Rides
    Including: *Grail Mission*

Edited

Pegasus in Pinfeathers: Collected Poems 1919-1928
    - by Betty Ford

Dedicated to my Mother:

Lady Marian Dorothy Elisabeth Ford of Rachane
Priestess of Set

who gave me life, love, and the wonder of wisdom

Table of Contents

Preface 2016

The Neutron Bomb was originally my dissertation for the Doctor of Philosophy degree in Political Science at the University of California, Santa Barbara. It consisted of the present Chapters #1-8 and an earlier (#9) version of the present Chapter #10. The dissertation version was completed in February 1980 and my Ph.D. conferred the following month.

While subsequently considering whether to publish the work commercially, I updated it through 1982 with the current Chapter #9 and appropriate annotations to (original #9) Chapter #10. Later that year I decided that it was too "research-intensive" to be viable commercially, so devoted no further time to it.

Revisiting it thirty years later, I think it does have additional and indeed timely significance, and thus have decided to publish it:

In the present "Age of Terrorism!" we live in a worldwide madhouse of emotional political grandstanding and immediate military overreaction. That major international problems could be addressed cooperatively and methodically seems anachronistic, even Quixotic; yet in 1977 et seq. that is indeed how friends, foes, and onlookers went about deciding what to do with a new nuclear-weapons technology that purported to kill people without contaminating land or damaging property. In an inexplicable way this seemed to make nuclear war more of a "thinkable option". The choice boiled down to either thinking it or removing it.

Researching the events of the national and international resolution of this issue presented its own problems. The neutron bomb was never supposed to have been made public in 1977 in the first place; despite its becoming a front-page media football for the next two years, many government officials seemed to be uncertain whether saying anything about it violated "classified information". So even when obtaining statements or documents, I found myself in much the same situation: How much of everything I had learned could I actually include in a [public] doctoral dissertation?

Not to mention that the research, or I should say "investigation", process began to resemble more a John le Carré spy novel than an armchair library exercise. Requests to the CIA resulted in fat envelopes from nonexistent persons with non-Langley return addresses. Various officials insisted upon anonymity or non-attribution when they did agree to answer questions.

Easily the most exotic resources were the Washington embassies of the Soviet Union and the People's Republic of China:

At the Soviet embassy I was greeted by Igor Neverov, a young man about my own age, who had only recently arrived in the United States and was still astounded by our overflowing supermarkets and long escalators [in the Washington Metro]. He assured me he was just a minor agricultural bureaucrat, a facade which his remarkable familiarity with the neutron bomb quickly dissipated. Whatever the Soviets' blandness about making many N-bomb comments on their own, they were easily the best source of world opinion on the subject: I left the embassy loaded down with copies of newspapers and magazines from every continent. When at one point I asked Igor why his country was so upset about a clearly defensive-only weapon, he obligingly brought out a magazine from the U.S. Air Force's Air University containing an article about how neutron warheads could be fitted to cruise missiles targeting Moscow. Oops![1]

Nevertheless my experience at the Soviet embassy paled nest to that of the People's Republic of China. I had an appointment with one Brigadier General Wang Qiming, whom I supposed would be as stony as most general officers. Imagine my surprise when General Wang turned out to be not just a woman, but one as drop-dead gorgeous as the Dragon Lady from *Terry and the Pirates*. She - or rather her snap-of-the-finger aides - served us tea and delicacies while she graciously shared with me many of the supersecret/forbidden documents which other governments had denied. Evidently China's spy apparatus was on a par with SPECTRE's. Sadly, or perhaps fortunately, the Dragon Lady declined to give me any take-away copies. Nevertheless I left her audience having a far clearer behind-the-scenes picture of the neutron bomb.

Otherwise on the embassy circuit, well, the Germans were predictably cautious and nervous, as they were generally about Cold War intrigue, while the British were ebullient and anxious to reinforce their image as international arbiters.[2]

And despite that fact that I was making my research rounds as a humble civilian U.C. graduate student, my "other hat" as a U.S. Army Reserve Major with a Top Secret/SCI clearance caused the Pentagon some vague heartburn. Despite our not being at war with either the

---

[1] In the precarious world of Soviet officialdom, Igor proved to be a survivor, bearing out my impression of him. He rose to ambassador assignments and continued as one of his country's principal diplomats following its transition from the U.S.S.R. back to Russia.

[2] "You have to admire Sir Arthur; he always manages to give the impression that God must be an Englishman." - The German ambassador, regarding his British counterpart (David Niven) in *55 Days at Peking* (1963).

U.S.S.R. or the P.R.C., why had I gone knocking on their doors? [A copy of the final dissertation appeased concern. "But please don't do it again."]

What you are about to read is something of a time-capsule. I have resisted the temptation to do any further factual updating, or even to tinker with my 1980-82 opinions and conclusions to enhance their "wisdom" with 2016 hindsight. Part of the present value of *The Neutron Bomb*, I think, is precisely its "snapshot" of its topic from a research-vantage-point just past the events in question. Thus it serves to illustrate just how much information could be discovered, correlated, and analyzed that quickly. In today's "Internet age" it is not unusual to be inundated by data about a given topic before it has had time to cool even a little. In 1980-82 a scholar determined to get to the bottom of a research topic still needed to wear out both shoe-leather and library cards![3]

As for *The Neutron Bomb* today, I think it still stands the test of time as a close-look into how an international issue, not quite of "crisis" proportions, came to be addressed and [sort of] resolved in the late 1970s. It is part history, part James Bond adventure, and part soap opera - and I daresay the latter two elements help to make it entertaining as well as informative. I hope you enjoy it, and perhaps learn a bit more about the mysteries of politics as well.

Finally, as upon my initial research and writing, I must recall with appreciation the many individuals and offices without whose gracious time and helpfulness this

---

[3] As an incidental curiosity, *The Neutron Bomb* was, as far as I know, the first dissertation at U.C.S.B. to be prepared and printed on a computer - a PolyMorphic #8813 named "Glinda" - long before IBM and Apple entered the personal-computer market. I still remember the astonishment in my doctoral committee's eyes when I presented them with a pristinely-retyped revision of the text only a day or two after receiving marginal annotations on the previous draft from them!

study never could have been written. Among these I owe particular gratitude to:

President Jimmy Carter and Mr. Landon Kite, Staff Assistant to the President.

Senator Mark O. Hatfield of Oregon and Mr. Jack Robertson, Foreign Policy Advisor.

Senator Edward M. Kennedy of Massachusetts.

Major General Bjorn Egge, Norwegian Army, Deputy Commandant of the NATO Defense College, Rome.

Professor Dr. Helga Haftendorn, Institut für Internationale Politik und Regionalstudien, Fachbereich Politische Wissenschaft, Freie Universität Berlin.

Dr. Erwin von den Steinen and Dr. Peter Schöttle of the Office of Central European Affairs, U.S. Department of State, Washington, D.C.

Mr. Mark Parris, Office of Soviet Affairs, U.S. Department of State, Washington, D.C.

Dr. Hans von Plötz, Counselor, Embassy of the Federal Republic of Germany in Washington, D.C.

Colonel A.J.B. Stagg, Assistant Military Attaché, British Embassy, Washington, D.C.

Brigadier General Wang Qiming, Assistant Military Attaché, Embassy of the People's Republic of China in U.S.A.

Igor S. Neverov, Research Assistant, Embassy of the U.S.S.R., Washington, D.C.

Inge Godenschweger of the German Information Center, New York City.

The Senate Armed Services Committee, Washington, D.C.

The Senate Foreign Relations Committee, Washington, D.C.

Commandant of the U.S. Army Command and General Staff College, Fort Leavenworth, Kansas.

- 14 -

Commandant of the U.S. Army Institute for Military Assistance, Fort Bragg, North Carolina.

Commander of the U.S. Army Foreign Science and Technology Center, Charlottesville, Virginia.

Mr. John M. Fisher, President of the American Security Council, Boston, Virginia.

The Central Intelligence Agency, Langley, Virginia.

The Defense Intelligence Agency, Arlington Hall Station, Washington, D.C.

The Consulate of the Federal Republic of Germany, San Francisco.

The Goethe-Institute, San Francisco.

The World Affairs Council of Northern California.

The Academic Senate of the University of California, Santa Barbara.

The Library of Congress, Washington, D.C.

The Brookings Institution, Washington, D.C.

An especial remembrance to Professor Michael Gordon, Chairman of my Doctoral Committee, and to Professors Peter Merkl and Stanley Anderson, Members of the Committee, for the inspiration they were to me in my undergraduate and graduate studies.

And with love to my wife Lilith, and to my parents Michael Aquino Sr. & Betty Ford, for their encouragement, suggestions, and tolerance throughout the years of this project.

And finally with fondness to my Irish setter Brandy, who was always there to keep me company in my study during those long evenings of work.

Michael A. Aquino
San Francisco, 2016

Chapter One:
The 1977-1978 Neutron Bomb Episode

On June 6, 1977 the *Washington Post* printed a story with the provocative title "Neutron Killer Warhead Buried in ERDA Budget".[4] Thus began a year-long controversy on the subject of what are technically called enhanced-radiation weapons, but what the press, the public, and the diplomatic community came to know simply as the neutron bomb.

The issue - whether or not the United States should produce and deploy the bomb in NATO and particularly in West Germany - became a subject of prime concern for President Jimmy Carter, who saw it become a test of his administration's humanitarianism on one band and an issue of defense preparedness on the other.

In Congress Senator Mark Hatfield led a fight against introduction of the bomb, which for a time became one of the most highly-debated subjects in both legislative houses, and in Germany Chancellor Helmut Schmidt tried to walk a tightrope between offending factions in the Bundestag by making an unpopular decision, damaging his rapport with Carter by refusing the bomb outright, and crippling Germany's promising *Ostpolitik*_successes with the Soviet Union and eastern Europe by accepting it.

From Moscow Leonid Brezhnev issued letters to virtually all NATO heads of state warning against the introduction of the bomb, whipping up an international propaganda barrage that pictured the new weapon as barbaric and inhumane beyond the acceptable limits for modern warfare. And the Soviet Union's concern was of all the more interest to Germany because of an important

---

[4] *Washington Post*, June 6, 1977 and June 24, 1977.

state visit of Brezhnev's to that country, scheduled for early May 1978.[5]

Aside from the purely political considerations, there was the question of the bomb's tactical effectiveness both as a deterrent and as an actual battlefield device for combat. Would it solve the growing problem faced by NATO - that of confronting an increasingly well-armed Warsaw Pact with seemingly inferior resources? As a "usable" nuclear weapon - a device whose collateral damage would be substantially less than that of existing tactical nuclear weapons - would its deterrence be greater, thereby discouraging the Warsaw Pact even more from attempting a westward attack? Or would its impact on deterrence be insignificant, in which case its presence might serve primarily to encourage NATO to cross the nuclear threshold that much earlier in any conflict? [That, of course, could be interpreted as a deterrent factor from the Soviet point of view.]

But the issue went deeper than simply the introduction of a new and more efficient weapon into the NATO arsenal. For the first time the United States was asking states that had renounced both the production and the use of nuclear weapons (most conspicuously Germany) to participate in a decision regarding the production and deployment of a new and potentially significant nuclear device. In Germany feelings ran high on the subject of nuclear warfare and nuclear weapons, and expecting the Bonn government to commit itself even prior to a U.S. decision was expecting a great deal.

And there was time pressure, since Congressional approval of funds for production and deployment was sought by the Carter Administration in 1977 for use during fiscal 1978. Yet when the funds were finally

---

[5] *Strategic Survey 1978*. London: The International Institute for Strategic Studies, 1979, page #107.

approved after tortuous Congressional debate, President Carter delayed making a production decision, waiting for endorsement from other NATO governments.

Not until April of 19178 did Carter announce a decision, and then it was neither a firm commitment to the neutron bomb nor a firm rejection of it. Production and deployment were "deferred" only, with the options remaining open should appropriate disarmament/arms control measures not be forthcoming from the Soviet Union and the Warsaw Pact.[6]

In trying to please all parties, and in trying to achieve a deterrence/disarmament victory with the absence of the weapon rather than its presence, Carter left a good many people confused, dissatisfied, and angry - and few pleased. Yet no one seemed to be able to suggest a better answer, nor did any party to the issue show great inclination to pursue the matter further. Official, media and public attention soon shifted to other, more novel subjects such as Senate ratification of the Basic Panama Canal Treaty, new Soviet-Chinese border incidents, and the UN Special Session on Disarmament.

As a subject for detailed examination, the 1977-1978 neutron bomb episode is interesting from a number of standpoints:

> First, like the Cuban Missile Crisis or the *Pueblo* incident, it took place over a fairly limited and demarcated period of time. Thus it can be examined more comprehensively than a more indefinite, ongoing issue could be.

> Second, it was an issue which highlighted the decision-making processes relative to

---

[6] Statement by the President on Enhanced Radiation Weapons, April 7, 1978, recorded in the Presidential Papers: Administration of Jimmy Carter, 1978, page #702.

international issues of two domestic political systems - those of the United States and the Federal Republic of Germany - when faced with the same, highly-controversial problem from slightly different perspectives.

Third, the issue serves to illustrate both the cooperative and the conflicting aspects of the American-West German military defense relationship within the more comprehensive NATO framework.

Fourth, the debate brought out contemporary strengths and weaknesses in NATO as perceived by both American and German governmental and military leaders.

Although the Reagan Administration's Secretary of Defense criticized Carter for his decision not to deploy the neutron bomb, it is not yet possible to pass final judgment on the handling of the 1977-78 proposals by those involved.[7] The decisions that were made were based upon forecasts of the probable medium- and long-range consequences of one course of action or another, and enough time to see whether one or more of those forecasts has been borne out has not yet passed.

The value in this decision-making study, aside from its possible use as a compendium of the historical facts most relevant to the episode, lies in the focus which it may bring to the ongoing process of politics and international relations. It shows "the system at work" - perhaps in an unusual, "crisis" situation rather than under "normal" circumstances - but upon reflection it is

---

[7] "Weinberger Pushes Neutrons for NATO" in *Washington Post*, February 11, 1981, page #A1.

difficult to say just what would constitute "normal" circumstances. Statesmen are employed to deal with the unusual as well as the usual, and this case study may highlight some aspects of the United States, NATO, West German, and even Soviet leadership which are not illustrated elsewhere.

The neutron bomb controversy began in the United States and then spread first to NATO and then to West Germany in particular, with a gradual international protest being mounted by the Soviet Union all the while. The format of this analysis reflects this sequence. It is of course not a strict sequence, since many events in different contexts were proceeding simultaneously during the entire episode. But I think that the topic is best understood if considered as follows:

In Chapter Two the stage is set for the neutron bomb episode as it developed within the American political system and climate of 1977-1978. Any political event must be considered in context for its actual significance to be appreciated, and this chapter attempts to define that context.

In the first few months of 1977 a number of factors were coalescing in the United States' international political perspective. A new President had just assumed office - a President whose campaign had emphasized an informal, humanitarian approach to governing, but also a President who was determined that the country should make positive progress towards regaining that reputation for leadership of the free world that it seemed to have lost under the intolerant Johnson, the sinister Nixon, and the lackluster Ford.

Jimmy Carter did not enter the White House amidst the messianic euphoria that heralded John F. Kennedy's inauguration, perhaps, but he did begin his Presidency with a minimum of holdover problems from previous administrations and was therefore relatively free to create a positive image for his administration rather than spend the first few months - or years - putting out fires that he had inherited from a predecessor. In early 1977 only the Panama Canal treaties, SALT-II, and ongoing oil/energy difficulties appeared as problems of unusual significance, and the public seemed to be willing to give Carter a reasonable opportunity to deal with them.

The North Atlantic Treaty Organization had not been a focus of critical Presidential attention for some time, with the most recent high-tension incident remaining the Soviet incursion into Czechoslovakia in 1968. Since that time the trend bad been towards reconciliation and *détente*, per Mutual and Balanced Force Reduction (MBFR) negotiations [beginning with NATO's "Rome Declaration" in 1970 and leading to the start of negotiations at Vienna in October of 1973], the September 1971 quadripartite agreement and 1972 Four Power Declaration on Berlin, the Conference on Security and Cooperation in Europe (CSCE) at Helsinki in 1973-1975, and, of course, SALT-I and progress towards SALT-II. The infamous "German Problem" seemed to have been alleviated, if not entirely solved by the post-1970 FRG/GDR agreements, and no country appeared to have a vested interest in destabilizing the situation.

There was, unfortunately, a complication. Since the time of the Cuban Missile Crisis, the Soviet Union had been modernizing and strengthening the Warsaw Pact's forces to the point where, by the mid-1970s, they seemed rather too powerful for purely-defensive purposes. In the west there were various interpretations of this, ranging from predictions of eventual westward invasion to speculations that the U.S.S.R. was simply interested in "Finlandizing" capitalist Europe by maintaining a threatening presence alongside it.

In his Annual Reports of 1974 and 1975, Secretary of Defense James Schlesinger called attention to the Warsaw Pact augmentation, provoking a gradual disgruntlement in Congress and among the general public that subsequently manifested itself in what some might consider a disproportionate degree of attention lavished on the neutron bomb.

Chapter Three defines the bomb. One of the more illuminating discoveries of this research project was the realization that major decisions concerning the bomb had apparently been made either in ignorance or in disregard of the actual properties of the weapons system in question. The image of the bomb as a political and ethical football, in other words, became the substance of the issue. After the reader becomes familiar with the neutron bomb's technical aspects, the discussions of the weapon that are brought out in succeeding chapters will be that much easier to understand and to criticize.

The neutron bomb was conceived and intended as a device for introduction into NATO as a tactical weapons system. It was not designed to be used as a strategic weapon, and no serious thought was given to its possible deployment or use anywhere else besides NATO. Chapter Four therefore "sets the stage" with regard to NATO, discussing the current military posture of the alliance, the precepts under which it operates that would be relevant to the neutron bomb proposal, and the possible effect of the new weapon on the alliance's effectiveness. Emphasis is accorded the military status of NATO rather than upon the political factors bearing upon that status, the intent being to present a tableau against which the political action would subsequently take place.

Chapter Four is thus the last of the "situational" chapters; subsequent sections of the study focus rather on the sequence of events that transpired and on their interrelationship with one another.

Chapter Five presents a sequential overview of the United States political decision-making process relative to the neutron bomb during the June 1977 - June 1978 period. Apart from post-mortems on the Carter deferment decision, the neutron bomb was not to become an item of political interest until its potential was reconsidered by the Reagan administration in 1981. The 1977-78 debate brought into focus the same questions now being raised anew, so it would seem helpful to have a summary of how the the earlier debate was resolved.

Assembling an accurate and comprehensive account of the neutron bomb's journey through the American [and the international] political system proved to be unusually difficult. Unlike many topics for political science analysis, this one presented problems of information gathering comparable, perhaps, to Watergate. Before June of 1977 the neutron bomb's existence, characteristics, and proposed uses were all classified at the highest levels. When the information began to become available, it was not because the United States Government, any other national government, or NATO evidenced particular enthusiasm about shining a spotlight on it; it was because accusations in the Congress and in the news media had to be answered if the program were not to be peremptorily destroyed by a wave of public indignation. Again not unlike Watergate, however, each new revelation of facts concerning the bomb only seemed to make matters worse and the controversy more bitter.

So as I sought facts and accounts concerning the episode in Washington by mail and during research in the capital in October 1979, I encountered a mixture of cooperation and hesitation in those I interviewed. Many seemed to be somewhat confused about whether they were discussing classified or privileged information or not; and indeed there are, as far as I have been able to discover, no clear guidelines on this.

What appears in Chapter Five is a piecing-together of a variety of accounts which, according to quotable and non-quotable sources of mine, are essentially accurate. But it must be acknowledged that a great deal of information concerning the neutron bomb is still highly classified, and therefore there were limits to the research that could be done if this paper were not to be classified itself. I make this point because, beginning with Chapter Five, it may seem to the reader that some of the accounts and discussions of events come to a halt just when they are becoming most interesting!

Chapter Five is in many ways the most essential part of this study. It illustrates how greatly the American political process affects the course of events elsewhere, at least with regard to certain issues. One is struck by the attention that NATO, the Soviet Union, and indeed all the major governments of the world paid to what was happening in Congress and the White House on this particular subject. It seems improbable that the American leadership would devote as much attention to the decision of the U.S.S.R. to develop the SS-21 missile, for example, or that we would be comparably fascinated by the Germans' development of a new Leopard tank.

The course of events in Chapter Five suggests that the United States feels free to pass judgment on adjustments to the East-West balance of power - to determine. whether certain changes are destabilizing or not. In this instance President Carter elected to allow other NATO governments a say in the decision, but it is evident that he was not required or even expected to do that. Quite the contrary, he seems to have surprised and dismayed NATO by such a policy.

As the United States Government moved towards resolution of, if not consensus on the neutron bomb issue in late 1977, the political climate in NATO was just beginning to heat up. Chapter Six focuses upon the part that the alliance's decision-making machinery played in the ultimate neutron bomb decisions.

Forearmed with a brief of the military situation as described in Chapter Four, one is in a position to assess NATO's perception of the neutron bomb and its strengths and weaknesses in dealing with the political controversy that surrounded it.

The neutron bomb issue confronted NATO just as that alliance had embarked upon a showy, ten-year modernization program, designed, among other things, to impress the Soviets and the Warsaw Pact. The antics over the neutron bomb obviously did not enhance NATO's image in this respect. The bomb's proponents seemed to imply that the alliance would be impotent without this new wonder weapon, while critics argued that the bomb was being put forward as a "quick fix" to NATO's weakness and was thus a dangerous substitute for more difficult conventional modernization. Either way NATO did not look any the more impressive.

As the neutron bomb became an item of debate within NATO, all eyes soon shifted in the direction of West Germany, where it was obvious that the new weapon would be principally deployed. Until now Germany had managed to avoid serious political crises resulting from the stationing of tactical nuclear weapons on her territory, and it was obvious that the Germans were in no hurry to get themselves entangled in the neutron bomb debate. To date in the 1970s the Federal Republic had achieved major breakthroughs in the "iron curtain" of the 1950s and 1960s, and the Schmidt government did not want to see this good work undone by a flare-up of nuclear weapons tensions.

Moreover the subject of tactical nuclear weapons in Germany is a delicate one for another reason: Were NATO to use those weapons, it would be in the event of a westward attack by the Warsaw Pact - in which case the targets would probably be located on West German soil. It is not a prospect which the Germans like to think about, nor is it a prospect which other NATO countries like to bring up to Germany.

So the question of the neutron bomb was a difficult one. On one hand the bomb was "more usable" [which was bad]; on the other band it was more usable precisely because its collateral damage to non-military targets in West Germany, such as towns near advancing columns, would be minimal [which was good].

Chapter Seven recounts, therefore, the tortuous trip of the neutron bomb through German politics. Again I think it helpful to introduce the account with some historical perspective, because Germany is a country whose postwar legacy seems to weigh very heavily upon its present political dispositions. In selecting the illustrations I sought to identify those whose relevance to German behavior in the case of the neutron bomb would be the most evident. It would be easy to conclude that the extraordinary reticence of the Germans in coming to grips with the neutron bomb, for example, evidences simple cowardice on their part. When one bears in mind the national and international. forces with which Germany has had to deal since World War II, however, this unusual sensitivity is perhaps more understandable.

Existing reference works on the German political system, when correlated with the case-study data presented here, would yield a much more thorough picture of the situation. Here I seek to highlight the arguments and considerations that were involved in the decisions that were reached, the object being to relate them to the supranational picture rather than to factional interactions within Germany.

Any discussion of the neutron bomb would be incomplete without some attention to the opinions of the presumed targets of that device - the Soviet Union and the Warsaw Pact. Chapter Eight, consequently, examines the situation from the Soviet point of view. I have found no evidence to suggest that the opinions of the other Warsaw Pact countries differed significantly from that of the U.S.S.R.

In the neutron bomb episode the Soviet Union perceived both a threat to its potential designs in Europe and an opportunity for a propagandistic victory against NATO and the United States. Therefore the statements and actions that originated in Moscow evidence a blend of motives and objectives, most of which should be apparent to the reader after having been exposed to the arguments and tensions of the debate in the West.

Again the account ends somewhat inconclusively - not only because the neutron bomb problem was never really resolved, but also because the Soviets themselves are not certain whether they "won" or "lost" the contest. Nor is the Soviet Union overly inclined to communicate whatever doubts it may have on the outcome of the event. But the data presented in Chapter Eight may be of use to the scholar who is interested in considering the possible "outside" pressures on the American, German, and NATO decision-making processes.

Chapter Nine - an update to the original 1979 research project - surveys the 1981 events revealing the Reagan Administration's renewed interest in the neutron weapon.

Chapter Ten, finally, is an attempt at summary and assessment. After consideration of all the previously-presented data, it seems apparent that the factors which made President Carter's decision a prudent one have not changed, and that any new effort to deploy the weapon in the 1980s must be accompanied by a serious rethinking of the United States' international strategic goals, to say nothing of its tactical combat doctrines in both NATO and such other environments as the enhanced radiation warhead may appear.

Chapter Two:
The Political Setting - The United States

The immediate, overwhelming, and inescapable problem with any analysis of American foreign policy is the sheer vastness of American involvement with the rest of the globe in both the public and the private sectors.

Within this ocean of interaction the political scientist enjoys considerable latitude in selecting the data that seem most significant to him in a given problem. Frequently the result is a plethora of explanations and interpretations by various analysts, many if not most at odds with one another.

And the difficulty of approaching truly objective analysis is a continuing problem not only for political scientists, but also for political officials, departments, legislatures - and the citizen who is asked to vote for Presidents, Senators, and Congressmen based, among other things, upon their presumed abilities to address and solve foreign policy questions. Accordingly it is virtually impossible for American foreign policy to be cohesive, much less for all of its components to be mutually consistent and complementary.

I emphasize this point at the outset of this study because a commonly-heard criticism of the Carter Administration's handling of the neutron bomb episode is that it was awkward, characterized by indecision as to the worth of the weapon and by incompetent diplomatic maneuvering within NATO that proved unjustly embarrassing to the governments of other member nations.

Superficially the sequence of events may indeed appear almost haphazard, but a more detailed examination suggests that deliberate and informed decision-making did occur at the key points of the process. Carter's insistence on receiving NATO-nation endorsement of production and deployment, for example, had a practical as well as a diplomatic basis. If the United States were to produce an extremely unpopular weapon - as the neutron bomb showed signs of becoming - deployment of that weapon in Europe in general and Germany in particular might have been extremely difficult, with various governments refusing permission out of fear of domestic political unrest. Before investing the substantial funds required for the bomb's production, therefore, it would seem prudent to secure advance acceptance of it.

Another aspect of this involves consideration of national sovereignty issues, which become more complex than usual when nuclear weapons questions are involved. Some nations, like Denmark, are NATO members and participate in the Nuclear Planning Group, yet do not permit the stationing of nuclear weapons on their own territory. Others, like Germany, have rejected manufacture or use of the weapons but do permit their stationing under NATO/United States control. For an American President to deploy an unpopular weapon in seeming disregard of the host nation sentiment, then, would be politically damaging if not strictly unprecedented. In considering the neutron bomb episode, one must remember that it was not the first time that nuclear weapons modifications for Europe bad been proposed - but it was the first time that such a proposal had been so visible and so subject to open governmental decision-making processes.

When the neutron bomb controversy began in 1977, the United States had been out of Vietnam for only two years and was torn between a desire for domestic harmony by cultivating political neo-isolationism and a simultaneous urge to "do something good and powerful" to correct its self-perceived "Vietnam image" of oppressiveness and foreign policy ineptitude.

This is not a new impulse in American political culture. George F. Kennan described the phenomenon as a characteristic of the egocentrism common to embattled democracies, i.e. the tendency - aggravated by inflammatory propaganda - to portray international power struggles in moral terms highly favorable to one's own nation. The enemy of the moment then becomes a moral criminal rather than simply another culture with a different perspective and a different set of political goals.[8]

The United States had enjoyed the luxury of considering itself the champion of truth and liberty in the twentieth century - against the Kaiser, against imperial Japan and Hitlerian Germany, and then against the communist threat. Now, after Vietnam, it found itself cast as the villain by both foreign and domestic opinion, and so there was impatience in the country for a return to the idealism of an earlier time. Spasmodic demonstrations of American power - such as the *Mayaguez* incident and American blasts at the Soviets during the Angola crisis - evidence this mood. And the electorate's rejection of President Ford in favor of Jimmy Carter may well have been fueled as much by Carter's call for a return to traditional morality as by revulsion at the Watergate- and Vietnam-tainted Republicans. [By the early 1970s Vietnam had become "Nixon's war" and no longer "Lyndon Johnson's war".]

But despite his cheerful candor, homespun enthusiasm, and disassociation from the Washington establishment, Jimmy Carter proved unable to make as much progress against the the evil image as he had hoped. Energy costs were continuing to climb, the

---

8 Kennan, George F., *Russia and the West*. New York: The New American Library, Mentor Book, 1961, page #11.

Mideast situation [in the aftermath of two 1976 clashes in Lebanon] remained critical, and domestic political passions were afire over the Panama Canal treaties that the new administration had inherited from its predecessor [though Carter himself was not deemed responsible for them].

In any event the return of the Democrats to power had brought a return neither to the seemingly clear-cut moral posture of the Kennedy "Camelot", nor even to the tough, self-assured leadership of the Johnson Administration. Instead there gradually developed a political climate of confusion and frustration. Carter soon acquired an image as an indecisive and even incompetent leader as a consequence of his inability to find and proclaim quick, dramatic, and triumphant solutions to domestic and international issues.

To what extent he deserved such blame is conjectural; it is certain that - again as a consequence of Vietnam and Watergate - Presidential prerogatives were no longer what they had been. Congress had sought to strengthen both its theoretical powers relative to the Executive Branch and its practical exercise of them - especially in the areas of foreign policy and military affairs.

Encumbered by an estimated staff of 20,000 and its own complex decision-making process, Congress was not an effective substitute for a strong Presidency. This would be glaringly illustrated by the neutron bomb episode, wherein Congress would "intrude" on a traditionally Presidential decision to an extraordinary degree. To a great extent the problems relative to the bomb derive from this Congressional impulse, which caught both the

Carter Administration and the United States' NATO allies unprepared for public debate of such questions.[9]

As the situation in Vietnam became increasingly critical in the late 1960s and domestic pressures pro or con U.S. involvement in southeast Asia became more intense, the Cold War in Europe received correspondingly less attention, both politically and militarily. There was a certain amount of ritual indignation over the Soviet invasion of Czechoslovakia, but the NATO consensus seemed to be that the Soviet Union had remained "on its side of the fence".

The old atmosphere of Cold-War crisis was further dissipated by the signing of the Non-Proliferation Treaty on Nuclear Weapons in March 1970, the Warsaw Treaty between Germany and Poland in December 1970, the Four Power Agreement on Berlin in September 1971 and June 1972, and the Basic Treaty between East and West Germany in December 1972. SALT and MBFR talks continued, and it seemed that Europe was, on the whole, no longer a danger area.

After Vietnam, however, the United. States suddenly "discovered" that the Warsaw Pact was expanding and improving its military capabilities at a high rate - an arms modernization program that in actuality had been proceeding since the early 1960s. NATO's deterrent abilities began to become a subject for popular debate and concern at the same time that the United States Government was proceeding with SALT-II negotiations.

The essence of the problem was that the Soviet Union and the Warsaw Pact seemed to be expanding their forces substantially beyond the levels conceivably necessary for defense in eastern Europe, at the same time that the Soviet Union was increasing its strategic

---

[9] *Strategic Survey 1978*. London: The International Institute for Strategic Studies, 1979, page #9.

capabilities beyond the previously-assumed goal of second-strike massive retaliation.

In his *Annual Defense Department Report, FY 1975* Secretary of Defense James Schlesinger took note of these trends, criticized the Soviet Union for failing to provide a satisfactory explanation for them, thereby making it necessary, so to speak, for the United States to assume the worst, and proceeded to cite what he felt were the most serious developments.

First there was the simple question of initiative. Schlesinger argued that the Soviets were now proceeding with arms development and deployment in advance of United States capabilities rather than by way of reaction to them. This, he implied, could constitute evidence of Soviet intentions to abandon arms-reduction goals in favor of the sort of sabre-rattling power politics indulged in during the 1960s.

Schlesinger went on to describe the size and power of the Warsaw Pact forces in eastern Europe as far greater than necessary to meet any conceivable invasion threat by NATO, even were NATO logistically equipped or task-organized for an eastward offensive, which was and is not the case.

The Secretary said that SALT-I was intended to allow the Soviets a quantitative advantage in ICBMs and SLBMs in exchange for the United States' qualitative lead in those same strategic systems. The Soviets, however, were now flight testing four new ICBMs, beginning production of the Backfire bomber, and developing new MIRV systems for their larger throw-weight ICBMs that would permit the eventual deployment of as many as 7,000 nuclear warheads. Moreover they had now achieved better than numerical parity with the United States in terms of strategic nuclear launchers (bombers and missiles combined).

Schlesinger said that an assessment of Soviet objectives in light of this armament effort would be premature, but he warned of its exploitation for political advantages as well as of its more direct military threat to the United States' strategic arsenal. [10]

Turning specifically to the situation in the Center Region of NATO - in which the neutron bomb would subsequently be proposed for deployment - Schlesinger identified two perceived threats. The first was the danger of a surprise attack launched by the deployed forces of the Warsaw Pact, and the second was the possibility of an assault after a period of mobilization and deployment by the Pact.

Already deployed in East Germany, Poland, and Czechoslovakia by the Pact were 27 U.S.S.R. divisions and 31 additional divisions of those countries' own military forces, together with some 2,800 tactical aircraft, the majority of which were air-to-air fighters. Schlesinger laid particular emphasis on the more than 8,000 tanks which he estimated the Soviet forces to possess, pointing out that tank-heavy forces are designed for offensive rather than holding or defensive operations.

NATO in 1975, by way of contrast, had in the Center Region of Europe about 29-1/3 divisions and more than 2,700 aircraft in a roughly comparable area of Western Europe. The total included five French and 4-1/3 United States divisions, but not the United States Berlin brigade or two armored cavalry regiments. Manpower in ground forces amounted to about 777,000, including French forces in Germany. Around half of the NATO tactical aircraft were fighter-bombers.

Schlesinger concluded that in terms of deployed forces in the NATO Central Region, there existed an

---

[10] Schlesinger, James R., *Annual Defense Department Report, FY 1975*. Washington, D.C.: U.S. Government Printing Office, 1974, pages #25-45.

approximate parity between the immediately available forces of NATO and the Warsaw Pact. Against the Warsaw Pact's advantage in the number of men in ground forces and numerical superiority in tanks (about 15,500 opposed to NATO's 6,000), NATO possessed important quantitative or qualitative advantages in antitank systems and in its logistics network. The Warsaw Pact's logistics system was not at the state of readiness that it would need to be for active combat. NATO's deployed fighter aircraft were also considered to be technologically more advanced than those of the Pact.

If the Warsaw Pact were to mobilize the reserve assets available to it, said Schlesinger, it could field a total of 80-90 divisions in the Central Region within a few weeks. While such a massive force "would have a significant probability of breaking through NATO's forward defense", its mobilization would necessitate a shifting of Soviet assets away from other critical areas, specifically the Sino-Soviet border.[11]

It is important to bear in mind that Secretary Schlesinger's analysis reflects relative force estimates in 1974-1975, which remained essentially applicable at the time of the neutron bomb episode two years later. Hence it is cited here. Also significant is the tone of the analysis, which many took to be belligerent and a return to the confrontation philosophy of the Eisenhower/Dulles era. Hence the term "Schlesinger Doctrine", whose influence persisted past the Defense Secretaryship of Donald Rumsfeld into the Carter Administration.[12]

---

[11] *Ibid.*

[12] For a detailed discussion of the "Schlesinger Doctrine", see Section 3 "Strategic Doctrine: Official Documents and Statements" in Robert J. Pranger and Roger P. Labrie (Eds.), *Nuclear Strategy and National Security: Points of View*, pages #85-202.

When Dr. Harold Brown became Secretary of Defense under President Carter, he inherited an American commitment to NATO of gigantic proportions. At the time there were about 300,000 Army and Air Force military personnel in Europe, together with 250,000 dependents, 18,000 U.S. civilian employees, and 70,000 foreign national civilian employees - all stationed on or near 139 principal U.S. military bases throughout Europe. The tactical nuclear weapons force in NATO consisted of 7,000 warheads and 2,000 delivery systems, being the lance missile, tactical-support aircraft, and 8-inch artillery.[13]

The cost to the U.S. of maintaining its NATO forces is difficult to fix, given the complexity of the entire alliance's accounting system and the existence of classified figures in certain areas such as that of nuclear systems. For fiscal year 1975, however, the Defense Department estimated that the Europe-based forces themselves cost some $8.8 billion, to which could be added an additional $26 billion in "primary contingency" and "secondary contingency" forces oriented on NATO.[14] To that $35 billion figure can then be added a major portion of the $10 billion spent annually on research and development by the Defense Department, together with roughly $21-25 billion of the $30 billion in new weapons systems acquisition costs.[15]

These figures are significant in that they evidence the inertia of NATO as a going concern. No matter what the ideology of the Carter Administration, it could not

---

[13]   Johnson, David T., "U.S. Forces for Europe and the MBFR Talks" (Chapter 2) in Johnson, David T. and Schneider, Barry R. (Eds.), *Current Issues in U.S. Defense Policy*. New York: Praeger Publishers, 1976, page #18.

[14] *Ibid.*, page #19.

[15] *Ibid.*, page #20.

make major changes in NATO structure or development and acquisition programs such as the neutron bomb without simultaneously encountering major budgetary and international exchange problems.

The military and economic inertia of NATO, sane observers feel, is countered to a certain extent by the political tensions that have arisen in the alliance from time to time. So much attention has been given to the picture of NATO as "the troubled partnership", in fact, that it is easy to form the impression that the alliance is and has been for some time in serious trouble as a viable international entity.

In 1961 Robert Osgood wrote that the complications to the problem of effective strategic collaboration in NATO are reflected in significant doubts and apprehensions in four general areas: the credibility of America's massive retaliation policy as a deterrent, the role of ground forces, the role of specific nuclear and conventional weapons, and the control of nuclear weapons.[16]

To this Robert Pfaltzgraff later added the possibility that NATO's overall effectiveness might not be appreciated by all of its members to the extent of inspiring their continued support.[17]

And in *The Troubled Partnership* Henry Kissinger had also argued this point, suggesting that NATO would have to be transformed from a defensive concept into a "political arrangement [with] positive goals" because

---

[16] Osgood, Robert E., *NATO, The Entangling Alliance*. Chicago: The University of Chicago Press, 1962, page #26.

[17] Pfaltzgraff, Robert L. Jr., *The Atlantic Community, A Complex Imbalance*. New York: Van Nostrand Reinhold Company, 1969, page #13.

"defense against a military threat will soon lose its force as a political bond".[18]

Such problems admittedly exist in NATO, but it is easy to overestimate their significance. The first question that must be asked is: Are these problems symptomatic of extraordinary deficiencies in the basic concept of the alliance, or are they not rather inevitable given the complexities of NATO's existence? The latter seems to be more necessarily the case. The fact that NATO must deal with the control, cost, and concept of its arsenal on a continuing basis, making "best politically possible" modifications from year to year, ought to be taken for granted. Perfect solutions will rarely if ever be possible - particularly in such a heterogeneous atmosphere as that of western Europe - but the fact remains that NATO has successfully engineered working compromises to its major problems since its founding and has fulfilled its primary function of deterring to some extent Soviet expansion into western Europe.[19]

As for seeking to justify the alliance on grounds other than those of military deterrence and defense, one

---

[18] Kissinger, Henry A., *The Troubled Partnership*. New York: McGraw-Hill Book Company, 1965, page #10.

[19] In 1976 the NATO Information Service published a major history of the alliance and description of its working machinery entitled *NATO Facts and Figures*. Although presumably written to present the alliance in the most favorable and harmonious light, this book nonetheless details and justifies a great many more positive accomplishments of NATO than one would tend to suspect from the more prolific critical texts. Particularly when compared to the record of just about any other alliance in history, NATO seems to have dealt with its problems reasonably and systematically. The neutron bomb episode proved no exception to this, as the decision-making machinery that NATO had created to deal with such issues appears to have fulfilled its function. Problems arose principally in the contexts of national, rather than alliance politics, though of course those problems did ultimately reflect upon NATO's access to the bomb and upon the effectiveness of its deterrence posture.

may note that Kissinger's forecast of a lessening perception of threat has failed to materialize. While it is true that sane of the more "primitive" types of Cold War confrontation in Europe - water-cannon fights at the Berlin Wall, etc. - have subsided in favor of efforts towards *détente*, the presence of the Warsaw Pact's military machine is not ignored. NATO's costs and periodic problems may be mildly and even significantly irritating, but they are obviously preferable in the members' eyes to no NATO at all. In fact the prevailing question of the 1980s is not whether NATO's existence is necessary, but rather whether the alliance as it is currently configured is as strong as it should be.

There is the other part of Kissinger's proposition - that an "unthreatened" NATO would have to find some other, positive justification for its existence. The way in which such a question as this is answered depends upon the respondent's theory of international organization - whether "more" or "less" is a good thing.

At the time when *The Troubled Partnership* appeared, international involvement was in vogue; the United States was the non-communist world's leader, inspiration, and policeman. Fifteen years later we are not so sure about that [neither, perhaps, is H.A.K.]. The public sentiment now seems to be towards minimum necessary binding alliances and a more flexible approach to specific international developments by the United States. If we didn't think NATO necessary and justifiable as a war-deterrent, we probably wouldn't want it - in which case it would fade away from serious attention after the fashion of SEATO, CENTO, and ANZUS. But it is perceived to be necessary, and so we do our part to preserve it.

Osgood's four problem areas were going to come into play again in the neutron bomb affair. As a tactical, Europe-based nuclear weapon, the neutron bomb was conceptualized as another alternative to strategic nuclear retaliation by the United States. It struck squarely at the heart of the two force-composition questions: How much of NATO's power should be nuclear and how much should be conventional? And finally it brought up the issue of nuclear weapons control by forcing NATO's member nations to take official positions on its manufacture and deployment.

The episode would raise other questions as well. There was the issue of NATO modernization as a war provocation in itself. A sudden, dramatic rush to strengthen NATO might influence the Soviets to seize what advantage they have and strike peremptorily - or, more likely, to retaliate by increasing their military and/ or paramilitary efforts elsewhere in the world as they had done in Angola. And even if that did not happen, and NATO's forces were expanded successfully, how would NATO know when it had enough in the way of arms and armies to be a completely effective deterrent in the face of the Warsaw Pact's growing strength? Would the neutron bomb be a solution or an illusion? And would it decrease or increase the probability of either nuclear or conventional war in Europe at some future time? Or would it have no effect at all save to cost American taxpayers a considerable amount of money?

These questions were debated between the summer of 1977 and the spring of 1978, but of course they were not resolved. It was improbable that they would be. NATO's primary *raison d'être* is deterrence, and one can never be certain how much deterrence is enough - or even why the present posture is effective in this regard, because the Soviet Union and the Warsaw Pact have been disinclined to be specific as to their goals, motives, fears, and frustrations.

We can be sure that the League of Nations failed as a war-deterrent because World War II took place despite the League's efforts, but there are many reasons why the Warsaw Pact might choose not to attack westward, and fear of NATO might not even be the principal one. For example, disruption of existing trade between the NATO countries and the Warsaw Pact would have a seriously damaging effect on the Pact, and it is problematical how quickly and effectively such trade could be restored in a Pact-conquered Europe. Economically it may be to the advantage of the Pact to have access to capitalist trading partners.[20]

Before examining the sequence of national and international events comprising the neutron bomb episode, it is necessary to understand something more basic - the nature of the neutron bomb itself.

---

[20] See in particular Karl-Heinz Narjes, "Striving for Security and. Economic Factors" and Jacques Billy (Director of NATO's Economic Directorate), "Economic Consultation Within NATO in 1977" in *NATO Review*, April 1977 (Brussels: NATO Information Service). Billy observes:

> Trade with the communist countries represents only a small proportion of the NATO countries' overall foreign trade; in 1975 it accounted for about 5% of exports and 3% of imports worth $22.6 milliard and $14.6 milliard respectively ...
> But the Eastern countries have hardly any option but to trade with NATO nations, and the statistics highlight the degree of relative dependence. In 1975 26.9% of exports from the East European countries and 29% of those from the Soviet Union went to the industrialized market economy countries, while the East European countries and the Soviet Union obtained respectively 35.8% and 39.5% of their imports from the West ... By Spring 1976 the Soviet and East European debt had reached some $40 milliard, [which has] only been made possible by increasing recourse to the Euro-currency market ...

Chapter Three:
The Neutron Bomb Defined

What is the neutron bomb? Described most simply, it is a thermonuclear device which kills by "enhanced radiation" (ER), i.e. a relatively more deadly emission of radiation during the initial detonation of the warhead.

The advantages of such a warhead are twofold: It is theoretically a clean nuclear weapon, and it is theoretically a surgical nuclear weapon.

As a clean nuclear device which does not contaminate the areas around the target with residual radiation or fallout, the neutron bomb could be used to kill or incapacitate a large attack formation of enemy soldiers, whether on foot or in armored vehicles. Minutes after the detonation, friendly forces could enter the target area without risk to themselves - something quite impossible in a situation in which old-style "dirty" tactical nuclear warheads were used.

The second advantage of the neutron warheads is also related to the limitations of their effects. Since the bomb kills with a single burst of radiation, and since the size of that burst of radiation can be controlled, field commanders could use the weapon under conditions containing restrictions on "collateral damage", i.e. the incidental effects of a nuclear explosion on nearby population centers and/or structures. This controlled-burst aspect of the neutron bomb is hereafter referred to as its surgical characteristic.

The term "thermonuclear" refers to bombs incorporating the fusion principle, as opposed to the fission principle of Hiroshima-style atomic bombs.

Both the familiar hydrogen bomb and the neutron bomb fall into the fusion category. Whereas fission bombs utilize isotopes of uranium and plutonium at the high end of the periodic table, fusion bombs employ instead the heavier isotopes of hydrogen - hydrogen-2 and hydrogen-3 - for fuel. H-2 and H-3, known respectively as deuterium and tritium, explode with many times the force of TNT. Since tritium in particular is expensive and highly radioactive, it is generally stored in warheads as lithium-6 - a less-expensive and non-radioactive substance that is converted to tritium when the fusion process begins. When a warhead's charge of fusion fuel is struck simultaneously on all sides by a fusion tamper set in motion by the initial fission (atomic explosion) process, it is compressed and heated, causing the lithium-6 to be converted into tritium, and then the bulk of the fusion fuel to explode.

This is the essential functional sequence of the hydrogen bomb:

$$n + Li \rightarrow \alpha + T \begin{cases} \alpha : \text{helium particle} \\ T : \text{tritium} \end{cases}$$

The fusion process also releases large quantities of high-energy neutrons:

$$D + T \rightarrow \alpha \qquad + n$$
$$(3.5 \text{ MeV}) \quad (14.1 \text{ MeV})$$

... and these neutrons have been utilized in two ways:

- In a hydrogen bomb they virtually double the explosive power of the warhead by inducing fission in the uranium-238 casing of the fusion fuel, making it possible to create hydrogen weapons a thousand times more powerful than the Hiroshima atomic bomb.

• The second use of the neutrons is as a killing system themselves - the neutron bomb.

Refinements in nuclear engineering have made it possible for the second-stage fusion process to be triggered by smaller and more controlled first-stage fission explosions. In the case of the neutron bomb, the fusion-fuel casing is made of high-density metal other than uranium-238 - tungsten alloyed with nickel, iron, and rhenium - so that there will be no "dirty" third-stage fission explosion and consequent fallout. The same design factors, however, require a neutron warhead to incorporate a greater quantity of tritium, because the warhead's weaker fission trigger lacks the power to convert as much lithium-6 into tritium. [21]

The importance of the neutron bomb to a field commander, particularly in a high-density environment such as that of West Germany, becomes apparent when it is understood that existing tactical atomic weapons in NATO have a roughly coincidental blast and radiation kill-radius. To destroy an advancing enemy force, in other words, the defending NATO commander would have to accept blast, residual radiation, and fallout effects proportionate to the size of the target area. The following statistics from the airburst explosion of a single one-megaton warhead illustrate those effects:

> Within a radius of 1.5 miles from ground zero, overpressure would be 20 pounds per square inch (psi), winds would exceed 500

---

[21] Black, Brigadier General Edwin, "The Realities of the Neutron Bomb" in *Washington Report* #77-8. Boston, Virginia: American Security Council, September 1977, pages #1-2. See also Morland, Howard, "The H-Bomb Secret" in *The Progressive*, November 1979, Volume 43, Number 11. Madison, Wisconsin: The Progressive, Inc., pages #14-23.

mph, reinforced-concrete type (i.e. the most strongly constructed) buildings would be destroyed, and virtually all people would be killed.

Within a radius of 2.9 miles, winds would. reach 300 mph, overpressure would be 10 psi, and buildings up to the stone wall-tearing type would be destroyed. Heat of the explosion would cause third-degree burns and spontaneous ignition of clothing.

At a radius of 4.2 miles, overpressure would be 5 psi, winds would be 160 mph, and buildings up through brick and wood-frame construction would be destroyed. Again there would be third-degree burns and spontaneous clothing ignition, and. spontaneous building combustion would extend out to about 4.9 miles. Second-degree burns and substantial building damage would extend to a radius of at least 8.5 miles.

To put such statistics in perspective: If a 1-megaton bomb were detonated directly over the White House, virtually the entire District of Columbia would be destroyed by the initial blast, and the fallout pattern, assuming a normal eastward wind condition, would extend across Maryland and Delaware out into the Atlantic Ocean.

The point to be taken from this illustration is that "surgical" employment of conventional nuclear bombs is impractical if not completely impossible. The blast effects are too great and vary markedly depending upon the environment, and the residual radiation is too disproportionate. The use of existing tactical nuclear weapons in combat, accordingly, would mean near-certain extinction for nearby population centers. [22]

An ideal tactical nuclear weapon, therefore, would minimize the blast and residual radiation effects and enhance initial radiation effects. Thus its application would be primarily antiforce and not anticity. As it was originally conceived, the neutron bomb was intended to meet this requirement by incorporating the following characteristics:

> • Its neutron emission would be enhanced to a level sufficient to penetrate all armor or built-up structures in a predetermined area, sparing only persons in cellars or A-bomb-type shelters.
> • Its blast and heat effects would be substantially less than those of a normal atomic weapon of equivalent power.
> • Residual radiation would be eliminated or at least greatly reduced.
> • The size of its neutron emission could be controlled precisely enough to enable it to be used surgically against targets of varying size such as troop formations, enemy supply centers, etc.
> • The neutron emission would have the practical capacity to neutralize (i.e. destroy all life in) an area larger than that of a non-nuclear weapon of equal weight.
> • The non-thermonuclear effects of a neutron warhead could possibly enable it to be regarded as a weapon whose use would not be

---

[22] U.S. Arms Control and Disarmament Agency, "The Effects of Nuclear War". Washington, D.C., April 1979, pages #1-15.

subject to the Presidential-level controls of existing tactical nuclear weapons.

• The neutron bomb's development and production costs would be competitive with those of comparable tactical nuclear and conventional warheads.

That the neutron bomb was not developed until now is understandable because of the obvious difficulties involved in achieving some of these seemingly-paradoxical conditions - for example the disassociation of different types of radiation and the production of an inexpensive warhead which would require proportionately larger quantities of the expensive tritium fuel. If tritium is used instead of lithium-6, however, a given detonation will release about ten times as great an emission of much more energetic neutrons (14.1 MeV as against 2 MeV on the average), blast and heat energy will be four times as small (20% as against 80% of the total energy), there will be an absence of radioactive fallout; and there will also be an absence of the critical mass condition and hence of a lower limit of power. The basic problem then becomes that of the cost of the tritium, details of which are not publicly available.[23]

Once the technological and economic problems of the neutron bomb are understood and resolved, a closer look can be taken at its actual characteristics of tactical employment.

The instantaneous radiation of a nuclear explosion consists of (a) primary gamma radiation, most of which is absorbed within the trigger process, (b) neutron emission, and (c) secondary gamma radiation, resulting from the impact of the neutrons on the atmosphere

---

[23] David, Colonel Rene, "The Neutron Bomb: Myth or Reality" in *Revue de Defense Nationale*, July 1972, pages #1160-1173.

(inelastic radiation diffusion and radiation capture). Thus the initial radiation of the bomb is almost exclusively a function of the neutron emissions.

The neutron flux is almost instantaneous, with most of the neutrons being emitted within a few millionths of a second of the initiation of the warhead's detonation.

The neutrons themselves are heavy, neutrally-charged particles normally found within atomic nuclei; their mass and high energy give them great penetrating power. Neutrons radiated into the atmosphere will eventually be captured by nitrogen atoms, but until such capture they are unstoppable and highly lethal.

A W79 8-inch artillery 1-kiloton neutron warhead will deliver a neutron dose of 5,000 to 8,000 rads at a half-mile from ground zero, with the radiation falling to 600 to 700 rads at a range of three-quarters of a mile. As it penetrates a human body, the neutron flux is invisible and cannot be sensed except as a momentary tingling sensation when high-dose rates are absorbed:

> • At 5,000 to 8,000 rads, damage to the brain and the central nervous system causes 100% fatalities within 24 to 48 hours. Incapacitation occurs within five minutes of the detonation, and there is no possible medical treatment other than sedatives.
> • At doses of 3,000 to 5,000 rads, exposed troops will be incapacitated within five minutes to an hour. The intestines and the blood-producing cells will suffer severe damage, and death will occur in four to six days as a result of massive infection and circulatory collapse. Again there is no effective medical treatment.
> • At a dosage of 650 rads, functional impairment occurs within one to two hours. Symptoms include vomiting, nausea, loss of

appetite and fatigue. Medical treatment includes blood transfusions and antibiotics. Fatalities may be 50 to 80 percent of those exposed. The causes of death are hemorrhaging and infection. Death will occur within four to eight weeks. Convalescence for survivors will take a month to a year.

   • At dosages of 200 to 300 rads, functional impairment and casualties will. be minimal. Doses of 100 to 200 rads or less will have little effect. The treatment required is limited to medical observation and reassuring the patient that he has not absorbed a lethal dose.[24]

Four to five inches of armor plate will stop 90 percent of the gamma radiation from a nuclear explosion, and so Warsaw Pact anti-nuclear radiation preparations are based upon the supposed protection offered by their tanks and armored personnel carriers. But the same thickness of steel will stop only about 20 to 30 percent of the neutrons which strike it. The rest "shine" through the armor. And the neutrons which are captured by the nuclei of the atoms of the armor cause those nuclei to become unstable, emitting excess energy almost instantaneously as gamma radiation. The result is that armored vehicles not only offer little protection against neutron radiation; they actually become sources of additional lethal radioactivity themselves.

Effective shielding against the effects of a neutron bomb would incorporate dense, thick substances capable of capturing the neutron flux. Damp earth and thickly-layered concrete are two such materials and, of course,

[24] FM #100-5: *Operations*. Washington, D.C.: Department of the Army, 1978, page #10-4.

would be more suited to defense than to attack. Ten inches of concrete or fifteen inches of damp earth will screen out 90 percent of the neutron flux, and twenty inches of concrete or thirty inches of damp earth will stop 99 percent. Such fortifications are not difficult for troops in a defensive posture to prepare. [25]

The current generation of neutron warheads, however, may not have succeeded in eliminating the problems of fission-triggering. The explosive yields of the subkiloton and 1-kiloton enhanced-radiation warheads for the 8-inch artillery shell are roughly 50-50 fusion-fission, and the neutron warhead for the Lance guided missile is about 60-40 fusion-fission. The 2-kiloton 8-inch neutron shell is between 70 and 75 percent fusion.

The energy released from the Lance and the lower-yield 8-inch neutron weapons is divided into approximately 40 percent blast, 25 percent thermal radiation, 30 percent prompt radiation, and 5 percent fallout. The highest-yield 8-inch enhanced radiation shell produces about 10 percent more prompt radiation and slightly less blast, thermal radiation and residual radiation.

In short, the neutron bomb is only a relative improvement in its present state of development and is not yet the "clean" bomb portrayed by its proponents. [26] This point should be kept in mind, since, as crucial as it was to the actual worth of the new weapon, it appears to have been inadequately recognized or considered by those involved in the 1977-1978 decision-making process.

---

[25] Rogers, Patrick F., "The Neutron Bomb" in *Army Magazine*, Vol. 27, No. 9. Washington, D.C.: Association of the United States Army, September 1977, page #33.

[26] Kaplan, Fred M., "Enhanced-Radiation Weapons" in *Scientific American*, May 1978, Volume 238, Number 5, page #47.

There are also unresolved questions pertaining to the neutron bomb's "surgical" capabilities. For one thing, the rad-level damage/injury estimates cited above - reflecting the standard guide used in U.S. armed forces nuclear combat manuals - were formulated with regard to gamma radiation, not neutron radiation. The threshold rad levels for biological damage have not been completely verified for neutron radiation, and some scientists are of the opinion that there is no safe threshold.

And the known genetic damage potential of neutron radiation is about six times that of gamma radiation, with neutron doses of only one or two rads being sufficient to cause leukemia or eye cataracts. Exposure to a mere five rads could double the mutation rate in the progeny of those exposed. If a single neutron collides with a strand of DNA in a sperm or egg cell, the probability of irreparable long-term genetic damage is high.

Thus, for the "surgical" potential of the neutron warheads to be realized, the bombs would have to be so employed that virtually no neutron radiation at all reached friendly troops or civilians. This is not an insurmountable problem, since neutron radiation does dissipate rapidly as the distance from ground zero increases. But insufficient data exist to indicate that this problem has been recognized and that utilization procedures for the neutron warheads have been adjusted accordingly.[27]

The utility of neutron radiation as a weapon has been questioned on still another count. Since enemy personnel other than those within a short distance of ground zero could conceivably continue to function for times varying from a few hours to a few weeks after exposure to radiation, it has been argued that they could still continue to fight - even more aggressively, perhaps,

---

[27] *Ibid.*, pages #49-50.

because of their resignation to death. This presumes extraordinary rationality on the part of the soldiers, however, and I think that unlikely under such psychologically shocking circumstances. More probably the attack would cease - not from the soldiers' physical incapacitation, but because discipline and control would be shattered.

Another problem with the "surgical" doctrine involves its actual usefulness in the event of a Warsaw Pact strike. Soviet tactics call for concentrated "breakthrough" formations against conventional defenses and widely-dispersed formations in a tactical nuclear environment. If NATO should not resort to nuclear [including neutron] weapons until after a Warsaw Pact penetration of conventional defenses, then the opportunities for effective "surgical" strikes would be minimal.

Summarily we have a technical picture of a tactical nuclear weapon which at first would seem to be an improvement over existing fission warheads deployed in the NATO Central Region, but which, upon closer examination, displays radiological side-effects that at least partially negate its advantages. It could still have certain tactical applications, but it cannot be said to be the definitive answer to NATO's growing problem with the combat power of the Warsaw Pact.

As the sequence of the 1977-1978 dialogue concerning the bomb unfolds in Chapters Five through Eight, it is noteworthy that these technical problems with the neutron bomb were addressed either perfunctorily or not at all; the criteria being applied to the bomb's acceptance or rejection were almost exclusively ethical and emotional.

Chapter Four:
NATO - The Strategic Context

What are the military implications of the neutron bomb for NATO? How, if at all, would the picture have changed had the weapon been introduced into the inventory?

NATO is intended primarily as a deterrent to Soviet/ Warsaw Pact aggression, and secondarily as a military alliance to combat that aggression should it actually occur, i.e. should deterrence fail.

A fundamental problem with any sort of "deterrence" scheme, of course, is that - short of an explicit statement by the opponent that he is being deterred - there is no way to tell if the absence of war is the result of the deterrent measures in whole or in part, or whether that absence derives primarily from other pressures upon or desires of the opponent. As long as the Warsaw Pact does not attack, in other words, NATO can claim some deterrent influence; but it cannot define that influence very clearly.[28]

Accordingly NATO faces the continuing problem of justifying its existence and its cost to its member nations,

---

[28]   For a discussion of the history and implications of NATO deterrence theory, see Robert Hunter, *Security in Europe* (Bloomington: Indiana University Press, 1969), pages #83-132. See also W.S. Bennett, R.R. Sandoval, and R.G. Shreffler, "A Credible Nuclear-Emphasis Defense for NATO" in *Orbis*, Vol. 17, No. 2 (Summer 1973), pages #463-479. See also Chapter #3: "Deterrence Analyzed" in Helmut Schmidt, *Defense or Retaliation: A German View* (New York: Frederick A. Praeger, 1962). See also André Beaufre, "Nuclear Deterrence and World Strategy" and Philip E. Mosely, "Requirements for   a European Deterrent in the 1970s" in Karl H. Cerny and Henry W. Briefs (Eds.), *NATO in Quest of Cohesion* (New York: Frederick A. Praeger, 1965). See also "Part III: NATO Strategy" in James L. Richardson, *Germany and the Atlantic Alliance* (Cambridge: Harvard University Press, 1966.

and it also must come up with reasonable estimates as to its own effectiveness as a deterrent. Though there is a great deal of opinionated discussion in the West about NATO's deterrence ability, the Soviet Union and the Warsaw Pact - whose opinions, after all, are the only ones that really count - are not inclined to be helpful on the subject. Western analysts must grope for signals from and indices within the Pact nations indicating their actual opinions of NATO's effectiveness.[29]

NATO in 1977 was becoming increasingly concerned about its actual deterrence ability in the face of increasing Warsaw Pact modernization measures. Problem areas included the numerical weakness of NATO's deployed military forces, poor organization and morale within

---

[29] For a discussion of the evaluation of international relations in terms of signals and indices, see Robert Jervis' *The Logic of Images in International Relations* (Princeton: Princeton University Press, 1970). Jervis defines his two key terms as follows [pages #18-19]:

> Signals are statements or actions the meanings of which are established by tacit or explicit understandings among the actors. As all actors know, signals are issued mainly to influence the receiver's image of the sender. Both the sender and the perceiver realize that signals can be as easily issued by a deceiver as by an honest actor. The costs of issuing deceptive signals, if any, are deferred to the time when it is shown that the signals were misleading. Signals, then, can be thought of as promissory notes. They do not contain inherent credibility. They do not, in the absence of some sort of enforcement system, provide their own evidence that the actor will live up to them. Signals include diplomatic notes, military maneuvers, extending or breaking diplomatic relations, and choosing the shape of a negotiating table.
> In contrast to signals, indices are statements or actions that carry some inherent evidence that the image projected is correct because they are believed to be inextricably linked to the actor's capabilities or intentions. Behavior that constitutes an index is believed by the perceiver to tap dimensions and characteristics that will influence or predict an actor's later behavior and to be beyond the ability of the actor to control for the purpose of projecting a misleading image. Examples of indices include private messages the perceiver overhears or intercepts; patterns of behavior that disclose, unknown to the actor, important information (e.g. a pitcher's mannerism revealing what he will throw next); and major actions that involve high costs.

those units, and difficulties in the multinational logistics network on which NATO depended for its supplies. The question seemed to be not whether a Warsaw Pact strike would succeed, but rather how quickly and at what cost. Belgian Major General Robert Close, commanding a NATO tank division in West Germany, estimated that an attack would reach as far as the Rhine within 48 hours.[30]

A more systematic study was undertaken by retired U.S. Lieutenant General James Hollingsworth for a report on NATO readiness issued in February 1977 by Senators Sam Nunn and Dewey Bartlett. Hollingsworth's conclusion was also that NATO would be unable to halt a Warsaw Pact invasion short of the Rhine, which he estimated the Russians would reach in six days.[31]

There were no indications that the Soviet Union or its allies were actually contemplating such an attack, but the psychological and political implications of the Pact's capabilities were not difficult to appreciate. "Their strategy is simple," said a NATO defense minister. "Moscow and its allies are striving to achieve such manifest superiority that Europe's decision makers will gradually acquire conditioned reflexes of appeasement whenever political demands are made."[32]   In short, the Soviet Union's efforts in eastern Europe were intended to cultivate an increasing climate of "Finlandization" in the West - an atmosphere in which the NATO countries would be inclined to cooperate with even the more disliked Soviet demands due to fear of what the Warsaw Pact could do.

---

[30] De Borchgrave, Arnaud, "Nightmare for NATO" in *Newsweek*, February 7, 1977, pages #36-38.

[31] *Ibid.*

[32] *Ibid.*

Recent tests of NATO's own combat efficiency had not produced favorable results. In the fall of 1976 a series of large-scale maneuvers named "Autumn Forge" had revealed that sane units would run out of ammunition after only half a day of intense fighting. Combat loaded tank and motorized rifle elements of the Warsaw Pact, by contrast, carry enough ammunition for two to three weeks of intense fighting. On the first day of "Autumn Forge" NATO units "destroyed" 20 to 30 percent of the enemy's armored units, but still the "Soviets" were able to overrun NATO's forward lines of defense within twelve hours.[33]

The key to NATO's effectiveness as a deterrent, accordingly, had to be its tactical nuclear arsenal of approximately 7,000 warheads [as against roughly 3,500 for the Warsaw Pact]. According to a high-level Soviet intelligence paper acquired by NATO, the alliance's tactical nuclear weapons were regarded as an "objective to be eliminated as a matter of absolute priority" in the event of war. General Alexander Haig, the NATO Supreme Commander, was evidently sufficiently sensitive to both the alliance's nuclear strength and its conventional weakness so that he remarked to friends that be would resign if the nuclear weapons were negotiated away.[34]

The essential question, then, was whether NATO would have the prerogative or the resolve to employ nuclear weapons in the event of an invasion. Not to do so would apparently mean defeat; to do so would risk nuclear retaliation - possibly at the strategic level against targets in the United States - by the Warsaw Pact. This issue is not a new one - it was the rationale for Charles de Gaulle's independent *force de frappe* some years earlier -

[33] *Ibid.*

[34] *Ibid.*

but it was now lent new urgency by the new and growing conventional capabilities of the Pact.

The neutron warheads for the Lance missile and 8-inch artillery, it will be recalled, were envisioned by proponents as devices to halt just that sort of "Soviet blitzkrieg" of tank-heavy forces discussed above. The argument was that they were more "surgical" in their effects; i.e. they could be detonated against military targets fairly close to built-up areas (German cities and towns) without the risks of blast-effect or residual radiation contamination that would accompany the older, "dirtier" tactical nuclear weapons now deployed in NATO. The "suicidal" side-effects of the present weapons, the argument continues, makes them virtually unusable because of the risk to the German civilian populace.

In all the governmental, military, news-media, and political literature available concerning the neutron bomb, the "cleanliness" of the neutron warheads seems to have been questioned only once - by the *Scientific American* magazine article cited as a source in Chapter Three. Intranational and international debate centered on the political effects of introducing any sort of "new" nuclear weapon into Europe. If anything, the "clean" qualities of the bomb were taken for granted and used as an argument against the bomb's introduction: "A bomb that destroys lives and not property is barbaric", etc.

In Washington, D.C. Senator Mark Hatfield's foreign policy advisor, Jack Robertson, commented in 1979 on the "cleanliness" of the neutron bomb, citing the *Scientific American* article's contention that the weapon had significant non-neutron side effects. Robertson said that, when investigating the facts concerning the weapon for Senator Hatfield, be had been unable to obtain either documents or factually-supported statements from Defense Department or Administration officials on that subject.

He was advised by confidential sources that the person from whom a reliable answer might be obtained was J. Carson Mark, former Director of the Los Alamos Nuclear Testing Facility. Contacting Mark, Robertson was told that the actual neutron warheads were not in fact significantly cleaner than existing nuclear warheads, a fact which he promptly relayed to Hatfield for the Senate's information. A day or so later Robertson was called to the Senate lobby, where he met Mark, accompanied by three Army generals. "You have misquoted me," said Mark, who bad presumably been brought to the capital by the Defense Department to make that statement!

During the 1977 Congressional debates on the neutron bomb, however, Hatfield and Robertson came to the conclusion that a discussion of the bomb based upon such technical considerations as its blast or residual radiation characteristics was too complicated to be effective. Robertson did not pursue the matter further, concentrating rather on issues related to the bomb's psychological "usability" if in fact it were manufactured and deployed. On the subject of the bomb's actual effects, Robertson observed that "cleanliness" arguments for the neutron bomb would in any case hold true only if the neutron warheads were to be used in the absence of existing nuclear warheads. In fact, he said, NATO contingency plans called for simultaneous use of both neutron and existing warheads in the event of an attack - thus making the "clean" characteristics of the neutron bomb, assuming that they did exist, something of a moot point.[35]

If, as some critics argued, one of the dangers of the neutron bomb would be that its "clean/surgical" qualities

[35] Interview with Jack Robertson, Washington, D.C., October 26, 1979. See also the NATO Single Integrated Operational Plan (SIOP) and General Strike Plan (GSP).

would make its use in war all the more probable, mention should be made of existing NATO and Warsaw Pact attitudes towards nuclear war in Europe.

The Soviet Union's tactical doctrine, for instance, does not draw a sharp distinction between the use and non-use of nuclear weapons in combat. Such influential Soviet strategists as Marshal Sokolovsky (author of the standard reference work of the 1960s *Soviet Military Strategy*) have viewed nuclear and chemical weapons as complementary to conventional weapons and essential for the successful prosecution of an offensive in Europe.[36]

How such a doctrine may be altered by Soviet perceptions of NATO's conventional weakness and self-proclaimed adherence to a "nuclear threshold" is conjectural. It is conceivable that, while the Soviets would have no theoretical reservations about withholding use of their tactical nuclear weapons in a conflict, they would do so in the hopes that NATO would thereby lack an excuse - or simply be locked in indecision until it was too late - to bring its own tactical nuclear weapons into play.

On the other hand, the nature of modern tactical nuclear warfare is such that critical advantages accrue to the side that strikes first, particularly since the most important targets are the other side's tactical nuclear artillery. In the words of Soviet tactician A.A. Sidorenko: "The side which first employs nuclear weapons with

---

[36] Menaul, Air Vice-Marshal Stewart W.B., "The Shifting Theater Nuclear Balance in Europe" in *Strategic Review*, Fall 1978, pages #35-36. Menaul was Director-General of the Royal United Services Institute for Defence Studies in London from 1968 to 1976. During his distinguished career in the Royal Air Force, he served as Director of Bomber Operations and Nuclear Affairs in the Air Ministry, Commander of the British atomic task forces in Australia, Senior Air Staff Officer at Headquarters Bomber Command, and Commandant of the Joint Services Staff College. He is Vice-President of the Military Commentators Circle and a member of the Council of the Foreign Affairs Research Institute in London.

surprise can predetermine the outcome of the battle in his favor." V.Y. Savkin, discussing nuclear weapons in direct support of land forces, said: "Skillful employment of nuclear weapons in conjunction with artillery, aviation, and the fire of tanks permits delivery of a decisive defeat on the enemy on the axis of attack and creation of favorable conditions for friendly troops to advance swiftly into the depth of his defenses and move into operational space."[37]

The question ultimately becomes one not of military capabilities, but rather of military intentions as to desired goals and acceptable risks and losses and perceptions of the opponent's strategy.

Soviet tactical doctrine also envisions the possibility of fighting either a nuclear or a non-nuclear war in Europe without its necessarily escalating to a strategic-level nuclear conflict. This viewpoint is shared at least to some extent by the United States, and the fact that it is shared is one of the major concerns of the other NATO countries; they are prone to view it as an indication that the United States would not consider an attack on NATO as an attack on itself, and that it might thus abandon Europe rather than risk nuclear escalation to the strategic level.

The psychological profile of NATO's nuclear weapons has always been one of deterrence rather than contemplated use. This is due to the fact that the use of such weapons in the case of an invasion would almost certainly involve targets in western Europe, and also to the presumption that any move which would make Soviet use of nuclear weapons more likely is to be avoided as much as possible. West Europe's population density is high, and the effects of even a few nuclear detonations there would be catastrophic.

---

[37] Ibid.

Another crucial distinction between the two alliances lies in the area of nuclear weapons control. At least in theory, the prerogative to initiate the use of nuclear forces in the Warsaw Pact is in the hands of the Soviet military commanders at front and army level. Such decentralization of authority implies a readiness to use the weapons fairly early in a conflict and without exhaustive authorization procedures involving many higher command echelons. It is of course possible - and in fact probable - that this is an illusion meant to intimidate NATO all the more, and that in truth the decision to go nuclear would be reserved to the highest policy-making levels.

In NATO's case, controls on tactical nuclear weapons are highly centralized. A request to use nuclear weapons would normally be initiated at corps level, and that request would then go to CENTAG (3 hours), to AFCENT (3 hours), to SHAPE (1 hour), to the NATO Ministerial Council (3 hours), to the National Command Authority (the U.S. President) (1 hour), to SHAPE (1 hour), to AFCENT and CENTAG (1 hour), and to the originating corps (1 hour). Beyond this initial 14-hour delay, an additional ten hours would be required to deliver the authorized warheads on target.[38]

Both Warsaw Pact tactical doctrine and the variance in NATO and Pact nuclear control systems argue against the seemingly taken-for-granted notion that NATO would have the privilege to initiate the use of nuclear weapons in the event of a Pact invasion.[39] Pact commanders might delay their own use of such weapons only if they felt that they could win without them and that NATO would fear

---

[38] FM #100-5: *Operations*. Washington, D.C.: Department of the Army, 1978, page #10-9.

[39] Menaud, *op. cit.*

to use its nuclear weapons without Pact nuclear provocation.

At the present time, incidentally, NATO doctrine does call for the first use of tactical nuclear weapons in the event of invasion, though once again it is problematical whether such a statement is more substantive than it is a device of psychological warfare.

The proposition that the notion of a mutually-honored "nuclear threshold" is simply a comforting NATO illusion and has no basis in Warsaw Pact doctrine necessitates, in my opinion, sane reconsideration and refinement of "deterrence theory" as it is currently discussed in Western scholarly circles. That theory is based upon the presupposition that conflict will not take place if the opponent fears the probable effects of one's weapons; in the U.S./U.S.S.R. context this is generally taken to mean nuclear weapons.

In *On Thermonuclear War* Herman Kahn proposed two "types" of deterrence: Type I - deterrence of a direct attack due to the probability of an immediate, automatic retaliation; and Type II - the use of strategic threats to deter an enemy from engaging in very provocative acts, other than a direct attack on the United States.[40] That the premises of Kahn's Type I and Type II deterrences were accepted by NATO is evidenced by passages in NATO Ministerial Guidance statements - for example that of 1975 with reference to tactical nuclear weapons in particular:

> The purpose of the tactical nuclear capability is to enhance. the deterrent and defensive effect of NATO's forces against large-scale conventional attack, and to provide a

---

[40] Kahn, Herman, *On Thermonuclear War*. Princeton: Princeton University Press, 1960.

deterrent against the expansion of limited conventional attacks and the possible use of tactical nuclear weapons by the aggressor. Its aim is to convince the aggressor that any form of attack on NATO could result in very serious damage to his own forces, and to emphasize the dangers implicit in the continuance of a conflict by presenting him with the risk that such a situation could escalate beyond his control up to all-out nuclear war. Conversely, this capability should be of such a nature that control of the situation should remain in NATO hands.[41]

There are at least two critical problems with this attitude:

First there is the presumption that, if a European war should begin, both sides would have ample time to consider the nuclear option and could conceivably fight and finish the war without resort to it - a sort of "Korean War in Europe" scenario. In fact, however, even a short delay of the decision by NATO to utilize its nuclear weapons would probably rule out the later option to exercise that decision - due to the forward positioning of the alliance's nuclear warheads and the increasing collateral danger to friendly populations as the Warsaw Pact targets move west. So if the war should begin, and if the United States and NATO were not too intimidated to use nuclear weapons at all, those weapons would be used quickly, if not immediately by both sides.

And the option to use or not to use those weapons would not likely be a NATO prerogative. Even if the Warsaw Pact forces believed that they were winning a

---

[41] *NATO Facts and Figures.* Brussels: NATO Information Service, 1976, page #347.

conventional victory without resort to nuclear weapons, doctrine would still call for their use as a preemptive measure against increasingly probable NATO use of its nuclear weapons.

In short, the time pressure on both sides in the event of a Warsaw Pact strike would be so overwhelming that merely delaying the introduction of nuclear firepower could constitute a fatal error.

The notion of preemption is crucial to an understanding of Soviet and Warsaw Pact doctrine. Soviet strategic planners, being sensitive to the way in which a given force balance in peacetime can yield widely varying outcomes to war depending on the details and uncertainties of combat, are tasked to develop and pursue ways of waging war that tend to push outcomes in favorable directions. In Soviet military doctrine, accordingly, there is great emphasis laid on the virtues of the preemptive strike. In part this may be a reaction to the "lesson" of June 1941, when Soviet failure to foresee and counter Hitler's Operation Barbarossa cost the U.S.S.R. frightful losses in the years that followed.

Should the Soviet Union again sense itself on a course in which it believes war to be "inevitable", its philosophy concerning the factors that determine war outcomes would place a high premium on seizing the initiative and inflicting the greatest possible damage on the enemy's forces and options in the prosecution of the war. The highest likelihood of limiting damage and coming out of the war with intact forces and a surviving nation is achieved, the Soviets feel, by a first strike, and the advantages of such a first strike are considered to be not marginal but substantial and even critical.[42]

---

[42] Ermath, Fritz W., "Contrasts in American and Soviet Strategic Thought" in *International Security*, Fall 1978, Volume 3, Number 2. Center for Science and International Affairs, Harvard University: MIT Press, 1978, page #152.

Assuming again that the neutron bomb is deployed in its theoretically "clean and surgical" design, how would it affect NATO's warfare capability within its present contingency plans?

Dr. Hans von Plötz, Counselor at the West German Embassy in Washington, D.C., stresses that any conflict, should it break out, would almost certainly take place on West German soil since there would not be much question of NATO's taking ground to the east. In view of West Germany's high population density, with towns often only 2-5 miles apart, any measures that could be taken to restrict the side-effects of NATO nuclear weapons would lessen the "hostage" value of the German civil populace against the use of those weapons - particularly if the Warsaw Pact drew that same conclusion [in other words, if the Warsaw Pact determined NATO use of nuclear weapons to be all the more probable because of decreased collateral risk to the West German civil populace]. Then, if German cities and towns suffered nuclear damage, the onus would be entirely on the Warsaw Pact.[43]

It is difficult to estimate just how much, if at all, that onus would bother the Pact. Twentieth century wars in Europe and Asia have been accompanied by considerable damage to civilian population centers, and it is unlikely that this prospect per se would bother the Soviet Union. It could, on the other hand, bother other elements in the Warsaw Pact, most notably the East Germans.

The essential deterrent effect would not lie in this onus, however, but rather in a Pact belief that NATO had found a nuclear weapon it had few qualms about using. Pact propagandists could argue that NATO employment of its neutron weapons, no matter how "clean and

---

[43] Interview with Dr. Hans von Plötz, West German Embassy, Washington, D.C., October 24, 1979.

surgical", would force the Pact to use its dirtier and less-accurate nuclear weapons, but such a rationalization would probably not be very convincing, particularly if there were in fact major damage to civilian areas.

Considering that (a) the neutron bomb may not in fact be as surgical or clean as its advocates believe it to be, and (b) it is not now scheduled for NATO deployment, are there other options for NATO that could approximate its benefits? The two most generally cited are low-yield, precision-guided fusion-atomic and conventional weapons and precision anti-tank guided missiles (ATGM).

With modern technology tactical nuclear guidance systems have been developed for cruise, Lance, and Pershing II missiles that have the potential for 90 percent destruction of the target - this being an improvement from the 20 percent probability of first-generation tactical nuclear systems. The improved accuracy makes it possible to use lower-yield warheads, thereby decreasing the danger of collateral damage. Yields of 1 kiloton or less are now available and militarily practical, whereas older capabilities might have called for 10 kiloton yields under similar conditions.

In the field of conventional munitions, the last ten years have seen a significant increase in options. Some of the bombs developed for B-52 delivery during the Southeast Asian war are powerful enough to substitute for nuclear weapons on some target assignments. Once again, the effectiveness of such munitions is increased by heightened accuracy and reliability in delivery systems and targeting techniques.

On a tactical level, the infamous MIRV technology has been adapted to what are termed "submissiling" weapons. Such payloads are designed to disperse prior to detonation, with the result that the multiple detonations blanket a larger area than would be covered by a single explosion. Submissiling is thought to be especially effective against "soft" targets, such as troops in the open or involved with rear-area logistics activities.

Similar development has taken place with regard to two other destruction-enhancing techniques: controlled fragmentation (wherein explosive casings break up into predetermined patterns for maximum effectiveness) and shaped or hollow charges (in which explosive energy is focused in one direction for maximum armor-penetrating power).

There are also fuel-air explosives (FAE), which are up to twenty times per pound more effective than ordinary high explosives. An FAE mixes with ambient air at the target; thus no oxygen in the payload is necessary. Also, since the explosion is more widely dispersed due to the spread of the mixing process, lethal effects are increased. Again the development of FAE weapons is a result of the use of such weapons in Vietnam. [44]

Cruise missiles, of course, are reputed for their pinpoint accuracy and would thus be ideally suited for low-yield, precision munitions. And at this time modernization of both the Lance and the Pershing II missile systems is in fact proceeding with an eye to increasing their accuracy - thus enabling them to carry lower-yield fusion-atomic weapons as well as the higher-strength conventional payloads - and, to be sure, neutron warheads should they be subsequently introduced. This particular option, therefore, seems to be receiving priority attention by NATO after the neutron bomb decision. In December 1979 the North Atlantic Council formally decided to develop and deploy 572 Pershing II and cruise missiles in West Germany, Britain, and Italy,

---

[44] Cane, John W., "The Technology of Modern Weapons for Limited Military Use" in *Orbis*, Volume 22, Number 1, Spring 1978, pages #222-223.

with two-thirds of the new missiles based in the Federal Republic.[45]

Such analysts as Stanley D. Fair, Kenneth Hunt, and James F. Digby have contended that the contribution of anti-tank guided missiles (ATGM) to NATO deterrence and defense would be substantial. [46]

So much attention has been given to ATGMs after their spectacular use in the Vietnam War and 1973 Arab-Israeli Conflict that the Strategic Studies Institute of the U.S. Amy War College (the senior strategic institution of the Army) issued a Research Memorandum on the subject (*Precision ATGMs and NATO Defense*) in September 1978. Despite the impressive record of ATGMs to date, the War College feels that NATO should expect no immediate or radical shift in the balance between offense and defense because of their introduction. A surprise attack at a moment when many NATO units were positioned in garrison areas could overrun much of West Germany before ATGMs could be brought up for positioning.

Such weapons, because of operator vulnerability, require considerable cross-positioning and camouflaging to be efficiently employed - particularly against the massive combined-arms (armor, mechanized infantry, artillery, and tactical air) attack the Warsaw Pact would be likely to employ. Moreover battlefield saturation

---

[45] *Time*, December 24, 1979, pages #30-31.

[46] See Stanley D. Fair, Precision Weaponry in the Defense of Europe, Military Issues Research Memorandum, Carlisle Barracks, Pennsylvania: Strategic Studies Institute, December 15, 1974. See also Kenneth Hunt, "New Technology and the European Theater" in *The Other Arms Race*, ed. by Geoffrey Kemp, Robert L. Pfaltzgraff, Jr., and Uri Ra'anan. Lexington, Massachusetts: D.C. Heath & Company, 1975. See also James F. Digby, *Precision-Guided Weapons* (Adelphi Paper #118). London: International Institute for Strategic Studies, 1975.

weapons, such as war gasses and smoke, would severely hamper ATGM operators. The Warsaw Pact has an advanced chemical warfare capability and regularly trains to fight in a chemical environment.

If precision ATGMs have a specific application in NATO, it would most likely involve the slowing and attriting of Warsaw Pact armored forces should an invasion lose its forward momentum. This would be especially applicable to mountainous areas on the flanks, in the rolling hill country of central Germany, and possibly on the North German Plain if employed in villages and towns as part of an interlocking defensive grid.

Additional problems constraining the use of ATGMs in a NATO context include limited visibility caused by darkness or adverse weather (clouds, fog, haze, etc.). Such adverse conditions would be all the more likely if the Soviet Union were to attack during the winter months. And Employment of ATGMs in interlocking defense networks in and around urban areas on the North German Plain would require the use of villages, towns, and cities into strong points (combat positions deliberately strengthened with the purpose of halting or delaying a Warsaw Pact advance). This would increase the probability of extreme damage to each strong point, of course, and thus the West Germans do not favor such options.

The conclusion of the War College study, therefore, was that while the inclusion of ATGMs in NATO would somewhat improve the conventional balance in Europe, the introduction of such weapons would not in itself restore NATO's complete conventional effectiveness. "Flexible response" doctrine, including the use of tactical nuclear weapons "to deter" a Soviet conventional attack, would still be required.[47]

While there are advantages to be found in high-yield, nonnuclear warheads and precision ATGMs, then, neither would seem to be a substitute for the neutron bomb - the former because they are not yet sufficiently developed or deployed [nor is their anti-armor capability resolved], and the latter because they have a variety of battlefield vulnerabilities not shared by the neutron bomb.

Since the April 1978 "deferment" decision, many NATO analysts have proceeded on the assumption that the neutron bomb is a dead issue, and that it would not have solved that many problems for the alliance in any case had it been introduced. In an extensive analysis of NATO modernization and combat power in the September 1978 issue of the influential *Armed Forces Journal International*, Justin Galen commented that the "improvement" in theater nuclear posture generated by the "neutron bomb" bad been subjected to intense debate throughout NATO. Among the key issues involved he included the following:

> • The neutron bomb would cost $2-$3 billion to fully deploy, or roughly the projected cost of all of the improvements the U.S. is now making in prepositioning.
> • The "bomb" actually consisted of warheads for the limited numbers of Lance forces in Europe (75 mile range), and nuclear artillery (presently 13 miles maximum range, but planned for 20 miles in the future).

---

[47] Kennedy, Robert, *Precision ATGMs and NATO Defense* (Military Issues Research Memorandum). Carlisle Barracks, Pennsylvania: Strategic Studies Institute, U.S. Army War College, September 11, 1978, pages #27-30.

• The bulk of the warheads were for artillery weapons which presently have deployment and vulnerability problems. A major reason for recent efforts to increase the range of nuclear artillery, said Galen, is that present weapons must now be deployed so far forward in combat that they can easily be overrun or suppressed by longer-range Warsaw Pact artillery, and it is unclear that even extending their range to 20 miles will solve this problem.

• Deploying the "neutron bomb" would mean continuing reliance on nuclear artillery in spite of these problems and in spite of the fact that longer-range tactical missiles might be more cost-effective. Galen specifically deplored the fact that 60 percent of NATO's 7,000 nuclear weapons must now be delivered by artillery systems with ranges of less than 15 miles.

The purported advantages of the "neutron bomb", concluded Galen (to destroy more armored units while reducing collateral damage), might then prove illusory:

If the U.S.S.R. shoots back with more weapons and higher yields, an ER warhead could have little real impact. However, its proponents assert that the deployment of ER weapons would seem to convince the Warsaw Pact that NATO would have a more credible war-fighting capability, thus adding to deterrence.

Unfortunately the Carter Administration fully evaluated these factors only after it (a) built the bomb into a major political symbol in

NATO, (b) made it a test of wills with the U.S.S.R. over SALT-II and the SS-20, and (c) got the German, Belgian, and British prime ministers to commit themselves to endorse the weapon and propagandize. it in NATO at some political cost.

As has been all too publicly documented, it then singularly mismanaged the political handling of its cancellation notice to our allies and managed to personally insult Chancellor Schmidt in the process. Needless to say, the overall result was to arouse both European antagonism and European fears that the U.S. might sacrifice NATO capability for a SALT-II agreement.[48]

Let us examine Galen's comments in light of previously-presented facts concerning the neutron bomb:

The $2-$3 billion price tag for the neutron bomb: Presumably Galen took this estimate from the fiscal 1978 Energy Research and Development Administration authorization bill, which authorized $2.6 billion for 1978 ERDA military programs. The exact amount of money within that bill earmarked for the neutron bomb's development, however, is classified information. And so are official cost estimates concerning the scope and time-span of neutron weapon provision to NATO units.

The entire subject of NATO funding is itself a grey area, it being difficult to assess just what effect each member nation's contributions have [see Chapter Two]. What value, for example, should a European nation place upon land that is being used permanently or temporarily for NATO operations?

---

[48] Galen, Justin, "Restoring the NATO-Warsaw Pact Balance: 'The Art of the Impossible'" in *The Armed Forces Journal International*, September 1978, page #46.

And even if the neutron warheads were to be assembled wholly in the United States and delivered exclusively to U.S. military units in NATO, would the entire process not result in cost-adjustments, including increases caused by appropriate tactical reconfigurations, by other NATO countries?

Then, too, it is not known what amount of funds from general NATO resources might be drawn upon for neutron weapon deployment, if not development or manufacture.

The cost argument against the neutron bomb, then, is a weak one - at least in an unclassified forum. And the fact that the neutron bomb has been the subject of discussion in an unclassified forum will be returned to in a later chapter, since consideration of this fact is crucial to an understanding of the entire episode.

Range-limitations of the Lance and 8-inch delivery systems: A 13-20 mile range for division- or corps-level 8-inch artillery and a 75-mile range for the Lance missile may seem disappointingly minimal to the reader who has been accustomed to the impressive ranges of modern IRBMs and ICBMs. However Galen fails to consider two important aspects of these range limitations: (a) their significance to the Warsaw Pact and (b) the concept of forward defense warfare in Germany in which such close-support weapons would be used.

As has been brought out in the more recent debates concerning the cruise missile, it is important to the Warsaw Pact in general and to the Soviet Union in particular just how far eastward a weapons system can reach. The moment that NATO begins arming itself with weapons - particularly nuclear weapons - which can threaten major damage to East European or Soviet territory, the alliance's proclaimed defensive rationale becomes all the more suspect - and the odds for a Warsaw Pact preemptive action against it become all the greater.

Increased ranges of NATO weapons would also impact on SALT negotiations, with the Soviets claiming them to be "strategic" rather than "tactical" weapons - in somewhat the same way that the United States is doubtful about the "tactical" nature of the Backfire bomber. Hence range-limitation of weapons in NATO is not necessarily a liability - and is in fact an asset in deterring preemptive war.

Forward defense warfare - which is official NATO policy - is another way of saying that NATO intends to stop a Warsaw Pact invasion as far forward as possible, in which case the range-limitations of nuclear weapons would not present a problem and, once again, would suggest to the invaders that NATO would be inclined to commit them before they could be overrun. The following excerpt from *White Paper 1979: The Security of the Federal Republic of Germany and the Development of the Federal Armed Forces* is germane:

> An essential element of NATO's strategy is the principle of forward defense. Forward defense is defined as a coherent defense conducted close to the intra-German border with the aim of losing as little ground as possible and confining damage to a minimum. This includes the recapture of lost territory.
>
> For the Federal Republic of Germany there can be no alternative to forward defense; in view of her geostrategic situation, her population density near the border to the Warsaw Pact, and the structure of her economy, any conceptual model of defense involving the surrender of territory is unacceptable. Thirty percent of the population live in a 100 kilometer-wide zone this side of the intra-German border, and twenty-five

percent of our industrial capacity is located in that zone.

These geographic circumstances rule out any defensive operations conducted flexibly in the depth of the area and accepting the loss of territory. Such a concept of operations would not be in accordance with the mission to preserve the integrity of our territory.

The presence close to the border of our own and allied forces in German territory demonstrates effectively to the Warsaw Pact the Alliance's deterrence and defense capabilities.[49]

Galen's strongest point is with reference to the "purported advantages of the neutron bomb". It has already been brought out that there are three problems with the "clean/surgical" characteristics of the ER warheads: First, are the warheads themselves really all that "clean" and "surgical"? Secondly, if they are, would not their advantages be negated if, as seems the case, they would be employed together with old-style, "dirty" atomic weapons? And thirdly, wouldn't nuclear retaliation by the Warsaw Pact - using "dirty" weapons - also negate any effort on the part of NATO to conduct a tactical nuclear war away from population centers and undamaging to German territory?

The answer to question #1, as Jack Robertson found out, is hard to find out. At this time, in fact, it appears to be unanswerable through unclassified material.

The answers to questions #2 and #3 are obvious: The neutron bomb's theoretical advantages would be

---

[49] The Federal Minister of Defense, *White Paper 1979: The Security of the Federal Republic of Germany and the Development of the Federal Armed Forces.* Bonn: Federal Minister of Defense, 1979, page #126.

instantly negated if other, "dirty" nuclear weapons came into play - as they almost certainly would. Translated into practical terms, this means that the combat advantage of the neutron warheads over the old-style atomic warheads would be minimal - except in some hard-to-imagine case in which NATO alone resorted to nuclear weapons - and then of only the neutron variety.

As for Galen's condemnation of the Carter Administration for the way it handled the entire neutron bomb affair, I think it will be shown in this paper that it was no more a "bungle" than it had to be, given the accidental circumstances in which the entire matter came to light and the delicacy of resolving nuclear-weapons questions in NATO at all. And if Helmut Schmidt did in fact suffer embarrassment, it was neither by design of the Carter Administration nor even by ineptitude on its part, but rather by the awkward pressures and deadlines surrounding the entire international episode.

Galen, I think, moves a touch too quickly to blame NATO problems such as this on the United States. Many of them are simply unavoidable due to the complexity of the alliance.

The judgment that was ultimately rendered on the neutron bomb, of course, was not a function of scientific fact, nor of military practicality, nor of dispassionate logic - though elements of each were present in some degree. The judgment was a factor of political perception, manipulation, and opinion. In this study the historical, scientific, and military facts are introduced not so much to critique the judgment as to see how and why the political processes involved used or did not use various factors.

What is already apparent is that the neutron bomb was highly politicized - so much so that its actual characteristics were almost beside the point. Consider, for example, the way it was discussed in a U.S. Senate

Hearing in July 1979 by someone who presumably had the greatest possible knowledge of the weapon's characteristics:

Senator Exon: In that regard I want to return to a question that I have asked you before when we have been in more informal sessions than this about the neutron bomb. I continue to be confused by the political and military leadership in Europe who I agree were concerned or outraged, or whatever you want to call it, about some of the concessions that they thought we had made not in our interest in SALT and yet at the same time such a fundamental weapon as a neutron bomb historically they have been against deploying in Europe. How do you justify that?

General Alexander Haig: First, Senator, let me premise my remarks with the observation that there were no medals to be awarded on either side of the Atlantic for the handling of the neutron bomb issue. Secondly let me assure you that after many months of intense consultation between ourselves and those members of the Alliance who were involved in a decision for deployment a consensus had in fact been formed to accept the neutron bomb.

It was only after that consensus had been formed, and I may add at great political cost to some of the political leaders involved, that they were informed that there was a reversal on what had been the consulted thrust of the American approach to the neutron issue. In the wake of that disappointment and the embarrassment that it caused these political leaders, the kind of reluctance that we are running into today as we talk about theater nuclear modernization is directly traceable to that. They are very fearful that the American Administration will again change course on them at a very critical moment.

Senator Cannon: If a land mass invasion of Europe were attempted, it no doubt would be accompanied by thousands of Soviet tanks. Could we and our allies contain such an effort with our firepower from our helicopters, A-10s, and our tactical aircraft, as well as the ground forces available? Or do we need the neutron bomb to do that job?

General Haig: Senator, I would have liked to have had the neutron bomb not so much because of its ability to do that job, although it is certainly a very efficient vehicle for doing so, but more importantly because the other side would see that we had that capability and hopefully we wouldn't have to be faced with the contingency that your question poses. [50]

Here General Haig's response to Senator Exon seems somewhat inaccurate:

• In point of fact no consensus had been reached in NATO to accept the neutron bomb. By April 1978, when President Carter made his deferment decision, Turkey had agreed to host the new warheads and Germany had agreed to

---

[50] Committee on Armed Services, U.S. Senate, "Military Implications of SALT-II Treaty" 79-128, Statement of General Alexander Meigs Haig, Jr., USA-Ret., Stenographic Transcript of Hearings, Thursday, July 26, 1979, 2:30 PM, pages #46-47.

admit them if they were not stationed on German territory alone.

• Nor was there actually a "reversal" of Administration policy, since Carter had maintained since September of 1977 that he would not approve the stationing of the weapons in Europe without a clear mandate from the rest of the NATO membership to do so.

• Finally, as has been brought out in this chapter, the neutron bomb is not necessarily a "very efficient" vehicle for containing a Warsaw Pact attack. Its "cleanliness" is open to question; its "surgical" properties would stand to be negated by NATO and Warsaw Pact use of "dirtier", less-accurate tactical nuclear weapons; and its use could conceivably cause as much injury to NATO troops as to those of the Warsaw Pact.

It would be nice to be able to say that these factors were the real reason for the bomb's non-deployment, but, as General Haig's testimony and other evidence suggest, they were not.

Chapter Five:
The American Political Decision

Many political scientists assume that there is a predictable quality to the way in which governmental decisions are made; it is this assumption which permits patterns of behavior to be hypothesized and thus political science to be scientific in the strict sense of that term.[51] With regard to the neutron bomb decisions of 1977-78 there were two primary actors in the United States decision-making process - the Presidency and the Congress - influenced to a greater or lesser degree by such secondary actors as American public opinion, the news media, other NATO countries (particularly West Germany), and the Soviet Union. Depending upon the

---

[51] For a discussion of the proper use of such terms as "science" and "law" in an academic context, see Peter Achinstein, *Law and Explanation: An Essay in the Philosophy of Science* (London: Oxford University Press, 1971). See in particular Chapter VI: "Some Modes of Reasoning". See also J.R Lucas, *The Principles of Politics* (London: Oxford University Press, 1966). See in particular Section 6: "Political Reasoning".

approach favored by a given scholar, various models could be applied to the sequence of events.[52]

After examining the neutron bomb episode and discussing the decisions that were made concerning it with representatives of the two principal and of many of the secondary actors involved, however, I am not certain that the application of any particular model would particularly help to clarify what did take place and why.

Jack Robertson, Senator Mark Hatfield's foreign policy advisor, put it this way: "When you look at the way the neutron bomb business was handled, you have to remember that it was not a 'normal' thing for this town (Washington, D.C.). It came at an awkward time - when the fiscal 78 budget was being finalized - and almost nobody in the Congress or the Executive branch knew

---

[52] For example, Morton Kaplan in *System and Process in International Politics* (New York: Wiley, 1957) argues that the decision-making process is most strongly influenced by the systems for interaction that exist within it. In *Contemporary Theory in International Relations* (Englewood Cliffs, New Jersey: Prentice-Hall, 1960) Stanley Hoffman focuses rather on actors' goals, as does Arnold Wolfers in "The Actors in International Politics" [in William T.R. Fox (Ed.), *Theoretical Aspects of International Relations* (Notre Dame: University of Notre Dame Press, 1959)]. There are a variety of other system-or actor-oriented models as well, together with many different blends between them. See Wolfram Hanrieder, *Comparative Foreign Policy: Theoretical Essays* (New York: David McKay Company, Inc., 1971) for a discussion of these.

In the Comparative Politics sub-discipline of Political Science, stress is laid on decision-making as a dynamic process rather than as a static model in which actors either fulfill their functions or exercise their prerogatives. Dynamic-process models admit few constants, emphasizing rather the stream of variables entering the picture of a given case-study decision over a period of time. See Peter Merkl, *Modern Comparative Politics* (Second Edition) (Hinsdale, Illinois: The Dryden Press, 1977), pages #157-161, as well as the bibliography to Chapter #5 of that work. Differences within the dynamic approach hinge upon such factors as numbers of variables, timing of variable input, and strength of actors to influence the outcome of a particular process in view of the identified non-actor variables.

anything about it. And those who did know about it were not comfortable talking about it. So the sequence of events does not represent 'business as usual' in the way with which weapons and NATO defense questions are dealt. It was an ad hoc situation from start to finish."[53]

If this is in fact the case - that the neutron bomb episode was a unique event in American political decision-making rather than a type of event - then what is to be gained by studying it? An immediate comment would be that of course there were regular governmental functions involved with the episode - Congressional budgetary review powers, the military and foreign-policy prerogatives of the Presidency, etc. But the special significance of the neutron bomb episode, I think, does not lie in its ability to be used as an illustration of models, but rather in its illustration of the limits of competence in institutions and individuals. If anything it provides a clear example of how models cannot account for all the options; there is a haphazard element in government which defies systematic analysis.[54]

---

[53] Interview with Jack Robertson, Washington, D.C., October 26, 1979.

[54] Many models are so flexible that they can be "stretched" to cover even the most discrete events. An illustration of this is Graham Allison's "Conceptual Models and the Cuban Missile Crisis" in *Bureaucracy and Policy: Conceptual Models and the Cuban Missile Crisis* (Boston-Little, Brown, 1971). As Allison remarks in his Conclusion to that paper, "Formulation of alternative frames of reference and demonstration that different analysts, relying predominantly on different models, produce quite different explanations should encourage the analyst's self-consciousness about the nets he employs."

In the comparative/developmental field, see Gabriel A. Almond *et al.*, *Crisis, Choice and Change: Historical Studies of Political Development* (Boston: Little, Brown, 1973) for an illustration of the application of a single model to a variety of historical episodes. The efforts of the contributors to fit data to the governing master-model are apparent.

Is this a useful illustration - to show, in effect, certain limits of political science as a science? I think so, in that it exercises the responsibility of the political scientist to be an expert as well as a scientist - to appraise, as it were, a political event critically, correctly identifying its most meaningful components and their relative contribution to the whole without justifying such analysis on the grounds that it illustrates or refutes a given framework. The justification is to be found rather in the increased understanding of and appreciation for politics as a whole that results from such an appraisal - providing, of course, that the political scientist is successful in communicating his judgment. In such an undertaking models may be used as explanatory tools to clarify discussion, of course, but the political scientist, who is otherwise able to present his analysis need not feel uncomfortable in their absence per se.[55]

Treatment of the neutron bomb episode as a discrete political event is quite possibly crucial to an accurate understanding of the actual events in question. As was noted earlier, the Carter Administration came in for a good deal of criticism not just on the ethical and strategic

---

[55] In *The Statesman* Plato argues primarily for the statesman - but secondarily for any true expert [his examples are a doctor and a ship's captain] - using laws (established maxims) as guides but also having the prerogative to proceed in disregard of them without thereby sacrificing his professional integrity. The justification of such behavior, suggests Plato, is not to be found in the enforcement, application or demonstration of professional laws, but rather in the excellent exercise of that art which the laws only approximate. Judgment of the expert's expertise, therefore, would be primarily artistic rather than scientific, and thus would be based on criteria beyond the scope of existing law or custom in a specific discipline. Those criteria would involve the expert's impact on the larger social/political/cultural context which his discipline is actually designed to support. See *The Collected Dialogues of Plato* (Hamilton and Cairns Ed.) (Princeton: Princeton University Press, 1961), pages #1018-1085.

issues involved, but also on the seeming ineptitude with which it handled the entire sequence of events. A careful investigation of that sequence, however, reveals no indication of incompetence. Rather what appears is a situation in which the Administration's decision-making process followed no particular pattern to which the Congress or any other actor had became accustomed. Hence the accusations of "indecision" on the part of the President.

It would be more accurate to characterize the situation as a sort of "slow-motion crisis management" scenario in which the administration reacted to a situation in which it found itself rather than acted according to preconceived plans of its own. Viewed in this light, the neutron bomb episode, far from being the debacle most have supposed it to be, reflects favorably on the Carter Presidency. The record is one of "minimum necessary" decisions being taken carefully after extensive consideration of a great many opinions and options, including those from sources whose participation - at least publicly - in such decisions is unprecedented.

Accordingly a picture of Presidential decision-making emerges which is quite different from that of some of the more flamboyant Chief Executives of recent years - for example, Kennedy, Johnson, and Nixon. Instead of seeking to create an image of being a "man on a white horse" aggressively molding the course of events, Jimmy Carter chose an approach oriented towards national and international consensus - a solution that everyone could live with, if not one whose "sparkle" everyone would admire. [Accordingly one might characterize him as a passive-positive President per James Barber's case-study archetypes.[56]]

And that is essentially what transpired. After the neutron bomb issue had been resolved - to the extent that it was resolved - no one seemed particularly ecstatic about the outcome, but on the other hand it didn't mushroom into a Cuban Missile Crisis or U-2 incident either. And it was a situation which, if mismanaged, could have assumed crisis proportions - including touching off a Warsaw Pact strike if in fact the Pact has contingency plans for preemptive attacks in the face of radically-new technological change in NATO armaments.

Traditionally it has been the case that U.S. additions and modifications to the NATO nuclear arsenal have been made under high security classification and with minimum participation by other NATO governments, particularly the non-nuclear-armed ones. There have been four basic reasons for this:

  • The U.S. President controls the use of NATO nuclear weapons in the event of war.
  • NATO deterrence strategy includes providing as little information to the Warsaw Pact as possible concerning the exact types and characteristics of nuclear weapons deployed and the contingency plans for their use.

---

[56] Barber, James David, *The Presidential Character: Predicting Performance in the White House* (Englewood Cliffs, N.J.: Prentice-Hall, 1972), page #13: "Passive-positive: This is the receptive, compliant, other-directed character whose life is a search for affection as a reward for being agreeable and cooperative rather than personally assertive. The contradiction is between low self-esteem [on grounds of being unlovable, unattractive] and a superficial optimism. A hopeful attitude helps dispel doubt and elicits encouragement from others. Passive-positive types help soften the harsh edges of politics. But their dependence and the fragility of their hopes and enjoyments make disappointment in politics likely."

• Nuclear weapons are a sensitive topic in war-shy West Europe, and the governments there would just as soon not become embroiled in specific issues. They would rather leave the decisions - and the included public-relations fallout - to the United States.

• The United States is funding the research, production, and deployment of its own weapons - not an altogether minor consideration in view of the multi-billion-dollar costs involved.

The neutron bomb began as just such a "routine" modification to NATO armaments. It was not an entirely new development in nuclear warhead technology. Back in the 1950s two neutron bomb prototypes code-named "Dove" and "Starling" had been developed by the Livermore and Los Alamos laboratories, but the defense establishment had not endorsed their potential for practical use. In the early 1960s a neutron warhead was designed for use in the Sprint missile - a component of the U.S. Army's Sentinel antiballistic missile system. Again, however, it was not deployed; Defense Secretary McNamara wished to preserve a "firebreak" between nuclear and nonnuclear weapons and thus refused to develop low-yield nuclear weapons for deployment.[57]

After SALT-I placed restrictions on ABM deployment, the Sprint warhead was considered for adaptation to battlefield use. The result of this research was the neutron bomb of 1977-1978. Its proponents didn't consider it a major departure from NATO's existing nuclear posture. It was placed under the usual Top Secret security blankets, and funds for its development were

---

[57] Sharp, Jane M.O., "Is European Security Negotiable?" in Leebaert, Derek (Ed.), *European Security: Prospects for the 1980s*. Lexington: Lexington Books, 1979, pages #282-283.

included as a sub-category in the Energy Research and Development Administration's fiscal 78 budget request to Congress. This budget had passed the the House of Representatives Appropriations Committee and was before the House Rules Committee when, on June 6, the *Washington Post* published a front-page story entitled "Neutron Killer Warhead Buried in ERDA Budget" by a Staff Writer named Walter Pincus.[58]

In an editorial two days later the *Post* charged that the neutron warhead could be construed as another form of chemical warfare, argued that a "distinction between small, safe, and controllable neutron warhead and other nuclear weapons is false and dangerous", and urged President Carter to disapprove the warhead's production.[59]

Editorial support for the neutron bomb came from the *Atlanta Constitution*, which countered that it was important to develop new weapons systems in the absence of an effective SALT-II to the contrary.[60]

By mid-June the ERDA bill was on its way through the Senate Appropriations Committee, and Senator Mark Hatfield, disturbed by the descriptions of the "ER warhead", tried to find out more about it. As it turned out, no one in the Congress seemed to know - a matter of some in-house embarrassment since the House had just authorized $10-20 million [the exact amount remains undisclosed] for its research and development. Questions to the Executive Branch brought replies that neither

---

[58] *Washington Post*, June 6, 1977.

[59] *Washington Post*, June 8, 1977, page #22.

[60] *Atlanta Constitution*, June 12, 1977, page #22.

President Carter nor Defense Secretary Harold Brown knew anything about it either. [61]

In a contemporary *Doonesbury* cartoon strip, an ABC news correspondent inquires of a *Washington Post* reporter what is going on at the paper "since you guys overthrew the government". In June 1977 the answer might well have been "Neutrongate", because Walter Pincus promptly undertook to get the goods on the mysterious "ER weapon". And as I interviewed Congressional and Executive Branch officials in Washington, I was repeatedly - if unofficially - referred to

---

[61] Interview with Jack Robertson, Washington, D.C., October 26, 1979. As Hatfield remarked in the Senate on July 1:

> When it became apparent that this was in the budget, and some of the elementary and rather cursory facts became known concerning this weapons system, I called the. White House and I asked to talk to Mr. Stu Eizenstat, who is, as Senators know, a very close advisor to the President in his administrative family. I asked Mr. Eizenstat the question: "Simply what is the President's position on this weapon?"
>
> At the time it was apparent by comments made in response that Mr. Eizenstat was not aware that the President had a position, or that the issue even had been raised. He said he would get back to me and indicate what the President's position was. This was in the first part of June.
>
> In a few days we had another conversation, and it was then related to me that the President would be provided with a memorandum on this weapons system and, upon reading and studying the memorandum, the President would make known a position.
>
> Then a few more days passed, and I got another call from the White House that indicated they would not be able to get the response to me as soon as they had anticipated, but that the whole question was in the machinery and that there would be a response made. - *Congressional Record*, 95th Congress, 1st Session, Volume 123, No. 115 (July 1, 1977) pages #S11429-S11439.

Pincus' coverage of the episode for an accurate blow-by-blow account. By his own admission, even President Carter first learned of the subject when Pincus' first article appeared in the *Post*.[62]

This dependence upon the press for an accurate account of the neutron bomb episode is instructive, for it illustrates how compartmentalized the decision-making branches of government have become and how those same branches distrust their own intra-government communications media or simply regard them as inefficient or insufficient.

After Watergate, moreover, the *Washington Post* in particular seems to exercise a sort of "divine right" to interpret the intrigues of Washington, D.C. infighting. It - not the *Congressional Record* or the Presidential Papers or some State Department bulletins - was cited to me by individuals in those branches and departments as containing the single most comprehensive portrayal of events. The *Post* would regularly reveal facts that the Executive Branch or the Congress either did not know or did not wish advertised; then there would be a reaction to them; and so the episode would continue.

Contrast this, for example, to the aggressive "news media management" approach of the White House during the pre-Watergate Nixon Presidency, when the press was not so much a judge as a follower of events.[63]

As one of what Daniel P. Moynihan has termed "the two most important Presidential newspapers" (the other being the *New York Times*), the *Post* now became the

---

[62] Carter, Jimmy, "Remarks and a Question-and-Answer Session at a Town Meeting", Spokane, Washington, May 5, 1978 in *Administration of Jimmy Carter*, 1978, page #860.

[63] See Stephen Hess, *Organizing the Presidency* (Washington, D.C.: Brookings Institution, 1976), pages #129-130.

single most important link, it would seem, between all of the neutron bomb actors.[64]

It took Walter Pincus another two weeks to assemble the material for the first comprehensive story, "Senate Pressed for Killer Warhead", which appeared in the June 21 issue of the *Post*. In this article Pincus described the ERDA budget request for neutron bomb funds as being a maneuver of the Carter Administration to obtain Congressional sanction of the bomb even before Carter himself had decided whether or not to go ahead with it. The "cookie cutter", as the new device was called by its designers, was intended as a warhead for the 56-mile-range Lance missile, and was "the first publicly acknowledged tactical nuclear weapon designed specifically to kill people by radiation rather than destroy installations and equipment by heat and blast". This is a curious choice of descriptive terminology, since existing tactical nuclear weapons of comparable size are more destructive of human life than the neutron bomb; here, perhaps, is the germ of what would later become the anti-humanitarian argument against the new weapon.

The actual decision to build the warhead, continued Pincus, had been made in 1976 by the Ford Administration. President Carter and the new Defense Secretary Harold Brown bad not been aware of the significance of the "ER" entry in the ERDA budget until the original story had appeared in the *Post* and other papers two weeks previously.

With regard to the Carter Administration's position on the matter, Dr. Joseph Perry, the Director of Defense Research and Engineering in the Defense Department, had by now replied to the inquiry from Senator Hatfield. "To afford maximum flexibility, particularly if he

---

[64] Moynihan, Daniel P., "The President and the Press" in Tugwell, Rexford G. and Cronin, Thomas E. (Eds.), *The Presidency Reappraised*. New York: Praeger Publishers, 1974, page #155.

chooses" to go ahead with production, Perry asked Hatfield not to cut the warhead funds from the ERDA bill, promising that a Presidential decision would be made prior to the start of fiscal year 1978, which would begin on October 1, 1977.

Hatfield, however, refused to withdraw his amendment in the Senate Appropriations Committee to cut those funds. "This is backwards," he said. "We're supposed to respond to the President's request for funds. Here the President wants us to give him the money; then he'll decide if he wants to use it."

Declassification of the warhead's Lance application had been by ERDA authority, not that of the Defense Department, said Pincus, after ERDA Assistant Administrator Alfred D. Starbird had given testimony to a House Appropriations Subcommittee on the new weapon. Earlier in May the ERDA military applications authorization had received Senate approval, but the Senate Armed Services Committee report had mentioned only the name of the warhead and a decision to delete $3.2 million of the larger total amount being requested for production. It did not describe the type of weapon it was, nor say that it was the first of its kind being produced for use against people.

As the Senate Appropriations Committee continued consideration of the warhead, the House faced floor introduction of the ERDA military applications authorization. Representative Christopher Dodd (D-Conn.) was expected to lead House examination of the controversial issues involved.[65]

On June 22 the Senate Appropriations Committee voted on Hatfield's amendment; the result was a 10-10 tie, and the amendment was accordingly defeated. The committee then went ahead and approved production

---

[65] *Washington Post*, June 21, 1977, page #A-2.

funds for the warhead per the ERDA budget request. Opposition to the Hatfield amendment, which was discussed in closed session, was led by Chairman John C. Stennis, who refused to discuss his remarks with reporters. Saying at first that the new warhead was "a matter so highly classified" that the committee might break precedent if it released the Senators' votes on the amendment, he later changed his mind and made public the 10-10 figure.[66]

The following day Thomas Ross, Assistant Secretary of Defense for Public Affairs, gave a somewhat less than illuminating statement on the neutron bomb during a press conference. "This is a matter of legitimate high classification," he said. "There will be no comment." Contacting other Defense Department sources, Pincus and the other press representatives learned little more. "It's all 'Q' material," said one person, referring to the traditional "Q" clearance required of anyone working with highly-classified atomic weapons.[67]

The Pentagon was angry that ERDA had even declassified the fact that the 56-mile Lance warhead being funded in fiscal 78 was of the neutron variety. "That was not declassified by joint agreement," said a Defense Department spokesman on June 24. Another Defense Department official, who also declined to be identified by name, elaborated on the tactical rationale of the new weapon:

> [The Soviet Army in Europe] would have a major re-equipment problem to defend against this [neutron] weapon.
> The Soviets have equipped themselves to live on a present-day nuclear battlefield. [Their

---

[66] *Washington Post*, June 23, 1977, page #A-1.

[67] *Washington Post*, June 24, 1977, page #A-1.

tanks and fighting vehicles now deployed] now have protection against biological and radiological effects [of the type that would exist after tactical nuclear exchange with current weapons].

They can't handle the prompt radiation which would be delivered by the proposed new warheads. Introduction of the new generation of neutron shells and warheads would put the Soviets back twenty years in their new military acquisitions.[68]

At the same time information was beginning to come to light on the history of the original neutron weapon decision. In answer to reporters' questions, Robert Barrett, Executive Assistant to former President Gerald Ford, said, "He knew the concept and application of enhanced radiation to those weapons when he made the production decision [on November 24, 1976]."[69]

Meanwhile FRDA's Alfred D. Starbird replied to the Defense Department's comment on the Lance warhead declassification, saying that the release was made by the agency on guidelines jointly developed by Defense and ERDA. He refused to say why the declassification had been made, however, because "that would get into design" which itself was classified.[70]

On the same day (June 24) Presidential Press Secretary Jody Powell said that Carter would make a decision on whether to approve production of the neutron weapons "sometime this fall. [The President] has an abhorrence of nuclear weapons, period," continued

---

[68] *Washington Post*, June 25, 1977, page #A-1.

[69] *Ibid.*

[70] *Ibid.*

Powell, "as well as of other types of weapons. But if it [a nuclear weapon] has to be used ... there will be many fewer civilian casualties [with the neutron variety] than with the standard types of [tactical nuclear] weapons."[71]

As the neutron bomb issue headed to the floor of the Senate, a June 26 editorial in the *Washington Post* suggested that Gerald Ford had been only minimally briefed before he approved the original neutron warhead budget request. Furthermore no Arms Control Impact Statement, assessing the effect of the weapon on arms control efforts, had yet been sent to Congress as required by law. ERDA's disclosure that the neutron warhead was intended for the Lance missile was accidental, and word that a neutron artillery shell was also being planned was an unauthorized leak. Then, continued the *Post*, proponents of the weapon insisted upon closed-door hearings. The final approval was borderline: 10-10. And there was still no clarification from the Pentagon. "The whole thing," concluded the Post, "has the look of a black-bag job."[72]

After reviving some of the original objections to the principle of the neutron bomb - its similarity to chemical warfare and its dangerous image as an "acceptable" nuclear weapon - the editorial suggested that President Carter should have withdrawn the budget request instead of merely postponing his own decision on it. He was presumably under "fierce Pentagon pressure", and Congress could "do him - and the country - a favor" by eliminating the ER funds from the budget and putting the burden of proof for the neutron bomb on whoever the actual proponents might be.[73]

---

[71] *Ibid.*

[72] *Washington Post*, June 26, 1977, page #B-6.

[73] Ibid.

This is an interesting editorial from a number of standpoints. it represents an initial "solidification" of what had previously been a sort of vague disquiet concerning the neutron bomb. It is always difficult to make a case for or against a proposition when most of the key data are classified, but enough had now become known about the "cookie cutter" for the *Post* to feel emboldened to take a position. And it was not entirely a negative one, arguing rather for delay and reconsideration than for outright cancellation. The fireworks concerning arms control implications and chemical warfare are unconvincing, since not that much was yet known about ER effects to justify raising those specters. One can read this as a gauntlet flung down saying, in effect, "The effects of this weapon seem to go beyond those acceptable to the American ethic. Explain those effects so we can understand them and then justify them."

As was noted earlier, the U.S. Government had never before been in a position of being expected to justify nuclear weapons for NATO in a public forum. And there was still the question of the missing Arms Control Impact Statement on the neutron warheads, required by law since 1975. During the week of June 19-25 Senator Claiborne Pell, Chairman of the Senate Foreign Relations arms control subcommittee, sent a letter to the Arms Control and Disarmament Agency's Director, Paul C. Warnke, asking for an ACIS on the warhead. In the letter Pell asked specifically that the ACIS answer the question whether deployment of the new Lance warhead "would ... lower the nuclear threshold" and make "use of tactical nuclear weapons more likely."[74]

Commented a "key Administration official" on June 27: "Anyone trying to sell [the ER weapons] as more

---

[74] *Washington Post*, June 28, 1977, page #A-2.

usable is pushing a policy that is not that of the Carter Administration. They don't change the problem of the nuclear threshold. And if they did, that image would become a matter of public concern. [The decision on production rests] on whether it is cost effective to the military ... whether this is an option worth having."[75]

At this moment the neutron bomb was not the only defense budgetary consideration preoccupying the President, the Pentagon, and the Congress. On June 28th the House voted 243-178 to support the production of the controversial B-1 bomber, and Carter was expected to announce his own B-1 decision at a June 30th news conference. The overall appropriations bill would have provided the Defense Department $110.6 billion in fiscal 1977 - $3.3 billion less than the Carter Administration's initial request. Major cuts had been made in funds requested for the intelligence community (-$433 million) and for M-60A2 tanks (-$172 million), while the House had added $106.2 million for non-nuclear Lance missile production and A-7E attack aircraft production. B-1 opponents in Congress were fearful that the Congressional vote would enable Carter to approve the "wasteful and inadequate" bomber.[76]

During a closed session [the 76th in Senate history] on July 1 before the Senate's July 4th recess, Hatfield offered an amendment to the public works bill to delete neutron weapons funds, but Senator John Stennis succeeded in amending the Hatfield proposal to simply delay action on the funds until an Arms Control Impact Statement and Presidential certification had been filed. Stennis' version was passed 43-42. Hatfield then offered a second motion to make production subject to veto by either the House or the Senate; this was amended by

---

[75] *Ibid.*

[76] *New York Times,* June 29, 1977, page #1.

Senator Sam Nunn to make production subject to concurrent vetoes by both the House and the Senate.[77]

The ACIS had been delivered to the White House on June 28 but had still not been made available to Congress. The *Washington Post* said on July 6 that the Arms Control and Disarmament Agency had warned Carter that the neutron bomb might indeed endanger ongoing SALT-II talks, that production of such a second-generation nuclear weapon might also harm nuclear non-proliferation talks by provoking nations who bad not yet reached even first-generation level, and that deployment of the bomb would possibly interfere with NATO-Warsaw Pact proposals in the area of mutual arms reduction.[78] This account was denied the next day by Jody Powell, who said that the ACIS before Carter indicated that the neutron bomb's impact on SALT-II "will not necessarily be negative".[79]

First indications of the contemplated timetable for the neutron bomb came in a *New York Times* story on July 8, which reported that the ERDA had already conducted underground tests of the warheads in Nevada. "Virtually all fifteen" NATO members had endorsed deployment, and the Defense Department was planning to deploy the bomb in Europe within the next eighteen months.[80] Also on July 8 the *Wall Street Journal* came out in support of the bomb[81] , but a chilling *San Francisco Chronicle* account of the Defense Department's

---

[77] *New York Times*, July 2, 1977, page #1.

[78] *Washington Post*, July 6, 1977, page 1.

[79] *New York Times*, July 7, 1977, page #10.

[80] *New York Times*, July 8, 1977, page #5.

[81] *Wall Street Journal*, July 8, 1977, page #6.

estimates of neutron bomb lethality - illustrated on a map of San Francisco - brought renewed public criticism. [82]

Aware now that there was a real possibility that the Senate might kill the neutron warheads, President Carter sent a letter to Senator Stennis on July 12 formally requesting that the funds be approved:

> It is my present view ... [that the neutron weapons are] in this nation's security interest. An aggressor should be faced with uncertainty as to whether NATO would use nuclear weapons against its forward echelons. For these purposes [ER weapons would] present an attractive option.
>
> [ER weapons], by enhancing deterrence could make it less likely [that nuclear weapons would have to be employed at all]. The decision to cross the nuclear threshold would be among the most agonizing to be made by any President. I can assure you that these [neutron] weapons would not make that decision any easier.
>
> Whether or not the weapons have significant destabilizing aspects requires and will receive study [in an ACIS]. [83]

On the same day Carter held a press conference in which he reemphasized his appreciation of the dangers of atomic weapons use, but argued that those same dangers constituted a deterrence to major confrontation between nations who possess atomic weapons. Nations electing a first use of atomic weapons would be condemned by

---

[82] *San Francisco Chronicle*, July 10, 1977, page #1.

[83] Carter, Jimmy, letter to Senator John C. Stennis, quoted in *Washington Post*, July 13, 1977, page #A-1.

world public opinion "unless the circumstances were extremely gross, such as an unwarranted invasion into another country."

Carter reaffirmed his willingness to work with the other nuclear-armed countries to eliminate the need for such weapons. He indicated his belief that NATO could halt a Warsaw Pact invasion without resorting to atomics, citing the increased commitment and effectiveness of the forces of a defending nation fighting on their own invaded territory as compensation for the numerical superiority of the Pact forces. NATO-Warsaw Pact nuclear arsenals were now "roughly equivalent", he continued, but it was now necessary to ensure that there was similar equivalence in conventional forces as well.

The neutron bomb, said Carter:

> ... has been under development for fifteen or twenty years. It is not a new concept at all, not a new weapon. It does not affect our SALT or strategic weapons negotiations at all. It is strictly designed as a tactical weapon. I think that this would give us some flexibility.
>
> I have not yet decided whether to advocate deployment of the neutron bomb. I think the essence of it is that for a given projectile size or a given missile head size, that the destruction that would result from the explosion of a neutron bomb is much less than the destruction from an equivalent weapon of other types.
>
> The essence of the question is that if the neutron weapon or atomic weapon ever should have to be used against enemy forces in occupied territory of our allies or ourselves, the destruction would be much less.

Before I make a final decision on the neutron bomb's deployment, I would do a complete impact statement analysis on it and submit this information to the Congress.

But I have not yet decided whether to approve the neutron bomb. I do think it ought to be one of our options, however.[84]

A somewhat more colorful statement was given that same day by an official from the Ford Administration. In Los Angeles J.F. terHorst said that the neutron bomb was as American as the Constitution - that "because the bomb would not damage buildings, it reflects the Constitution's concern for the protection of property, which Jefferson, Adams, Hamilton, and Madison considered important." The neutron bomb, observed terHorst, "could be used in the United States and abroad to eliminate bothersome people."[85]   Also on July 12 the *New York Times* editorially endorsed deployment of the neutron bomb[86], and on the next day the *Washington Post* repeated its editorial condemnation of the bomb.[87]

While President Carter was making his position on the bomb explicit for the first time, Jack Robertson of Senator Hatfield's office, unable to get a clear answer from Executive Branch sources on the actual "clean" quality of the neutron bomb, had contacted J. Carson Mark, former Director of the Los Alamos Laboratories where nuclear weapons are designed [see Chapter Four]. Mark told Robertson that several neutron warheads used at the same time on a battlefield "would create high doses

---

[84] Carter, Jimmy, Press Conference, July 12, 1977.

[85] *Los Angeles Times*, July 12, 1977, page #11-7.

[86] *New York Times*, July 12, 1977, page #28.

[87] *Washington Post*, July 13, 1977, page #16.

of highly toxic isotopes which could endanger civilian populations" - an assessment which Hatfield promptly repeated to the Senate. As was recounted in Chapter Four, the Defense Department then flew Mark out to Washington to deny the assessment to Robertson.[88]

The day after the President's conference and letter to Stennis, the Senate moved towards final resolution of the public works bill and its neutron bomb provision. Support for Hatfield's position came from Senator Edward Kennedy, who together with Senators James Allen, H. John Heinz, and Dick Clark, bad come out against the bomb at the time of the closed-session debate.[89]

On July 13 Kennedy made a formal statement in the Senate endorsing non-deployment of the bomb. But, he continued, his more immediate concern was whether the Congress should consider approving the weapon before President Carter bad even decided whether or not he wanted it. "We are asked to suspend the judgment which we have been elected to exercise," charged Kennedy. "We are asked to tell the President, in advance of his sharing - let alone reaching - a full assessment with us, that any judgment his Administration reaches is fine by us."

Noting that the ACIS required by law had still not made the trip from the White House to the Hill, Kennedy called for a deferment of Congressional action until the Carter Administration's position had been made explicit. He raised the possibility that the Soviets might respond by developing neutron bombs of their own, or by retaliating against NATO use of neutron bombs by employing existing atomic weapons - thereby forcing

---

[88] Interview with Jack Robertson, Washington, D.C., October 26, 1979 and Hatfield, Mark quoted in *Washington Post*, July 13, 1977, page #A-14.

[89] *New York Times*, July 2, 1977, page #1.

NATO to use the more destructive nuclear weapons in its own inventory.

"I keep an open mind," said Kennedy, "about the possibility that the neutron bomb will have more of a stabilizing than a destabilizing effect, will strengthen rather than undermine deterrence. But this Administration has not yet reached this judgment and has not presented it to Congress. We should pause at even the slightest risk that our actions may increase the likelihood of nuclear war. We would shirk our Constitutional responsibilities if we were to leave a judgment of this importance to the Executive Branch. Let them first make the case; then let us evaluate it on its merits."[90]

As the July 13 Senate debate continued, it became evident that the continued absence of an ACIS was a problem with which the neutron weapon advocates were having some difficulty. As Jack Robertson later recounted it: "The Pentagon rushed over a 1-1/2 page ACIS that had apparently just been printed up. I remember Hubert Humphrey waving a copy triumphantly over his head in the Senate Chamber and saying, 'We, have the Arms Control Impact Statement!' as though it were the answer to the entire problem."[91]

That ACIS was perhaps not as helpful to the actual issues being debated as it might have been. It dutifully cited the basic pro and con arguments that had already been raised; it made no attempt to resolve them. It pronounced Soviet perceptions "difficult to analyze" and said that there was no evidence that NATO introduction

---

[90] Kennedy, Edward M., Statement Against Funds for the Neutron Bomb made in the Senate on July 13, 1977. Text provided by the office of Senator Kennedy, Washington, D.C.

[91] Interview with Jack Robertson, Washington, D.C., October 26, 1979.

of the ER warhead would change Soviet strategy at all. Nor, said the ACIS, did the neutron bomb have any arms control. advantages. At best it might enhance deterrence slightly. [The text of the ACIS is reproduced as an Appendix to this chapter.]

The arrival of the ACIS notwithstanding, the Senate debate lasted into the evening; Majority Leader Byrd later characterized the neutron bomb as "the most controversial and bitterly fought measure the Senate has had before it this year".[92] Hatfield's amendment prohibiting the use of any funds for neutron weapon production was defeated late in the afternoon by a 58 to 38 vote. Then Kennedy introduced a proposal that would have allowed one chamber to veto the President's decision to go ahead with the neutron missile warheads and artillery shells. After further highly-charged debate this too was rejected.

"We are being rushed too fast," said Senator Clifford Case at one point during the debate. "This is not a matter of prestige, but a matter for future generations."[93] Senator John Heinz agreed:

> There is simply no urgency to the matter. Before we give the go-ahead to what could ultimately cost the taxpayers billions of dollars, the President has an obligation to make a solid case, and we have the obligation to debate it thoroughly. Congress just does not know enough to be plunging into this new weapons technology. Even Mr. Carter, who prides himself in having been a nuclear engineer, is still studying the matter. Yet most Congressmen had never even heard of a

---

[92] *Washington Post*, July 14, 1977, page #A-2.

[93] *Ibid.*

neutron bomb a few weeks ago. This is no way
to run a government.[94]

Hatfield himself agreed, arguing that "almost hourly
or daily developments" showed there was a "knowledge
vacuum" in the Senate about the weapons. "To move at
this point," he said, "would be ill-timed and ill-advised."
Senator Charles Percy told the Senate the "most
powerful" and "most dangerous" suggestion in the impact
statement was that some foreign governments might see
U.S. deployment of the new type of nuclear weapons as a
"doctrine change" and that this "could have an adverse
effect on U.S. efforts to prevent further nuclear
proliferation."[95]

Some hours later the Senate approved 74-19 a veto
amendment jointly sponsored by Majority Leader Robert
Byrd and Minority Leader Howard Baker that would give
Congress 45 days to pass a concurrent resolution
disapproving production of the weapons if the President
chose to go ahead with them. "I am for the neutron
warhead, no ifs, ands, or buts," said Byrd in sponsoring
the amendment, "but I think Congress should retain for
itself a two-House role on this very important matter."
The veto amendment, added Baker, "would put the
matter to rest" without depriving the President of his
powers as Commander-in-Chief or chief architect of
foreign policy. "This is not intended to be a slam at the
President."[96]

Senator Hubert Humphrey, who two weeks
previously had voted against the neutron bomb, said he
had changed his vote "because. I have faith in the

-----

[94] *Congressional Record*, op. cit.

[95] *Washington Post*, July 14, 1977, page #A-2.

[96] *Ibid.*

President ... and I'm convinced he'll make the proper decision." Senator John Stennis, Chairman of the Armed Services Committee and floor manager of the bill, opposed the veto amendment on the grounds that the Senate had cast "a very decisive vote" against deleting production funds and "on a highly important international matter we should not put these crippling strings on the President. "[97]

The day after the Senate debate two major British papers commented favorably on the Carter Administration's evident resolve to proceed with the neutron bomb. The *Times of London* dismissed charges that the bomb was a "super capitalist" weapon [because of its destruction of people and not property] and suggested that NATO's nuclear posture should be modernized with "these less destructive, if highly lethal refinements".[98] The *Financial Times* added that the real cause for concern was the absence of effective international arms control arrangements, and that until such arrangements were reached, both the East and the West could be expected to continue modernizing their arsenals.[99]

In the United States the influential *Christian Science Monitor* refused to take a firm position but laid emphasis upon the neutron bomb's value as a deterrent and said that it was probable the United States as a whole would back Carter's decision.[100] And on July 19th the *Washington Post* quoted "informed sources" as saying that former Secretary of State Henry Kissinger had not known of the Ford Administration's plans concerning the

---

[97] *Ibid.*

[98] *Times of London*, July 14, 1977, page #15.

[99] *Financial Times*, July 14, 1977, page #20.

[100] *Christian Science Monitor*, July 15, 1977, page #28.

bomb. Kissinger, said the *Post*, believed the new warheads would cause difficult diplomatic problems in NATO because of their design for use on allied territory.[101]

On July 20 the Pentagon voiced its indignation over the treatment, such as it was, that it had received at the hands of Walter Pincus and the *Post*. Author of the blast was D.R. Cotter, Assistant Secretary of Defense for Atomic Energy. Via a letter to the newspaper he first addressed the allegation that the Pentagon had "hidden in the ERDA budget" the funds for the new warhead, as well as the Post's comment that "the whole thing has the look of a black-bag job."

Nuclear weapon developments in response to Defense Department requirements, said Cotter, are a proper concern of the ERDA, which is required by law to fund these developments. And as far back as April of 1975, he continued, the Defense Department had made official mention to Congress of neutron warheads in reports on "The Theater Nuclear Force Posture in Europe" provided specifically to the Senate Committees on Armed Services and Foreign Relations, and the Joint Committee on Atomic Energy. The extracts from the reports cited by Cotter make passing reference to "enhanced radiation" weapons, but the "neutron" designation is not mentioned and the meaning of "enhanced radiation" is not elaborated upon.

Cotter defended the "great secrecy" of the neutron warhead program as well. "The detailed military characteristics of warhead design information," he said, "are safeguarded under the Restricted Data Requirements of the Atomic Energy Act to deny our adversaries the details of critical nuclear weapon design information and to prevent the spread of any technology

---

[101] *Washington Post*, July 19, 1977, page #A-2.

that would likely result in the proliferation of nuclear weapons. The new weapons were accorded the required degree of classification - no more, no less." The *Post's* "unbalanced and, in many cases, inaccurate" accounts did not, concluded Cotter, "well serve the public or the Congressional debate of the past days." [102]

Comment from the world press continued to be heard. On July 24 David Fairhall of the *Manchester Guardian* held that the neutron bomb, because it would "blur the distinction" between conventional and nuclear warfare, would ultimately act to increase the danger of nuclear war breaking out in Europe. [103] In a companion article in the *Guardian*, James Cameron also attacked the weapon, quoting MP Reginald Maudling to the effect that it was "the ultimate insult that man can offer to the human race" - that it was "playing God" and that "only an ostentatiously God-loving man like President Carter would have the nerve to take on that responsibility." [104]

In the *U.S. News and World Report*, however, Joseph Fromm argued that Carter's production decision was based simply on the need to maintain the credibility of the U.S. nuclear deterrent in the face of current developments concerning the B-1 bomber and the time required for the cruise missile and MX programs to be implemented. [105] Andrew Greeley of the *Chicago Tribune* said in an article accompanied by photos of weapons from *Star Wars* that while there might well be tactical justification for the neutron bomb, it emphasized the "paradoxical lunacy of peace being maintained by ever-

---

[102] *Washington Post*, July 20, 1977, page #A-22.

[103] *Manchester Guardian*, July 24, 1977, page #7.

[104] *Ibid.*

[105] *U.S. News and World Report*, July 25, 1977, page #24.

increasing terror, and that leaves me - and everyone - scared." [106]

Not quite everyone, however; many people appeared to be just as confused as Congress and the President concerning the new bomb. The *New York Times* released the results of a joint *Times*/CBS poll on July 29. While 62% of the 1,447 persons interviewed approved of Carter's general performance during his first six months in office, only 33% felt they knew enough about the neutron bomb to reach an opinion on it, and that group was split evenly on the issue. [107]

A vote of evident public approval came from Texas, where Ross Durham, manager of the ERDA Pantex Plant that would be constructing the actual neutron warheads, said that there had been no adverse reaction at all to the project from residents of the nearby Amarillo area. [108]

Three weeks later pollster Louis Harris released the results of a survey on popular attitudes towards the neutron bomb. Among 2,510 adult Americans surveyed, a 44 to 37 percent plurality favored production of the weapon. Harris observed:

> The sharp public split over whether the neutron bomb should be built is evident in many ways. People on the east and west coasts, for example, oppose the neutron bomb, but those in the midwest and south favor it. Young people under 30 are against it, but those 50 and over favor it. Men favor the bomb by a decisive 56 to 32 percent, but women oppose it

---

[106] *Chicago Tribune*, August 2, 1977, page #7.

[107] *New York Times*, July 29, 1977, page #1.

[108] *Houston Chronicle*, August 2, 1977, page #1.

by 43 to 32 percent. Conservatives support it, while liberals don't.

The American people are also divided over many of the arguments that have been used to justify the bomb, although some positions are more acceptable than others:

• A 48 to 21 percent plurality agrees that the neutron bomb is the most effective defense in Western Europe for NATO against the threat of an attack by the Russians.

• By 45 to 34 percent, a plurality also believes "the neutron bomb is desirable, because it can be limited in its use against troops and not against civilian populations".

• By a much narrower margin of 39 to 33 percent, a plurality agrees that "the neutron bomb is such an effective deterrent that it will actually reduce the threat of war in Europe if it is given to NATO for use in its defense".

Although a plurality comes down in favor of building the neutron bomb, substantial numbers of the American people have real reservations about it:

• By 66 to 15 percent, a sizable majority agrees that the neutron bomb can lead to the use of other nuclear weapons and total destruction.

• By 47 to 26 percent, a plurality also feels that "the neutron bomb will more likely be used by field commanders as a substitute for conventional warfare, and that is wrong".[109]

On August 15 White House Press Secretary Jody Powell announced that President Carter would not make

---

[109] *Washington Post*, August 22, 1977, page #A-7.

a decision on either production and deployment until September so that be would have the opportunity to consult further with NATO. National Security Council spokesman Jerrold Schecter added that a Pentagon study on the subject had just been received by the NSC and was undergoing review. [110]

What that study may have contained was publicized in the *New York Times* five days later. According to C.L. Sulzberger, some NATO members had quietly indicated approval of U.S. plans for production and deployment despite public opposition in their countries. Their opinion was that, in the event of an invasion, neutron weapons might offer the opportunity for swift civilian evacuation and military retreat, followed by the chance to destroy invading forces without rendering the invaded territory useless for reoccupation. [111]

From Capitol Hill the most notable response to the White House August 15 announcement was a telegram to the President from five Senators and twenty-six Representatives on August 24, asking that production and deployment plans for the bomb be halted. The telegram contained no argument that had not already been made, emphasizing primarily the "risk of escalating nuclear exchange" as a consequence of the bomb's deployment. Hatfield was the only Republican to sign the telegram, and, if anything, it was probably interpreted by the White House as an indication of how weak the anti-

---

[110] *New York Times*, August 17, 1977, page #6.

[111] *New York Times*, August 20, 1977, page #21.

neutron forces on the Hill had become, at least in the absence of some further provocation.[112]

On August 27 there was an anti-neutron bomb demonstration at the Pentagon, but, despite the arrest of four persons involved, it did not elicit much public attention or interest.[113]

In due course the "provocation" appeared. By the last week in September the Carter Administration had still not achieved the consensus from the NATO allies it had hoped for, and the President had made no further move toward announcing a decision. As the month drew to a close, Representative Theodore Weiss and eleven other Democratic liberals introduced a bill in the House to eliminate the neutron bomb funds from the ERDA authorization bill. When the news about the neutron bomb first broke in June, of course, the ERDA bill had already gone through the House without the ER question being raised [much to the House's subsequent embarrassment]. Now, it would seem, the controversial weapon would undergo the floor test that it had missed earlier.

After a debate on September 28 that lasted most of the day, the House adjourned without taking a vote on the amendment. A succession of anti-neutron bomb Representatives spoke, but proponents of the program, confident that they had the votes to defeat the Weiss amendment, did not respond. The most heated exchanges, reported Walter Pincus, featured liberal Democrats against liberal Democrats:

---

[112] A synopsis of the telegram, together with the names of the Senators and Representatives signing it, was released by United Press International on August 25, 1977 and appeared in the *Washington Post*, August 25, page #A-23 and in the *New York Times*, August 25, page #II-7. I also obtained a complete copy of the telegram from the Soviet Embassy in Washington, D.C.

[113] *New York Times*, August 27, 1977, page #8.

Rep. Robert M. Carr, who normally opposes Pentagon programs, supported this one. At one point he was being questioned by three Democratic colleagues at once. "I haven't had so many liberal friends talking to me in a long time," Carr said. "I hope you cherish it," Rep. Elizabeth Holtzman shot back, "because it might not be repeated for a long time."

Carr at one point told his colleagues, "You're misinformed [about neutron weapons] because a lot of information was available to you only through newspapers ... and those accounts have been inaccurate." Carr said the proposed weapons would replace other tactical nuclear weapons that he said were more destructive.

Rep. Ronald V. Dellums made the most emotional plea, crying out that "Nuclear war is unthinkable." Neutron weapons, Dellums said, make nuclear war "thinkable, acceptable, possible, and," with his voice rising, "ultimately inevitable. Thinking like that ultimately goes into the building of this insane weapon."

Rep. Patricia Schroeder said that the neutron weapons "have a great potential in blurring the bright light between nuclear and conventional weapons." She added that those who term it a "clean weapon worry me a lot. Cleaner compared to what?" she asked. "Compared to conventional weapons it's not clean at all." [114]

After another day of heated debate, the House rejected the Weiss amendment 297 to 109. Congressional

---

[114] *Washington Post*, September 29, 1977, page #A-20.

emotions during the exchange ran from fervent support to fierce opposition to impatient irritation and even resigned boredom. The neutron weapons, observed Rep. Robert Leggett of California, were "not as lethal and diabolical as some may think. Scare headlines about a killer warhead set the parameters of the debate." Leggett called the decision to put neutron warheads "on the last 300 Lance launchers ... much ado about not much."[115]

Lest it be thought that all of the more considered exchanges in Congress on the neutron bomb took place in the House, the following is worth rescuing from the Briefings on SALT Negotiations in the Senate Foreign Relations Committee, November 29, 1977:

> Senator Stone: I read an account of our possibly offering to trade the concussion bomb weapon in all of its different formations for either Backfire or something else, or mobile missiles, or conventional limitations in the Eastern Bloc. What is the status of negotiations with regard to the concussion bomb, and what are we asking the Russians for if we don't deploy it in NATO?
>
> Mr. Warnke: I take it, Senator Stone, that by the "concussion bomb" you mean the enhanced radiation weapon?
>
> Senator Stone: Don't we call that the concussion bomb, even though it can be fired from a long rifle or whatever?
>
> Senator Church: Are you talking about the neutron bomb, Dick?
>
> Senator Stone: Excuse me, yes, absolutely. I mean the neutron bomb. The concussion is something else.

---

[115] *Washington Post*, September 30, 1977, page #A-4.

Mr. Warnke: The neutron bomb does not come into the SALT negotiations at all, Senator Stone, because it is not conceivably a strategic system. [116]

On October 11, satisfactory word still not having been received from other NATO governments, Defense Secretary Harold Brown flew to Bari, Italy to tell the NATO Nuclear Planning Group flatly that the U.S. Government would probably not deploy the neutron bomb to Europe unless there were a satisfactory consensus to that effect in the Alliance. [117] News observers quoted a "White House source" that it would be several months before decisions might be expected from the other governments, and with this development the neutron bomb ceased for a time to be front-page news. [118]

On November 3, 1977 the Congress gave President Carter authorization to go ahead with the development phase of the neutron bomb. The Senate passed a $476.4 million supplemental defense authorization bill and a $2.6 billion military energy authorization measure, approved by the House the previous day. Of these funds, $12.6 million were added to the funds already approved for the bomb. The bills elicited some controversial opinions while still in committee, but passed the House

---

[116] "Briefings on SALT Negotiations", Hearings Before the Committee on Foreign Relations, United States Senate, 95th Congress, First Session, November 29, 1977. Washington, D.C.: U.S. Government Printing Office, 1978.

[117] *Washington Post*, October 12, 1977, page #A-15.

[118] *New York Times*, October 12, 1977, page #8.

without protracted debate and passed the Senate by voice vote.[119]

Later the same month the Committee on Public Doublespeak of the National Council of Teachers of English gave its annual award jointly to the Pentagon and to ERDA for calling the, neutron bomb a "radiation enhancement weapon".[120]

After five months of diplomatic dialogue with various NATO governments [see Chapter Six], the Carter Administration abruptly canceled further NATO negotiations on the subject, and the neutron bomb was back on page one. "No final decision has yet been taken," an Administration official said on April 3, 1978 "but one way or another we expect it to happen this week."

The next day the *New York Times* reported that Carter had decided against neutron weapon production, acting against the advice of Zbigniew Brzezinski, Harold Brown, and Cyrus Vance. Carter's decision, said the *Times*, was reportedly due to his belief that development of the bomb would harm "prospects for disarmament".[121]

Editorials in the *New York Times*, the *Los Angeles Times*, and the *Wall Street Journal* promptly criticized the rumored decision. The Los Angeles paper said that the bomb was "too important a tactical weapon to be used by Carter as a 'bargaining chip' in SALT", and the *Journal* described the story as "frightening" and characterized the neutron bomb as "a handy thing to have in the event of a USSR tank attack in Europe". Existing criticisms of the neutron bomb should not be taken seriously, added the

---

[119] *Washington Post*, November 4, 1977, page #A-30.

[120] *New York Times*, November 23, 1977, page #10.

[121] *Washington Post*, April 4, 1978, page #A-1. See also the *New York Times*, April 4, 1978, page #1.

Journal, as they applied just as well to nuclear weapons already deployed in NATO. [122]

Even the *Washington Post* urged Carter to proceed with development and deployment of the bomb, based upon the evident unwillingness of the Soviet Union to slow augmentation of its own theater weapons in Europe. The neutron bomb should be abandoned, said the *Post*, only if the Soviets agreed to give up something comparable in return. [123]

On April 5 leaders of the House Armed Services Committee, who bad led the 1977 fight that ended with overwhelming House support of the neutron weapons, sent a letter to Carter arguing against the rumored production ban. Senate Majority Leader Byrd and Representative Bob Wilson, ranking G.O.P. member on the Armed Services Committee, said that Carter "would be mistaken to abandon the neutron [weapon] at this late date."

But Carter's mind seemed to be made up. Acting on advice from Hamilton Jordan, he was now considering what would happen if the program were ended before any weapons were produced. And there was the question of the United Nations special session on disarmament, scheduled for May. "Carter may have had a hard time thinking of himself up there talking about disarmament," one Administration source said, "and being the President who had ordered production of a new type of nuclear weapon."

Jody Powell also cited projected costs as another area of concern for Carter. According to informed sources, each 8-inch neutron shell would cost almost $1

---

[122] *Los Angeles Times*, April 5, 1978, page #11-4; *Wall Street Journal*, April 5, , page #18; *New York Times*, April 6, 1978, page #20.

[123] *Washington Post*, April 6, 1978, page #A-22.

million (twice the cost of the conventional nuclear shell), and the entire purchase would come to over $1 billion. That would include some $43 million just to cover the cost of building special production facilities for the shell.[124]

Another voice was that of ex-President Gerald Ford, who was asked his opinion in Palm Springs. He said he was surprised and disappointed by news accounts that President Carter had decided to abandon the project:

> The neutron bomb is a new weapons system that will help to preserve the peace in Western Europe as a deterrent against the Warsaw Pact nations, which we all know have more tanks, more guns, more artillery, more troops. The only way you neutralize that numerical strength is to have the kind of a weapons system such as the neutron bomb which aims at killing enemy soldiers and not tearing up the nations that are under attack.[125]

At a New York City Republican fund-raising dinner Henry Kissinger also criticized the decision, saying that it would have the net effect of weakening the U.S.[126]

On the afternoon of April 7 President Carter announced his decision in a statement issued at the White House:

> I have decided to defer production of weapons with enhanced radiation effects. The

---

[124] *Washington Post*, April 6, 1978, page #A-1.

[125] Interview with Gerald R. Ford in *Washington Post*, April 6, 1978, page #A-5.

[126] *New York Times*, April 7, 1978, page #1.

ultimate decision regarding the incorporation of enhanced radiation features into our modernized battlefield weapons will be made later, and will be influenced by the degree to which the Soviet Union shows restraint in its conventional and nuclear arms programs and force deployments affecting the security of the United States and Western Europe.

Accordingly I have ordered the Defense Department to proceed with the modernization of the Lance missile nuclear warhead and the 8-inch weapon system, leaving open the option of installing the enhanced radiation elements.

The United States is consulting with its partners in the North Atlantic Alliance on this decision and will continue to discuss with them appropriate arms control measures to be pursued with the Soviet Union.

We will continue to move ahead with our allies to modernize and strengthen our military capabilities, both conventional and nuclear. We are determined to do whatever is necessary to assure our collective security and the forward defense of Europe.[127]

Reaction to the decision was, as one might assume in view of the heat of the year-long controversy, decidedly mixed. Opponents of the bomb were disgruntled over the fact that modernization of the Lance warheads to enable them to accept the bomb was going ahead, and that Carter had decided only to defer, not cancel outright, the production of the bomb.

---

[127] Carter, Jimmy, Statement on Enhanced Radiation Weapons, April 7, 1978, in Administration of Jimmy Carter, 1978.

The Soviet Union, as is recounted in Chapter Eight, resented the attempt to tie the neutron bomb decision to what it preferred to consider "unrelated arms questions".

Some State Department officials later remarked off-the-record that "the President had really screwed that one up, and Helmut Schmidt was furious with him" [see Chapter Seven].[128]

Another NATO government reported to its embassies that it was essentially a case of Carter listening to Hamilton Jordan and Jody Powell, and rejecting the advice of Vance, Brzezinski, and Brown.[129]

On the Hill Senator Sam Nunn said:

> At this point we don't have a bargaining chip. We have an invisible chip with the Soviets. Why would they negotiate away a weapon they are willing to produce [the SS-20] for one we don't have the courage to produce? Europeans had reached a point where they were willing to support a production decision ... with a commitment that we would deploy the weapon if we did not get any agreement with the Soviets.[130]

In an April 13 letter to Carter, Senator S.I. Hayakawa commented:

> At this juncture I want you to know how very difficult it is for me to continue to support your foreign policies. I was appalled to learn in

---

[128] Interview with State Department officials, Washington, D.C., October 1979.

[129] Interview with a NATO government official, Washington, D.C., October 1979.

[130] Nunn, Sam, quoted in *Washington Post*, April 8, 1978, page #A-2.

the past three days of your decision to postpone (cancel?) the neutron bomb program - a humane weapon (if any war weapon can be said to be humane) in that it makes possible the destruction of enemy troops without at the same time killing tens of thousands of civilians, as was done in Dresden and Hiroshima. The postponement of the neutron bomb, along with the cancellation of the B-1 bomber program, has at least thrown away a valuable bargaining chip. It has also probably destroyed what technological advantages we had over the Soviets to offset their advantages in manpower, tanks, and. proximity to their major target, which presumably is Western Europe. [131]

Senate Majority Leader Byrd placed the "blame" for the deferment decision on the other nations of NATO:

First we need the decision [by the NATO nations] to deploy the enhanced radiation weapon. What good does it do to produce the weapon if we can't deploy it? We need a show of support from our European allies. Our European friends could have been more vocal in their support for going ahead. I think it is ironic, if not alarming, that our allies would be willing to play our trump card, one of the weapons most feared by the Soviets, as a throwaway in the high-stakes game of national security. If we're to depend on one another, our defense in Europe must be the stiff backbone,

---

[131] Hayakawa, S. I., letter to President Jimmy Carter, April 13, 1978.

and not the soft underbelly, of our protection. [132]

Jimmy Carter's own public explanation of the rationale for the deferment decision came on May 5, during a Presidential visit to Spokane, Washington. During a question-and-answer session at a Town Meeting, he said:

> As you may know, a decision to go ahead with the design of the neutron bomb was made before I became President. I didn't know about it until it was published in the newspaper. And at that time I began to assess whether or not we needed to go ahead to produce the neutron weapon itself.
>
> We have a serious problem in Western Europe and Eastern Europe. The Soviet Union has built up a tremendous quantity of tank force, military force of all kinds, nuclear weapons like the SS-20, which is 30 times more destructive than any neutron weapon that we've ever considered, and which has a range of more than a thousand miles, where the range of the kind of neutron weapon we're talking about is only 15 or 20 or 25 miles.
>
> There has never been any thought that neutron weapons, which are not bombs, but either shells or missiles, would be deployed on American soil. They're not feasible at all for use in this country or where Americans live. If ever produced, they would be deployed on the ground or in the lands of the West Germans or the Belgians or other Europeans.

---

[132] *Washington Post*, April 9, 1978, page #A-30.

Another factor to make is that if the Soviets did invade, then the lives that would be saved by a weapon with a very narrow destructive area would be West Germans, Belgians, those who live in Holland, perhaps the French, that are our friends and allies. I never had a single European country who told me that if we produced the neutron weapon that they were willing to deploy it.

West German leaders said that, "If other nations in Europe will deploy it, we will." So that's why I terminated any consideration of the neutron weapon for the time being.

If the Soviets continue to build up their own forces to a degree that increases the threat against the West Europeans, who are our NATO allies, and we have about 300,000 American soldiers in the Western European area, who would be directly threatened, then I would consider going ahead with the neutron bomb as one of the alternatives that faced me.

I would not want to close that option completely. But there is no plan now to go ahead with the neutron weapon.[133]

On May 17 the House of Representatives overwhelmingly approved the $2.9 billion fiscal 1979 Department of Energy national security program authorization bill, which gave Carter authority to go ahead with neutron weapon production should he consider it to be in the national interest. An amendment similar to the fiscal 78 one to provide Congress 45 days to override a Presidential decision to build neutron weapons

---

[133] Carter, Jimmy, Remarks and a Question-and-Answer Session at a Town Meeting, Spokane, Washington, May 5, 1978 in *Administration of Jimmy Carter*, 1978.

was proposed, but it was defeated 306 to 90. Under existing law, the President would then require only the approval of the House and Senate Armed Services and Appropriations Committees to go ahead with neutron warhead production.[134]

Results of a new Harris survey on the neutron bomb were published on May 25, and they seemed to suggest that public opinion inclined to the President's point of view. The poll showed that a 47% to 35% plurality of Americans opposed production of the bomb; in July 1977 a similar poll had been 44% to 38% in favor of production. Most notable on this new sampling was a 74% to 12% opinion that proceeding with the bomb's production might lead to renewed efforts to develop new and more deadly types of nuclear bombs.[135]

Coincidentally Dr. Donald Kerr, Acting Assistant Energy Secretary for Defense Programs, had announced on April 30 that teams at Los Alamos and Livermore were now working on a new nuclear device that would minimize residual radiation while producing more heat and blast. In other words, nuclear planners were now attempting to circumvent the "anti-people" image of the neutron warhead while still retaining its non-contamination characteristics.[136]

On June 16 the House of Representatives again turned back - 259 to 67 - an attempt to prohibit neutron warhead production under the fiscal 1979 public works bill, which contained funds for the Department of Energy's nuclear weapons program. The anti-neutron amendment, again offered by Ted Weiss, was debated for less than an hour before the vote was taken.

---

[134] *Washington Post*, May 18, 1978, page #A-1.

[135] *Chicago Tribune*, May 25, 1978, page #III-4.

[136] *New York Times*, April 30, 1978, page #18.

Four days earlier the Senate Armed Services Committee had released a report on the Department of Energy national security program in which it urged President Carter to begin stockpiling components for neutron warheads in the United States for quick shipment to NATO if a subsequent decision were made to deploy them. The report also asked the President to set a firm time for production of neutron weapons in the absence of any appropriate Soviet response. [Carter had not yet done so.] The message seemed to be that Congress felt it had made its moral points concerning the infamous neutron bomb; it had also seen the President evidently respect its opinion in his April 7 decision. Further decisions concerning the weapon would now be Carter's prerogative.[137]

The result of this somewhat confused political atmosphere was that the Carter Administration itself seemed equally confused over exactly how it should implement the President's decision. The key question was whether or not production of components should now begin, per the Senate committee's recommendation, or whether such a move would be in effect a violation of the intent of the President's decision, being interpreted by the Soviet Union [among others] as an outright effort to proceed with the bomb. Political aides to Defense Secretary Harold Brown, who had pressed for an outright decision to build the bomb, now voiced this caution on the grounds that component production would negate the constructive potential of Carter's decision.[138]

On June 23, however, the Defense Department announced that component production would begin, making it possible for new-generation tactical nuclear warheads in Europe to be converted to neutron warheads

---

[137] *Washington Post*, June 17, 1978, page #A-3.

[138] *New York Times*, June 17, 1978, page #1.

within the time space of a year were the President to make such a decision. This production plan, though not acknowledged as being approved by Carter himself, did carry the approvals of Brown and Zbigniew Brzezinski.[139] Funding ($2.97 billion for the fiscal year) for the components-building plan came before the Senate on September 30 and was approved 68-1.[140] Finally, on October 18, Jody Powell formally announced that President Carter had ordered production of the components.[141] The following day the Department of Energy confirmed that it had received an order from Carter to begin mass production of plutonium components for Lance missile and W-79 8-inch artillery neutron warheads at its Rocky Flats plant in Colorado.[142]

And there, it seemed, the saga of the neutron bomb's journey through the U.S. Governmental decision-making apparatus ended. Further developments on the subject were generally in the form of domestic and foreign speculation concerning future United States options and will be discussed as appropriate in chapters to come.

Was there a single, specific reason why official interest by the Administration and Congress seemed to fall off? In October 1979 Jack Robertson responded thus: "It was simply a case of other problems demanding attention. In the armaments field it was SALT-II, then the MX missile. We just haven't had the time or resources for further work on the neutron bomb issue." When asked if he felt that something worthwhile had actually been accomplished by the prolonged debate, he replied in the affirmative. "We may not have stopped the machine," he

---

[139] *New York Times*, June 23, 1978, page #1.

[140] *New York Times*, October 1, 1978, page #19.

[141] *New York Times*, October 19, 1978, page #5.

[142] *New York Times*, October 20, 1978, page #83.

said, "but we forced the Congress and the American people to take more personal responsibility for such a difficult decision. The President's decision reflected attention to Congressional and popular opinion, as well as his own."

On the key subject of the real reason for Carter's deferment decision, Robertson observed that the legislative and public expressions had all played some part, "but a source of ours close to Carter's personal administrative work tells me that it was at base Carter's own personal dislike for nuclear weapons in general and the 'inhuman' connotations of this one in particular. He just doesn't like it, and so he would rather it not exist. It is to a great extent as simple as that."[143]

Upon reflection, several features of Washington, D.C.'s encounter with the neutron bomb appear worthy of note, both favorably and otherwise. On balance it may be said that the system for dealing with problems such as this did work fairly well, if not without a few creaks and groans. Congress exercised its Constitutional right and responsibility to question Presidential policy (at the last minute); the President provided Congress with the information it required (at the last minute); and an eventual Presidential decision was made (several months after the. last minute) which did seem to reflect the sense of Congress and that of the United States people as well. The decision may not have been in keeping with the private desires of some other NATO governments, but it did enhance the face which they evidently felt it prudent to present to their own countrymen.

If a single fault appears most conspicuous, it is the almost comic-opera manner in which all of the U.S.

---

[143] Interview with Jack Robertson, Washington, D.C., October 26, 1979.

government decision-makers were anxious to have one another make the first decision.

The other side of this particular coin was perhaps the haste with which the press passed its judgments, to say nothing of the willingness of certain papers to almost reverse their positions from time to time. Most notable here, of course, is the *Washington Post*; after almost a year of more or less alarmist stories about the "neutron killer weapon", it called for preservation of the bomb when it suddenly appeared that the President might cancel it.

Who should have been first into the water? The difficulty in answering this question is due to the fact that the neutron bomb presented not one question but rather a series of them, ranging from research and development as envisioned by the ERDA to deployment in NATO. Congress did not want to answer the first question without considering the last, while the President did not feel able to make a recommendation concerning final use of the bomb while it was still in the earliest testing phases. The result was a certain amount of fumbling for a "picture" of what a 1977-1978 neutron bomb decision should actually be.

One can't help smiling at some of the Congressional oratory, to be sure, but it would appear that the final motions passed by that body were fairly reasonable under such nebulous circumstances. They neither abrogated Congress' responsibility to be critical of Presidential policy nor tied Carter's hands unnecessarily.

Though it is technically possible to do so, it does not seem altogether fair to criticize either Carter for his initial lack of familiarity with "his" budget nor the Congress for its near-rubber-stamping of a budgetary item about which it knew nothing. The federal budget is gigantic; it is not difficult for sub-sub-headings to receive only cursory attention as the legislature struggles to make an educated review of the whole. Once the "ER" entry was brought into the spotlight, a determined effort was made to define it to the satisfaction of all concerned, and that should be sufficient evidence of Congressional and Presidential conscientiousness.

Somewhat more disturbing, however, is the apparent readiness of Congress and the President to deal with the "image" of the neutron bomb as concocted by the news media rather than with the bomb as a technological reality. The foregoing account suggests that the Congressional and Presidential decisions were made for political reasons and did not stress the possible dangers of the neutron bomb to NATO troops as well as to those of an invader. Had the bomb been quietly deployed as a "black bag job", to use the *Post*'s quaint phrase for "Q"-classified modernization programs, U.S. and allied forces could now be armed with a new nuclear weapon which was almost as harmful to them - and to civilians - as to the enemy. And they would not know that to be the case. By contrast, the radiological side-effects of conventional nuclear warheads are known quantities and can be measured by such devices as field dosimeters and radiac meters.

This dangerous problem was effectively tabled by the deferment of the neutron bomb, but unfortunately there is no evidence to suggest that it was an acknowledged factor in the decision. If it should not be realized and addressed, a subsequent decision to introduce neutron weapons to Europe or any other locale could bring it again into significance.

The risks inherent in actual battlefield use of neutron warheads, presuming they are known and appreciated by the Pentagon, argue against the armed services' enthusiastic welcome of such a weapon. Such military endorsements of the bomb as have appeared seem once more to be based upon an idealization of its effects rather than an actual understanding of them. This may be understandable in comments by lower-ranking officers, many of whom rely upon the public media for their basic information, but it is more disturbing in the case of NATO's Commanding General as evidenced by his Senate testimony. One hopes that during the current postponement of neutron weapons a more thorough investigation will be made.

If there are grounds for skepticism concerning the military utility of the neutron bomb, wherein lies the impetus for the weapon's production? Who does want it to be built and why? No information along this line has appeared in Western sources; the only hint of ulterior (in this case monetary) motives is to be found in a Soviet *Izvestia* account cited in Chapter Eight.

Pursuit of this line of inquiry, however, is beyond the immediate focus of this examination and would open a Pandora's box of "devil" imperialism and conspiracy-theory hypotheses. It does seem appropriate to say here, however, that a purely military case for the bomb has not been proven and that, unpleasant as it may seem, the spectre of vested interest may arise to fill the gap. This is not to say that lobbying by defense contractors in Washington is anything new or even particularly shocking.

Appendix to Chapter Five

Arms Control Impact Analysis
Program Title: W-70 Mod 3 (Lance) Warhead

I. Program synopsis:

A. Descriptions:

The W-70 Mod 3 is being developed to satisfy an Army requirement for a low-yield enhanced radiation (ER) warhead for the Lance missile system.

Enhanced radiation is achieved by fusion reactions that produce high energy neutrons. When these neutrons are produced in connection with relatively low-yield fission reactions, the range of effect of the neutrons is greater than the range at which blast or thermal effects are lethal. At higher yields, blast and thermal effects predominate over both neutron and gamma radiation effects of any type. By employing ER as the target damage mechanism, a reduction in collateral damage is achieved since lower yields are required when personnel are the targets rather than equipment. For example a 1 KT (kiloton) ER warhead gives the same approximate damage expectancy of tank crew incapacitation through radiation effects as a 10 KT fission warhead does through radiation effects.

The Lance is a highly mobile surface-to-surface, ballistic missile system which can provide tactical nuclear artillery support to the battlefield through attacks on either fixed targets or non-fixed targets (e.g. tank battalions in staging areas). The nuclear lance missile has a maximum range of 130 kilometers with a CEP (Circular Error Probable) of 400-450 meters. Lance has replaced the Honest John and Sergeant in most NATO countries

(UK, FRG, Belgium, Netherlands, Italy) in both cases on a less than one-for-one basis, thus reducing the number of forward-deployed nuclear systems and weapons. [A total of 92 Lance launchers are now programmed for Europe.] Additionally two Lance Battalions will be based in the U.S., with one presently earmarked for deployment in the Pacific should the need arise. The Lance system is more survivable and more responsive than the systems it replaces, and it has a selectable yield capability. Its longer range allows it to remain further behind the forward edge of the battle area (FEBA) and thus contributes to its survivability. The longer range also facilitates targeting across Corps boundaries.

B. Rationale

An ER warhead provides increased kill capability, principally against personnel, and reduced collateral effects (blast and thermal). It has less effect on standard military equipment than a fission weapon of the same yield. With this weapon armored vehicles, which are relatively unaffected by blast effects except at close range, can be temporarily neutralized by radiation casualties of crew personnel. Requisite effects can still be achieved at much greater ranges, with less collateral damage, than could be expected from blast predominant weapons.

C. Funding

ERDA's total projected direct costs are $32.1 million for FY-77 through FY-80. [The ERDA Budget Estimate (as amended for FY-78) supplied to Congress cites a figure of $43.3 million for FY-78, of which $14.4 million are direct costs.]

II. Analysis

The ER warhead will kill tank crews by nuclear radiation. In covering the same intended target area with a non-ER fission weapon, casualties to civilians and damage to property from blast and thermal effects in a congested region would be greater.

It can be argued that the improved warhead may make initial use of nuclear weapons in battle seem more credible, which might enhance deterrence. However, by the same token, it can be argued that it increases the likelihood that nuclear weapons would actually be used in combat. In any event, the escalating potential is the same for this weapon as for any other nuclear weapon.

The political effects of deploying enhanced radiation warheads relate to characteristics which may be imputed to the entire class of enhanced radiation weapons rather than to the lance warhead alone. Potential effects on the nuclear threshold lie more in the gray area of perception - U.S., public, Allied, Soviet, and third world - than in judgments based on hard analytical criteria or weapons characteristics. This class of weapons is more dependent on radiation than on blast or thermal yields, but not entirely so. It is designed primarily against personnel and less against material and sheltering structures. Some will see this class of weapons as more plausible for battlefield use than other kinds of nuclear weapons and might infer a greater U.S. willingness to engage in nuclear war.

Soviet perceptions are difficult to analyze. There is no evidence that the development of this system would have any effect on Soviet doctrine for the initiation of nuclear war or that the Soviets would be less likely to escalate a nuclear exchange if ER weapons were used by the U.S. rather than standard fission weapons. They would presumably follow their own doctrines whether or not this weapon is introduced. The fact that the W-70 Mod 3 warhead may cause less collateral damage to civilians and property in NATO territory cannot be expected to moderate Soviet response. Its use would be no less likely than the present warhead to evoke Soviet retaliatory use of tactical nuclear weapons. Unless the Soviet forces are supplied with a comparable warhead, their response would create the kind of devastation that this warhead is designed to prevent.

Thus the President would be faced with a decision of the same nature whether or not this class of weapons or other tactical nuclear weapons are used.

If ER weapons are deployed, the Soviets will continue to accuse the U.S. of contributing to the arms race in Europe. There is little doubt that the Soviets would seize on publicized materials alleging that U.S. development of ER weapons make nuclear war more. likely by lowering the threshold.

In the U.S. case the prospect of escalation would remain a central component of a U.S. decision to use nuclear weapons regardless of the performance characteristics of this or other classes of nuclear weapons. Thus any U.S. decision to use nuclear weapons is in all likelihood insensitive to whether or not ER weapons were deployed.

There is no evidence that NATO governments would be particularly concerned about Lance deployment with this warhead. Nevertheless public discussion of the sort now taking place here could affect NATO attitudes.

The W-70 Mod 3 development and deployment would not be affected by the TTBT (Threshold Test Ban Treaty) since the underground testing of warheads under 150 KT is not prohibited.

A CTB (comprehensive test ban) would pose limitations on the further development of this class of weapons since over the long term further testing would be required. Conclusion of a test ban treaty with no PNE (peaceful nuclear explosion) exception during the next few years would limit the development and refinement of such weapons by both sides.

With regard to MBFR (Mutual and Balanced Force Reduction), the Western proposal does not affect Lance launchers. Neither does the Western warhead proposal select specific types of warheads for removal. Development and deployment of the W-70 Mod 3 could, however, be cited by the Soviets as evidence that the U.S. proposal would involve elimination of obsolete weapons while actual capability is being upgraded.

Some governments might couple a decision to deploy ER weapons with perceptions that U.S. doctrine has changed so as to make the use of nuclear weapons more likely in a tactical situation; such a coupling could have an adverse effect on U.S. efforts to prevent further nuclear proliferation.

In conclusion, this weapon system has no arms control advantages.

To the extent that it has any impact on ongoing arms control negotiations, the impact would be marginally negative.

A decision to cross the nuclear threshold would be the most agonizing decision to be made by any President. These weapons would not make that decision any easier. But by enhancing deterrence, they could make it less likely that the President would have to face such a decision.

Chapter Six:
NATO - The Political Sequence

Separation of the decision-making sequence of the neutron bomb episode into United States, NATO, and West German categories is admittedly something of a distortion. The actual situation involved considerable interrelationship between all three of these "actors" or, perhaps more accurately, "actor-environments". And, as was brought out in Chapter Five, the public forum of the problem brought other influences to bear as well, not the least important of which were public opinion and the press.

Yet there is some justification for focusing on the United States debate first and then proceeding in turn to NATO and Germany. The initial issue involved United States ethics in developing something like the neutron bomb at all; the utility of the bomb was not relevant. Then, when a sort of ethical stalemate developed, proponents and opponents began to be more interested in whether the bomb would actually do what it had been advertised as being able to to.

There was never really any doubt that the bomb was intended for NATO, and from United States dialogue it seems evident that it was envisioned de facto as a NATO cure-all even if this were rhetorically denied. The general feeling was that NATO was losing its cutting edge in the face of the Warsaw Pact's modernization, and some sort of highly-visible "wonder weapon" was needed to turn the tide. In theory the neutron bomb fitted that need perfectly - beginning with its very name, which quickly replaced the less-impressive "ER warhead" epithet and elicited the sort of "wonder weapon" image in 1977-1978 that the atomic and hydrogen bombs had in the 1940s and 1950s.

So the substance of the neutron bomb debate gradually shifted to NATO in the late summer and early fall of 1977, when President Carter made it clear that his production/deployment decision would reflect NATO input as well as domestic input. [144]And the considerations became almost totally NATO-oriented after October 1977, when Defense Secretary Harold Brown made a highly-publicized trip to Italy to discuss the neutron bomb with NATO's Nuclear Planning Group. Thereafter the neutron bomb issue reflected greater emphasis on NATO until spring of 1978, when there was once more a gradual shift of focus - this time to West Germany.

It may be useful to review some of the more important historical developments in NATO's involvement with nuclear weapons and then proceed to a discussion of the nuclear decision-making machinery in the alliance which was operative at the time of the neutron bomb episode.

Since the signing of the North Atlantic Treaty, there has been periodic discord among NATO member nations on the subject of the security priorities of Europe vs. those of the United States. The most celebrated instance of this was de Gaulle's 1966 decision to withdraw the French armed forces from the NATO integrated Military Headquarters, terminate the assignment of French forces to the international commands, and request the transfer from French territory of the International Headquarters, allied units and installations or bases not controlled by French authorities. On the subject of nuclear weapons there has been similar European nervousness about the reliability of the American "nuclear umbrella".

Movement of tactical nuclear weapons into bases in Europe under SACEUR control began in early 1958 after

---

[144] Statement by Jody Powell, August 16, 1977, quoted in the *New York Times*, August 17, 1977, page #6.

a meeting in Paris in December 1957 by the heads of the NATO governments. The decision was prompted by the newly-announced strategic concept of massive retaliation, and the heads of government agreed that the deployment of the nuclear weapons and the specific arrangements for their use were to be decided by agreement with the countries directly concerned. [145]

The first concrete formulation of guidelines under which nuclear weapons could be used was the "Athens Guidelines" resulting from a 1962 meeting of the NATO Ministerial Council in Athens. The language was understandably vague; both the United States and Britain committed themselves to "consultation with their allies, time and circumstances permitting, before releasing their weapons for use". [146]

During December 18-20, 1962 President Kennedy and Prime Minister Macmillan met in Nassau to discuss, among other things, a NATO nuclear force that would have some degree of joint member nation control. The result consisted of a series of American proposals for a Multilateral Nuclear Force (MLF) and a British counter-proposal for an Atlantic Nuclear Force (ANF).

Some interim modernization efforts were also made. In early 1963 SACEUR's obsolete Jupiter missiles in Turkey were retired[147], and he received direct control of the British V-bomber force and three United States Polaris submarines. In May 1963 at an Ottawa meeting of the North Atlantic Council, officers of non-nuclear

---

[145] *NATO Facts and Figures*. Brussels: NATO Information Service, page #106.

[146] *Ibid.*, page #107.

[147] This per the Kennedy Administration's secret "understanding" with the Soviet Union during the 1962 Cuban Missile Crisis that if the U.S.S.R. removed its missiles from Cuba, within a reasonable time thereafter the U.S. would remove its missiles from Turkey.

member countries were given broader participation in nuclear planning at Allied Command Europe and at the Strategic Air Command headquarters in Omaha.[148]

Perceived by other NATO governments as surface gestures rather than substantive offers, the MLF/ANF proposals never reached an implementation stage and were discarded by 1964. In the spring of 1965 a more positive step was taken by the establishment of an *ad hoc* Special Committee of Defense Ministers to study such problems as that of nuclear planning. In 1967 this arrangement was formalized by the establishment of the Nuclear Defense Affairs Committee (NDAC) and the Nuclear Planning Group (NPG).

The NDAC is a Ministerial-level committee under the chair of the NATO Secretary General, tasked to propose nuclear policy to the North Atlantic Council as a whole. The NPG, a subordinate agency of the NDAC, consists of representatives of seven or eight countries drawn from the membership of the NDAC.

From its inception in 1967 the NPG has been responsible for drafting the nuclear policy papers for review and approval by the NDAC and the Council. From 1967 to 1970 the NPG generated four basic nuclear policy documents dealing with tactical use of nuclear weapons, general consultation guidelines, concept of theater nuclear strike forces, and political guidance concerning the use of ADM (Atomic Demolition Munitions). Thereafter it proceeded to various detailed studies on specific issues, and in 1977 it was the NATO agency to which the United States turned regarding the neutron bomb proposal.[149]

Shortly before the June 1977 outbreak of publicity concerning the United States Government's neutron

---

[148] *NATO Facts and Figures, op. cit.*, page #107.

[149] *Ibid.*, page #110.

bomb plans, the NATO Defense Planning Committee in Ministerial Session met in Brussels on May 17-18 to discuss the NATO long-term defense program. In the official communiqués of that meeting, emphasis was placed upon immediate improvement of anti-armor capabilities (which would be cited as the essential justification for the neutron bomb in subsequent public debate).

The DPC communiqués reflected policies for improving NATO defenses which had been established in a more general way at the May 10-11 meeting of the North Atlantic Council in London. On that occasion the Ministers had directed the DPC in Permanent Session to prepare "a time-phased defense action program concentrating on a limited number of areas where collective action is urgently required, and to review means for strengthening NATO programming and implementing machinery, for Ministerial approval in the spring of 1978 and to be transmitted to Heads of State and Government at their meeting in Washington". Additionally the DPC was tasked to formulate a program of short-term measures in areas of anti-armor, war reserve munitions, and readiness and reinforcement. [150]

Specific guidance from the DPC May 17-18 meeting to the NATO military authorities began with a current assessment of the posture of the Warsaw Pact forces, which were described as being capable of projecting Soviet power on a global scale. Improvements in the Pact's nuclear forces were cited, with specific mention being made of the expected deployment of the SS-20 mobile intermediate range ballistic missile, a system capable of striking targets throughout western Europe. In the area of conventional forces, the DPC Ministers

---

[150] Ministerial Sessions of the North Atlantic Council, *Texts of Final Communiqués - 1977*. Brussels: NATO Information Service, page #14.

assessed the Pact as having the capability to stage a major offensive in Europe without reinforcement from non-deployed forces in the east.

Because of this situation, said the DPC, particular attention should be paid to NATO's ability to respond to an attack after very little warning. The deterrence aspect of such a force posture was also addressed. NATO governments, said the Ministers, would have to be able to take prompt political decisions in times of tension, "so that NATO can deploy its forces in a timely and orderly fashion".

No specific mention was made of the neutron bomb, and only two extracts from the DPC Ministerial Communiqué might be interpreted as indicating that it - or something like it - had been discussed at all:

> 11. New Technology: Efficient application of modern technology, while not offering any inexpensive solutions, can provide opportunities, if applied through cooperative and timely efforts, for substantial improvement to the deterrent and defense capabilities of the Alliance.
>
> * * *
>
> 17. Priorities: Priority should be given to those capabilities which contribute directly to deterrence and to NATO's ability to withstand the initial phases of attack and, in particular, to measures which will enhance readiness and reinforcement capabilities and promote a collective approach to equipping, supporting, and training Alliance forces. [151]

---

[151] *Ibid.*, pages #17-20.

On June 6, 1977 the *Washington Post* broke the story of the development of the neutron bomb by the United States. Although the *Post* articles did identify the neutron warhead with the Lance missile, a key NATO weapon, NATO was not yet disposed to comment on the subject - at least not directly.

On June 8-9, 1977 the NATO Nuclear Planning Group met in Ottawa, Canada. The official report of that meeting said that the Ministers discussed "current and potential improvements in NATO nuclear forces" and agreed "that the Alliance's nuclear capability as a whole continued to make a valid contribution to deterrence, and underlined their determination to maintain essential equivalence between the nuclear capabilities of NATO and the Warsaw Pact". Again the only mention made of the neutron bomb - this time ill-disguised - was again under the heading of "new technology":

> 4. Ministers also considered a report by a study group on new technology. Their discussion centered on the political and military implications of this new technology, and they agreed that its efficient application, while not offering a low-cost and easy means of maintaining a credible and effective deterrent, could enhance NATO's capability to implement its strategy if deployed in a timely, integrated manner and exploited imaginatively. They gave directions for further work in this area, taking into account work recently initiated in the Defense Planning Committee to develop a long-term defense program for the Alliance for the 1980s.[152]

---

[152] *Ibid.*, pages #20-21.

Via the same August 17th White House announcement containing President Carter's decision to seek formal approval from NATO governments before ruling on neutron bomb production, Jody Powell told reporters that Carter expected to take final action early in September 1977.

Although the next "official" meeting of the Nuclear Planning Group was not scheduled until October, the growing controversy over the now-public "new technology" - the neutron bomb - resulted in a special, secret session of the NPG on September 20 at the NATO Headquarters in Brussels. A detailed presentation of the neutron bomb's state of development and theoretical use in NATO was given by U.S. Defense Department and Energy Research and Development Administration officials. The official line, when the story leaked out in the *Washington Post* three days later, was that no pressure for NATO support had been applied. "We made no sales pitch," said one participant; another official commented: "They (the other NATO representatives) were asked for their views without forcing them to take a position right then and there." [153]

Another account of that meeting, as expressed shortly thereafter in the communiqués of one NATO government to its Washington embassy, indicates that considerable urgency for NATO endorsement was expressed - specifically that the United States wanted the NATO countries to endorse both the production and the deployment of the neutron bomb by October 1977, but in any event not later than December 1977. The reason was twofold: first that there was considerable political pressure on the Carter Administration to resolve the issue, and secondly that swift approval of the neutron bomb would have to be forthcoming if the weapon's

---

[153] *Washington Post*, September 23, 1977, page #A-2.

financing were to be continued to be tied to the current U.S. Government budget then undergoing Congressional review.[154]

Later both President Carter and General Alexander Haig would state publicly that no other European government besides that of Germany had been willing to accept deployment of the neutron bomb. At the secret September 20 meeting, however, the government of Turkey endorsed production of the bomb and agreed to have neutron weapons stationed on its territory. A short time later, according to the press, Greece made the same decision. No other government was willing to commit itself, though most seemed favorably inclined towards the innovation.

The most vocal resistance - which stopped short of refusal - came from the Netherlands representative, while a somewhat less emphatic expression of dissent came from Denmark, which, as a matter of general policy, does not permit nuclear weapons to be stationed on its soil and which therefore felt that the opinions of nuclear weapons-hosting nations should have greater weight, and from Norway.[155]

No official account of the secret September 20 meeting was included in NATO's published official communiqués for 1977.[156]

The next regularly-scheduled meeting of the NATO Nuclear Planning Group took place in Bari, Italy on October 11-12, 1977, and Defense Secretary Harold Brown flew to Europe on October 6th to lay some groundwork for the expected endorsements. Before departing from

---

[154] Interview with a NATO government official, Washington, D.C., October 1979.

[155] *Ibid.*

[156] Ministerial Sessions of the North Atlantic Council, *Texts of Final Communiqués - 1977.*

Washington, Brown made public the news that the Soviet Union had developed the "operational capability" to intercept and destroy United States satellites in space. Calling this development "somewhat troublesome", Brown indicated that the United States did not have a similar "operational capability" concerning Soviet satellites. [157]

Why did Brown choose this particular moment to make such an announcement? One reason could be that, since NATO depends heavily upon satellite reconnaissance for both intelligence and targeting information, such a negative revelation might prod NATO governments to be all the more receptive to the neutron bomb proposal. If so, however, Brown was in for a disappointment. The United States Government did not receive any further endorsements of neutron bomb development or deployment. The official statement of the meeting on the topic was the sort of thing that governmental officials issue when they haven't been able to get anywhere on that topic:

> Ministers discussed the handling of the nuclear aspects of NATO's overall Long-Term Defense Program initiated last spring at the London NATO summit meeting. They discussed in broad terms possible approaches for theater nuclear force modernization both with regard to the medium- and the long-term programs. They considered proposals for further work in the area of theater nuclear force planning in preparation for the next meeting and as part of the Long Term Defense Program. In the context of the modernization of theater nuclear forces, they had a further

---

[157] New York Times, October 5, 1977, page #11.

exchange on reduced blast/enhanced radiation weapons, which confine their effects to a more limited area for military purposes. They agreed that their governments would continue their consideration of this subject.[158]

In Bari on October 11 Brown reiterated the Carter Administration policy that the United States was unlikely to go ahead with the neutron warhead project unless there was a "consensus" among its European allies in support of it. United States officials said to the press that the neutron bomb had been developed exclusively for NATO use, that discussion of the weapon had been going on for five years, and that the Nuclear Planning Group had reached its own consensus in favor of the weapon some time previously.

The problem was that publicity about potential deployment had stirred uneasiness in West Germany, Belgium, Great Britain, and the. Netherlands - the countries most likely to host weapons with the new warheads. The same sources said that Carter had now postponed his date of decision on the neutron bomb indefinitely, awaiting the NATO "consensus".

At the Bari meeting the West German representatives said somewhat uncertainly that they would not oppose deployment, but an explicit position statement was lacking. None of the other nations with representatives present - Belgium, Greece, Britain, and Italy - took an official position. Commented one American official: "It is not our purpose to jam anything down anybody's throat. If the weapon is not desired, it will not be produced."

---

[158] *Ministerial Sessions of the North Atlantic Council, op. cit.*, pages #22-23.

There was no dissent at the conference about the military usefulness of the neutron bomb. European concern was rather of a political nature; worry was expressed about the bomb's possible impact on SALT and on domestic politics.[159]

On the other hand the European governments were less fearful about the political implications of the cruise missile; they criticized the Carter Administration's SALT offer to limit that missile's range to 360 miles. Brown assured them that the United States was not placing a "permanent" limit on the missile, and that the administration "does not take nuclear weapons lightly".[160]

Some positive results were forthcoming from the Bari meeting. The United States, Britain, and Germany presented a joint arms and troop reduction proposal to NATO which, if accepted by the alliance, would hopefully break the current deadlock over that issue with the Warsaw Pact. Included in the proposal was the U.S. offer to withdraw 1,000 nuclear warheads and 29,000 troops from central Europe; Carter Administration representatives said that the proposal could address the neutron bomb as well.[161]

Nevertheless there was disgruntlement on both sides of the Atlantic after the Bari conference. Jimmy Carter made a last-minute decision to delete mention of neutron bomb production from a speech that he gave at the United Nations, and European leaders complained that they should have been given better information

---

[159] *Washington Post*, October 12, 1977, page #A-15. See also *New York Times*, October 12, 1977, page #1.

[160] *New York Times*, October 13, 1977, page #1.

[161] *New York Times*, October 25, 1977, page #1.

about technical improvements made in United States nuclear weaponry in Europe beginning in 1974.[162]

British Minister of Defence Frederick Mulley and German Defense Minister Georg Leber said in answer to questions that their governments would not make any immediate decisions on the neutron bomb question.[163] In the *Financial Times* analyst David Buchan made public Turkey's willingness to host the bomb and said that Greece had also given its approval. Italy, said Buchan, was reluctant to take, a position but might follow a decision by Britain or West Germany.[164]

The official communiqués of the next two NATO high-level meetings - those of the Defense Planning Committee in Brussels on December 6-7, 1977 and of the North Atlantic Council in Brussels on December 8-9, 1977 - contained not a single mention of the neutron bomb.[165]

During the December 6 DPC meeting, however, Norwegian General H.F. Zeiner-Gundersen, Chairman of NATO's Military Committee, spoke out forcefully in favor of the bomb, noting that NATO modernization efforts were still failing to keep pace with those of the Warsaw Pact.[166] And shortly before the meeting Manfred Worner, Chairman of the Armed Services Committee of the West German Bundestag, publicly urged deployment of the bomb as well, pointing out that, in the event of a Pact attack, it would take at least three months for American reinforcements to arrive and that an effective, credible

---

[162] *New York Times*, October 13, 1977, page #8.

[163] *Manchester Guardian*, October 23, 1977, page #8.

[164] *Financial Times*, October 26, 1977, page #4.

[165] *Ministerial Sessions of the North Atlantic Council, Texts of Final Communiqués - 1977.*

[166] *New York Times*, December 7, 1977, page #3.

weapons system was needed to permit NATO to survive in the interim period.[167]

NATO sources said, however, that the official and unofficial positions taken at the secret Nuclear Planning Group meeting of September 20, 1977 did not change [and would not, with the exception of Germany, until the time when government endorsements were made superfluous by President Carter's April 1978 decision].[168]

The next major mention of the neutron bomb in a NATO nation took place in the British House of Commons on February 22, 1978, when Prime Minister James Callaghan defended the value of the weapon and accused the Soviet Union of launching an anti-neutron bomb propaganda campaign which completely ignored the greater destructive power of the SS-20 mobile missile which it had begun to introduce into the Warsaw Pact arsenal [see Chapter Eight]. Labour MP's responded, however, by urging Callaghan to denounce the neutron bomb.[169]

The following day the *Times of London* came out in support of Callaghan, saying that the real reason for the Soviets' campaign was not moral indignation but rather a fear that the neutron bomb would threaten the strategic value of their existing tank superiority in Europe.[170] On March 4th the *Financial Times* added its editorial endorsement, saying that public criticism of the bomb had subsided, that the weapon was not likely to increase

---

[167] *New York Times*, December 2, 1977, page #2. See also Manfred Worner, "NATO Defenses and Tactical Nuclear Weapons" in Wolfram Hanrieder (Ed.), *Arms Control and Security: Current Issues* (Boulder: Westview Press, 1979), page #262.

[168] Interview with a NATO government official, Washington, D.C., October 1979.

[169] *Times of London*, February 22, 1978, page #1.

[170] *Times of London*, February 23, 1978, page #17.

the probability of nuclear war, and that both Britain and West Germany should officially endorse it. [171]

A short time later, however, the neutron bomb suffered a setback on the continent. On March 6th Dr. Rölof Kruisinga, Dutch Defense Minister, announced his resignation following a difference of opinion on the bomb with other members of the cabinet.[172] Kruisinga was known as a strong opponent of the bomb, and the reaction of the Dutch Parliament three days later was to adopt a resolution opposing production of the neutron bomb and calling upon the government to communicate that position as policy to the United States and other NATO nations. Prime Minister Andreas van Agt refused, however, saying that the government's view was that further NATO talks would have to be held before an official position could be taken.[173]

On February 24th there was a secret meeting of NATO Ambassadors in Brussels, attended by Leslie H. Gelb, head of the State Department's Bureau of Political and Military Affairs. Gelb presented a proposal that the neutron bomb be used as a bargaining chip to get the Soviets to limit or halt deployment of their SS-20 in eastern Europe. The converse side of this move was to make it easier to proceed with neutron bomb production from a political standpoint, because a Soviet refusal would tend to place the onus on them. Some immediate doubt on the part of U.S. defense analysts surfaced, however; there was a problem of "symmetry" in the proposal. The SS-20, unlike the neutron bomb, is not a tactical battlefield weapon but a medium-range ballistic missile with three independent nuclear warheads.

---

[171] *Financial Times*, March 4, 1978, page #12.

[172] *Times of London*, March 6, 1978, page #4.

[173] *New York Times*, March 9, 1978, page #5.

Gelb introduced another option - for NATO to use the issue of the neutron bomb in the NATO-Warsaw Pact troop reduction talks currently stalled in Vienna. Once again there was a "symmetry" problem, though, because there was no obvious trade that the Pact could make.[174]

The NATO negotiations were discussed publicly by Defense Secretary Harold Brown in a Washington, D.C. news conference on March 10. He did not speculate on the reception of the proposal by other NATO members, though it was rumored after the Brussels meeting that the British and Germans had been favorable while the Dutch had not [on the grounds that formal introduction of the neutron bomb into negotiations would imply their government's a priori acceptance of its production].[175] In the Netherlands a strong anti-neutron bomb campaign organized by the Dutch Communist student and key leader Niko Schöten was under way; by April 16th more than one million signatures had been obtained for petitions against the manufacture or deployment of the weapon.[176]

The United States did not have to wait long for the Soviet response. Two days after Brown's press conference, *Tass* rejected the proposal.[177] On March 22 General Haig, NATO SACEUR, responded with a statement to the effect that the Warsaw Pact was now approaching parity with the United States' 7,000 nuclear

---

[174] *Washington Post*, March 10, 1978, page #A-1.

[175] *New York Times*, March 11, 1978, Page #4.

[176] *New York Times*, April 16, 1978, page #3 and April 19, 1978, page #4.

[177] *New York Times*, March 12, 1978, page #6.

warheads in Europe. The neutron bomb, said Haig, was essential to preserve NATO's lead.[178]

The next meeting of the NATO Nuclear Planning Group was scheduled for Denmark in mid-April. At the end of March officials of the Carter Administration were saying that an agreement would be reached at that meeting to allow the U.S. to begin production of the bomb immediately, delaying its deployment for up to two years while continuing efforts were made to reach arms control agreements based upon it.[179]   Meanwhile, said John Robinson of the *Washington Post*, "it is clear that the Americans want the decision on the neutron warhead out of the way before the NATO summit meeting scheduled for Washington May 30-3l."[180] On March 30th the *New York Times* editorially advocated that the NATO governments agree to deployment.[181]

Before the time arrived for the Nuclear Planning Group meeting, however, the U.S. Government's pressure on NATO suddenly eased. The preliminary negotiations in Brussels were abruptly called off by the White House during the last week in March. Administration sources told Walter Pincus of the *Washington Post* on March 27 that Carter had not yet made his final production decision. "That decision had been made some time ago, but now we are in a holding pattern." Amid speculation that Carter had once again reversed himself and was now inclined against production, one source told Pincus that he had only made "a decision to delay the decision".

"Because of the international political controversy that has developed around neutron weapons and the

---

[178] *New York Times*, March 22, 1978, page #8.

[179] *New York Times*, March 28, 1978, page #7.

[180] Robinson, John, *op. cit.*

[181] *New York Times*, March 30, 1978, page 20.

President's seven-month delay in making his promised production decision," said Pincus in a *Washington Post* article, "White House and other government officials are extremely sensitive about discussing the matter. Yesterday, for example, officials repeatedly requested during interviews that they not be quoted by name or even by agency."[182]

Similar apprehension was displayed by some officials of NATO - who also insisted upon their anonymity - over what they described as the "appearance" of the Carter Administration's vacillation on issues rather than the substance of those issues. Further postponement of a neutron bomb decision, they feared, might convince the Soviet Union that its propaganda effort against the weapon had in fact worked and that efforts in this area should be redoubled.[183]

The "holding pattern" lasted until April 7, 1978, when President Carter made the decision to "defer" production of the neutron warhead. Two days before Carter made his announcement, the Federal Republic of Germany announced its public endorsement of the deployment of the new warhead, subject to (a) a decision by the U.S. alone to produce the weapon, (b) linking of the neutron weapons to renewed arms control negotiations, and (c) stationing of the warhead in other NATO countries besides Germany. This support, such as it was, came too late - or was simply insufficient - to change Carter's assessment of the situation.

After the deferment announcement there was a certain amount of confusion in NATO, centering generally on the impact of the American decision on the German government in view of its endorsement of deployment. [This will be examined more closely in

---

[182] *Washington Post*, March 28, 1978, page #A-3.

[183] *New York Times*, April 1, 1978, page #5.

Chapter Seven.) But the Carter Administration did not make the deferment announcement without doing its best to explain the rationale to NATO. On April 7 Ambassadors of 15 NATO countries were informed of Carter's decision at a private meeting in Brussels. The United States representatives stressed that Carter intended to retain the option of producing the bomb at a later date rather than scrapping it completely.[184] NATO Secretary General Joseph Luns responded that "the move should inspire the Soviet Union to show restraint in its own troop and arms programs", and the Ambassadors, he continued:

> ... reiterated their concern about the increasing offensive capabilities of Soviet conventional forces and with the continued expansion and improvement of offensive Soviet nuclear forces. They therefore stressed the need to modernize NATO's military capabilities, both conventional and nuclear.
>
> In this connection, the allies noted that the United States intended to proceed with the modernization of the Lance [missile] system and of the 8-inch gun, leaving open the [option of] installing of enhanced radiation (neutron) elements.
>
> At the same time, the allies underlined the importance of contributing to European and world security through arms control and disarmament and through acts of mutual restraint as between NATO and the Warsaw Pact.
>
> The allies therefore expressed understanding for the U.S. decision to defer

---

[184] *New York Times*, April 7, 1978, page #1.

production of enhanced radiation weapons. The allies agreed that further action would be influenced by the degree to which the Soviet Union showed restraint in its arms programs and force deployments which affect NATO security."[185]

In London British Prime Minister James Callaghan's office issued a formal statement endorsing Carter's decision and calling on the Kremlin to "respond to the President's decision by measures to moderate the threat we see, from the scale of their buildup of both nuclear and conventional armaments."[186]   At the same time, however, the *Times of London* criticized Carter for his decision, saying that the security of Western Europe would be very much affected as a consequence.[187]   The *Financial Times* accused Carter of being "too erratic" in his dealings with the Soviets and said that his decision could reflect either domestic pressure in the United States or pressure from the Soviet Union.[188]   On April 10 these same criticisms were voiced in Canada by the *Toronto Star*.[189]

Focusing on Carter's statement that production could still be started in the future, however, the *Manchester Guardian* said that the neutron bomb's value

---

[185] *Washington Post*, April 8, 1978, page #A-2. See also *New York Times*, April 8, 1978, page #7.

[186] *New York Times*, April 8, 1978, page #6.

[187] *Times of London*, April 7, 1978, page #17.

[188] *Financial Times*, April 10, 1978, page #14.

[189] *Toronto Star*, April 10, 1978, page #8.

as a credible deterrent outweighed the risk of "adding another component to the nuclear stockpile".[190]

A few days later the *Financial Times* softened its earlier criticisms, saying that "if European governments cannot agree on what they want or are too afraid of their voters to say what they want", then they ought not to shift the blame to Carter. It is not wrong to expect leadership from the Americans, added the *Times*, but it is unreasonable for the alliance to expect the United States to assume responsibility for all alliance decisions.[191]

Again in Canada the *Edmonton Journal* praised Carter for the deferment decision, suggesting that the prospect that the neutron bomb might still be produced added an incentive for the SALT-II talks to proceed constructively.[192]   And the *Toronto Star* reversed its judgment on June 3, claiming that the neutron bomb "is no more insidious than the U.S.S.R.'s nuclear weapons, which have a 400-mile death range". The neutron bomb, added the *Star*, would force Soviet generals to radically change the "blitzkrieg" tactics to which they had become accustomed.[193]

Speaking for the Belgian government, Foreign Minister Henri Simonet said on April 28th that Carter's hopes of gaining concessions from the Soviet Union by deferring production were unrealistic.[194]

Canadian Prime Minister praised the Carter decision, calling it "far-sighted" and expressing the hope

[190] *Manchester Guardian*, April 9, 1978, page #10 and April 16, 1978, page #10.

[191] *Financial Times*, April 17, 1978, page #17.

[192] *Edmonton Journal*, April 25, 1978, page #4.

[193] *Toronto Star*, June 3, 1978, page #III-2.

[194] *New York Times*, April 28, 1978, page #12.

that the Soviet Union's response would allow the bomb to be deferred indefinitely.[195]

On May 1st *Atlas* magazine published a sampling of neutron bomb opinions from the press in France, the Netherlands, Britain, East Germany, Switzerland, Denmark, the Soviet Union, China, Mexico, and Canada. *Atlas* said that world opinion appeared to be thoroughly divided on the subject.[196]

And from France came word from General Guy Mery, French Chief of Staff, that France was considering developing its own neutron weapon.[197] An earlier report in *France-Soir* that France had detonated a subsurface neutron bomb on the Mururoa Atoll in the South Pacific and that France would have an effective neutron warhead in three to four years was not commented on by the. French government.[198]

On October 19 Harold Brown said at a secret session of the Nuclear Planning Group that there had been no sign of Soviet restraint in Warsaw Pact arms buildup since the April 7 decision.[199] Simultaneously Jody Powell announced in Washington that Carter had ordered production of components to begin[200], and on January 6, 1979, at a four-power summit meeting, Carter, Callaghan, Helmut Schmidt and Valery Giscard d'Estaing agreed

---

[195] *Toronto Star*, May 27, 1978, page #1.

[196] *Atlas*, May 1, 1978, pages #31-34 and June 1, 1978, page #13.

[197] *New York Times*, June 12, 1978, page #14.

[198] *New York Times*, April 20, 1978, page #10.

[199] *New York Times*, October 19, 1978, page #45.

[200] *New York Times*, October 19, 1978, page #5.

that "some kind of modernization" of the neutron bomb project would now be necessary.[201]

And there, for the time being, the neutron bomb's discussion in a principally-NATO context came to a halt.

Even with the advantage of hindsight it is difficult to judge the interaction because of the extensive security and carefully-phrased statements that surrounded the negotiations, but it can be said that the mechanisms of NATO itself do not deserve to be faulted on grounds of inefficiency. The consultation and planning groups served their designed purpose; the failure to achieve consensus was rather a political problem of the individual nations involved. It appears that each nation simply wanted the others to go first; on a more comprehensive scale there seemed to be a tacit polarization on this move between the United States and all of the West European NATO members.

Jimmy Carter could find no single solution acceptable to NATO. If he decided to proceed with the bomb unilaterally, he could have made himself the sole target of anti-neutron bomb sentiment in both the United States and abroad - even if European governments might secretly be relieved that NATO would have the new weapon. If Carter chose to await foreign ratification of the bomb, he would be accused - as he was - of abandoning America's position of leadership in NATO. His ultimate attempt at compromise probably drew the most favorable reaction that any solution under these circumstances could have achieved.

At the same time the entire episode reflected little credit to the West European members of NATO, who for years had been expressing dissatisfaction with their lack of influence over the American nuclear umbrella and

---

[201] New York Times, January 6, 1979, page #1.

who, now that they finally had a chance to participate in a key nuclear decision, got cold feet.

Why the cold feet? The most apparent explanation is simply that they were more sensitive to anti-nuclear and anti-neutron sentiment on the part of their respective populations than they were worried about the actual threat of a Warsaw Pact invasion of the west.

Dr. Hans von Plötz of the German Embassy in Washington stresses that the West Europeans' image of the Soviet Union and its allies is in many ways less intimidating than the image that many Americans have. They have learned to live with them as neighbors - somewhat bothersome but nonetheless human neighbors, whereas Americans tend to stereotype Russians in a somewhat fear-inspiring image - a holdover, perhaps, from the "Red scare" days of the 1940s and 1950s. Plötz' point is not that the Warsaw Pact presents no threat, but rather that it is not a threat which hangs constantly over West Europe. One might call this a kind of "reverse Finlandization" in the sense that the very fact of surviving so long in the face of the Soviet threat has tended to make many West Europeans complacent about that threat, foreboding military statistics notwithstanding.

In the absence of a "real" perceived threat, then, it is not altogether surprising that the European governments of NATO would be tempted to place their own stability and preservation as intranational political groups above measures to deter a "false" threat. It isn't the sort of attitude which any one of the countries in question would be anxious to announce; it would of course be offensive to Washington and possibly to the brunt-bearing European NATO members as well. But it would explain the European behavior in this instance.

Had "Finlandization" fears played a noticeable part, they would have been evident as comparatively extreme and emotional pro-deployment sentiment by various countries or interest groups within them. This was not the case; such pro-deploynent sentiment as was voiced was generally along the line of the reasoned, deterrence-oriented approach of the Carter Administration.

The European arguments against the neutron bomb because of its strictly-neutron characteristics do not tell the whole story either. The same reticence greeted the December 1979 proposal to introduce cruise and Pershing-II missiles into NATO, with the Netherlands, Denmark, and Norway again inclining against deployment. One must judge the "anti-neutron bomb" sentiment of 1977-1978, then, as "anti-nuclear weapons" sentiment or even just "anti-new weapons" sentiment, which casts the neutron bomb proper in at least a slightly less villainish image.

Does the neutron bomb episode teach any notable lessons applicable to future nuclear decisions in the alliance? With the perspective of hindsight some of the governments involved were probably less than elated with their showing, and quite possibly that residual embarrassment was instrumental in inspiring the alliance to reach a consensus in December 1979 on the Pershing-II and cruise missile question. [There was dissent, but the decision was made, and the entire membership formally agreed to stand behind it.] And to be fair it must be noted that the neutron bomb episode caught "public" Europe as much by surprise as it did the "public" United States, and under those circumstances governments tended to be more prone to caution than they might be in an instance where there were no sudden shocks.

Given the attendant circumstances, then, NATO receives reasonably good marks for its handling of the neutron bomb problem - particularly when one draws the distinction between functions of the alliance per se and functions of the individual countries that compose the alliance. In the chapter to follow a closer look will be taken at the key European country in the neutron bomb dialogue - the Federal Republic of Germany.

Chapter Seven:
Germany and the Neutron Bomb

The neutron bomb was of particular importance to the Federal Republic of Germany because, should the bomb be developed, it was in the Federal Republic that it would primarily be stationed. Though Germany's major contributions to the political exchange concerning the weapon did not take place until early 1978, the Germans' unofficial opinion - and their eventual official one - could later be seen to have a significant impact upon the Carter Administration's decisions on both development and deployment.

To understand why Germany acted as it did during the episode, it is first necessary to consider the cultural environment in which foreign policy and defense policy of the Federal Republic is formulated. It is not an environment which has come into being with the current administration; its roots are considerably deeper than that.

The history of twentieth-century Germany is a history of domestic turmoil and catastrophic international warfare - at least until the end of World War II, when the eastern and western subdivisions of the country effectively lost their prerogatives for independent action and came under the control of the Soviet Union and the United States respectively.

So devastating was the legacy of "politics" under the National Socialists - when virtually every facet of life was forcibly politicized - that the end of the war brought about an almost complete destruction of the established social strata. What began to arise in the Western zones during the period of reconstruction was, in the opinion of sociologist Helmut Schelsky, an almost complete leveling into a broad middle-class culture, with traditional values giving way to the consumer-gratification atmosphere of the United States.[202]

The postwar elite in the Federal Republic, according to sociologist Ralf Dahrendorf, is not dominated or even substantially influenced by the old aristocracy, but is composed of the leaders of various social and economic fields who attained their status by personal achievement and financial power. Because of its newness and pluralistic composition, this new elite does not possess class consciousness per se; rather it is a power-oriented sector of society.[203]

Patterns of political participation by the general populace reveal a similar lack of class solidarity. Eighty to ninety percent of the eligible voters cast ballots in German elections, but few people participate in political affairs more actively than that. In the early 1970s, for instance, German political parties included only about three percent of the people in their membership. About two or three percent of those who voted for CDU and FDP candidates were members of those parties, and only about six percent of SPD supporters were party members. In part this reflects the nature of the German party system, wherein the parties are regarded as nomination bases for political candidates rather than vehicles for the expression of popular opinion. When party leaders do attempt to deal with popular issues, it is generally through negotiation with major interest group leaders rather than through any attempt to seek grass-root input.

Politics in postwar Germany, then, is regarded as a specialty field - a career for professionals and not a forum

---

[202] Keefe, Eugene K. *et al.*, *Area Handbook for the Federal Republic of Germany*. Washington, D.C.: U.S. Government Printing Office, 1975, pages #124-125.

[203] Dahrendorf, Ralf, *Society and Democracy in Germany*. Garden City: Doubleday and Company, 1967, page #94.

for protracted popular involvement. In this one may say that it follows the example of the United States, wherein political parties are similarly remote from the average citizen and offices of major consequence are effectively reserved to a professional elite.[204]

If Germans shy away from active involvement in the formal political process, that does not necessarily mean that they are uninterested in political developments. They have of course undergone many years of seeing how directly and how crucially international and bloc political decisions can affect them. While many Americans may have been inclined to regard the Cold War environment of West Europe as something distant and "theoretical" - the stuff for spy novels and occasional "optional" crises - its significance for the German was [and remains - *détente* notwithstanding] something more immediate and practical.

At the best of times it has to do with the ease of commerce and individual travel; at times of tension it has reawakened the specter of another ruinous war - again fought in Germany and again contributed to by a number of other nations for their own political motives. Appropriately the German populace pays significant attention to it.

In *German Foreign Policies, West and East* Peter Merkl observed that West Germany's "attentive public" for foreign affairs is rather large. He cited a recent cross-national study by Daniel H. Willick as indicating that 27.1 percent of West Germans are "very interested in international affairs" as compared to 16.9 percent Englishmen, 11.9 percent Frenchmen, 8.7 percent Japanese, and 4.4 percent Italians. Richard Merritt and Ellen Pirro, he added, provided additional data to substantiate this variance. Moreover, said Merkl, the

---

[204] Keefe, *op. cit.*, page #235.

mainstream of this interest is in what Viggo Graf Blücher terms *grosse Politik* (foreign and world politics) as opposed to domestic issues. [205]

What this suggests is that the sovereignty and territorial integrity of the Federal Republic are substantially more immediate items of concern to the individual German than they are to the average American. They are not gambler's playing chips whose risk in the spirit of some ideological game is acceptable. If the stability of the current situation in Europe were to end, the Federal Republic's famous "economic miracle" and the relatively comfortable life-style enjoyed by its citizens could be obliterated in nuclear war potentially far more thorough in its destruction than World War II. This fact has become something of a *cliché* in U.S. politics due to its extensive propaganda use, but it is difficult for the inhabitants of Germany to regard it equally casually.

There are perhaps three general foreign policies of the Federal Republic which have a direct bearing on the way in which it reacted to the special situation posed by the neutron bomb question - (1) commitment to the future prospects for a united Europe, (2) commitment to a strong NATO, and (3) commitment to *détente* with the communist bloc. A brief illustration of the nationally-perceived significance of each of these general orientations may be helpful:

The commitment to a united Europe: This is technically both a German national policy and a supranational consensus in which Germany partakes. In his Memoirs Konrad Adenauer saw the German policy

---

[205] Merkl, Peter H., *German Foreign Policies, West and East*. Santa Barbara: ABC-Clio Press, 1974, pages #13-14. See also his "The Role of Public Opinion in West German Foreign Policy" in Wolfram Hanrieder (Ed.), *West German Foreign Policy 1949-1979* (Boulder: Westview Press, 1979).

principally in terms of the historic tension between Germany and other continental countries:

> I thought a great deal about the problem of a United States of Europe with Germany as a part. In a future United States of Europe I saw the greatest and most lasting security for Germany's western neighbors.
>
> The French fear of German resurgence which caused France to press for a policy of dismemberment of Germany seemed to be altogether exaggerated. After 1945 Germany lay prostrate - militarily, economically, and politically - and in my opinion this condition was a sufficient guarantee that Germany could not again threaten France.
>
> In the future United States of Europe, I saw great hope for Europe and thus for Germany. We had to try to remind France, Holland, Belgium, and the other European countries that they were, as we were, situated in Western Europe, that they are and will forever remain our neighbors, that any violence they do to us must in the end lead to trouble, and that no lasting peace can be established in Europe if it is founded on force alone.
>
> General de Gaulle had recognized this in his speech at Saarbrücken in August 1945: "Frenchmen and Germans must let bygones be

bygones, must work together, and must remember that they are Europeans."[206]

The supranational consensus presumably received its modern impetus from the European Congress of 1948 and reached realization in the European Community. In his political autobiography Willy Brandt said:

> The West witnessed a reawakening of the ancient dream of European unity, a distant vision which had continually fired the best minds in Europe. Though dispelled again and again, it survived in the internationalism of the labor movement, whose social democrats were natural Europeans from the very first.
> Meanwhile, responsibility for the fortunes of France, West Germany and Italy was initially entrusted to conservative politicians in the Catholic mold. Robert Schuman, Alcide de Gasperi and Konrad Adenauer translated Jean Monnet's ideas into reality and set to work to create the basis of a political union or federation, first through joint supervision of the coal and steel industries and later by means of an economic community.
> The French proposal that America's demand for the rearming of the Federal Republic within the framework of the Western Alliance should be countered by the

---

[206] Adenauer, Konrad, *Memoirs 1945-1953*. Chicago: Henry Regnery Company, 1966, page #37. See also Manfred Worner, "West Germany and the New Dimensions of Security" in Wolfram Hanrieder (Ed.), *West German Foreign Policy 1949-1979* (Boulder: Westview Press, 1979), page #41. Worner comments that under Adenauer West Germany made three "historical, irrevocable" choices: (1) to align itself with the West, (2) to seek a united Europe, and (3) to choose freedom rather than unification.

establishment of a European defense association might possibly have shortened the road to political unity. This plan was thwarted by the opposition of conservative and communist deputies in the French National Assembly, but also by the abstention of the British, who at first opposed all forms of integration under Churchill's aging leadership.

It turned out that national egoisms had yet to be wholly overcome. The road to European union has proved rough and arduous, yet the Treaty of Rome laid the foundations of a union which could and had to be developed further.

As fears of political and military pressure from the Soviet Union waned, so progress became slower. It has taken people time to bow to the realization that Europe can and must be more than a bulwark against the communist menace, in other words, a product of peace and constructive cooperation.[207]

Though the German government's motives for European unification may have changed - from fear of the German-French conflict to fear of the Soviet military threat to a positive approach towards economic opportunism - the policy itself has remained in force and has been actively promulgated.

There is also a continuing national/supranational security aspect to this European unification policy. This is described most succinctly in *White Papers on The Security of the Federal Republic of Germany and the Development of the Federal Armed Forces* issued

---

[207] Brandt, Willy, *People and Politics: The Years 1960-1975*. Boston: Little, Brown and Company, 1976, page #244.

periodically by the Bonn government. In the 1975/1976 edition of this document, for example, the object of the European Community was described as being not only economic cooperation in the short term but, as agreed upon in principle in Paris on October 19, 1972, progress toward a European Union before the end of the 1970s. The decade has now gone and Europe is still a long way from attaining fall political union, but what is relevant and important to this study is that the Germans appear to have undertaken - formally at least - a commitment to think of Europe's interests as a whole as opposed to those of Germany exclusively. [208]

This commitment would be tested in two ways in the neutron bomb episode. First there was the question of Germany's actual attention to the views and opinions of other NATO countries on a question which affected Germany more than any other nation, since the theoretical battlefield of a Warsaw Pact invasion would be located primarily on German soil. Secondly there was the question of German reaction towards the attitudes displayed by other NATO countries concerning the neutron bomb. Were they taking positions based on consideration for what use of the bomb might actually mean to the Germans, in other words, or were their policies determined rather by purely intranational considerations unrelated to Germany?

The 1975/1976 policy was reaffirmed in the 1979 *White Paper* with some specific emphases, most notably an expression of appreciation to the United States for its own encouragement of the European unity movement and a call for further Franco-German conciliation and cooperation. Such cooperation, stresses the *White Paper*,

---

[208] Press and Information Office of the Federal Republic of Germany, *The Security of the Federal Republic of Germany and the Development of the Federal Armed Forces: White Paper 1975/1976.* Bonn: Federal Minister of Defense, 1976, pages #46 and #54.

is "not directed against anybody. The main goal of Germany's European policy is to continue to develop, step by step, economic integration and political cooperation on the part of the member countries of the Community until European union has been achieved."

Special mention is also made of the European Council, a forum in which Heads of State and Government and Foreign Ministers work together, and of the first direct elections to the European Parliament on June 10, 1979. Anticipating the admission to the EC of Greece, Portugal, and Spain in the near future, the *White Paper* promises that the EC will enhance their efforts towards democracy, contribute to their economic prosperity, and thus ultimately help ensure their long-term stability. The European monetary system, it adds, is an important step towards the ultimate goal of an economic and monetary union. [209]

Emphasis is given here to this pan-European interest of Germany because the Germans themselves evidence interest in it. As one considers how they behaved in the face of the neutron bomb question, it may be helpful to assess their opinions and decisions according to their impact on this internationalist policy. It may not have been the deciding factor or even one of the more vital ones, but it probably was the case that a measure of Germany's reluctance to embrace the neutron bomb derived from her perception of other European countries' abhorrence for it.

The commitment to a strong NATO: On this subject the 1975/1976 *White Paper* is adamant and uncompromising. "The external security of our country," it begins, "is assured by virtue of her membership in the

---

[209] Press and Information Office of the Federal Republic of Germany, The Security of the Federal Republic of Germany and the Development of the Federal Armed Forces: White Paper 1979. Bonn: Federal Minister of Defense, 1979, pages #26-28.

Atlantic Alliance. Without the Alliance, peace would not be safeguarded."

This is true at face value, but what the *White Paper* does not say is that there is very little in the way of an alternative open to the Federal Republic. The rearming of West Germany in the decade after World War II was greeted with not a little apprehension by those neighbors who had suffered German occupation in that war, and Adenauer's willingness to put all German forces under NATO command - and hence to effectively place the responsibility for those forces' behavior in the bands of the United States - was probably the only way that rearmament could have taken place without a good deal of agitation in Europe as a whole.

Even so there was considerable ill feeling on the subject. Today NATO may be less necessary to the toleration of a German Army in the west, but the alliance's control of nuclear weapons is now just as indispensable to Germany. Having renounced national nuclear weapons, the Germans would be helpless in the face of a Warsaw Pact invasion using nuclear arms without NATO tactical nuclear arms to back them up. To support NATO, says the *White Paper* accordingly, the German Federal Government will continue to support a efforts aimed at ensuring the effectiveness of the Alliance, to include due contribution to alleviating the defense burdens of the economically weaker allies.

Finally the *White Paper* points out the role of NATO as the "forward defense line" of the United States, arguing that the global balance of power and the relative equilibrium in Europe depend upon NATO's effectiveness. "An expansion of the Soviet sphere of influence to include western Europe would have a decisive impact upon the security of the United States of America and its position as a world power." [210]

On the subject of Germany's own commitment to NATO, the 1979 *White Paper* praises the alliance as an effective peace-keeping instrument, a supranational defense community of free nations who have managed to solve NATO's periodic problems with a view to preserving its overall solidarity and security. "Solidarity in the Alliance does not exclude differing points of view on specific questions. But it does call for unanimous acknowledgment of the principle that the security of the individual is contingent upon the security of the whole. It is the security interest of the whole which makes possible freedom of action on the part of the individual while limiting it at the same time. "

The 1979 *White Paper* brings up the "troubled partnership" question and the consequent inclination of many observers to view internal NATO conflicts as more critical than they actually are:

> Ever since the Alliance has existed, it has had to cope with internal difficulty and tension. The multifarious problems which arise from the continually changing global balance of power, from the differing political and economic interests of the parties to the Alliance, and by no means least from the growing financial burden, will continue to beset NATO.
>
> To date the Alliance has settled its difficulties in a manner in keeping with the character of a voluntary association of sovereign states. Mutual aid, mediation in disputes, and ever closer consultation have

---

[210] *White Paper 1975/1976*, pages #46-47.

been the helpful means to that end. There are no grounds to doubt that this spirit of partnership will continue to determine the future of the Alliance.[211]

On the subject of *détente* the *White Paper* sees no inconsistency between the furtherance of peaceful cooperation and the preservation of a strong NATO. Chancellor Schmidt, it notes, made this point in a policy statement on June 1, 1978. "There is no contradiction," he said, "between limiting armaments and strengthening the Western Alliance, but an inherent logical association. It is a matter of complementary political goals; the assurance of the military balance is an indispensable prerequisite for durable *détente*."[212]

The commitment to *détente* with the communist bloc: A succinct and authoritative statement of this most crucial policy was given by Federal Chancellor Helmut Schmidt in an address to the Bundestag on December 16, 1976 - after the conclusion of the series of memorable treaties with Poland and East Germany and only six months before the neutron bomb controversy was to begin.

The German Federal Government, said Schmidt, had consistently pursued a policy of permanent integration within the community of free western democracies - a principal aim of West Germany since its formation. *Détente* is considered to be supplementary to that policy - a way of establishing good neighborly relations with the East - just as the Federal Republic also believes in a policy of "partnership based on equality" with the nations of the Third World.

---

[211] *White Paper 1979*, pages #12-14.

[212] *Ibid.*

However, warned Schmidt, "the steady increase of the Warsaw Pact's military strength continues, in spite of the fact that the military potential of that group of states has already reached a level far beyond that which is necessary for purely defensive purposes."[213] Germany, he hoped, would be able to play an active part in European disarmament efforts, particularly through the Mutual Balanced Force Reductions talks in Vienna. On a worldwide basis, he continued, Germany would encourage greater disarmament and arms-control efforts and was looking, forward with particular enthusiasm to the special session on disarmament of the United Nations General Assembly due to be held in 1978.[214]

The 1975/1976 *White Paper* from the Ministry of Defense takes a somewhat more pragmatic look at *détente*. The extent to which real *détente* is possible, it states, is delineated by the differing takeoff points and ideological designs of East and West. The communist interpretation of "*détente*" allows for international cooperation, mainly of an economic nature, but it also demands that the international class struggle between the social orders must continue. Hence the effectiveness of *détente* is inevitably limited to nation-to-nation relations and cannot be taken to include genuine efforts to reduce tension between or reconcile social orders.

The German government, said the *White Paper*, was willing to work toward better relations with the East despite these difficulties. Some progress could be made toward preventing war, improving economic cooperation, affording greater freedom of movement of people, and facilitating the exchange of information between East and West. There would be the risk that efforts toward *détente*

---

[213] *Ibid.*

[214] Auswärtiges Amt, *Abrüstung und Rüstungskontrolle: Dokumenten.* Bonn: Köllen Druck & Verlag, 1978, page #95.

might be taken for *détente* itself - that the negotiating process might provide an illusion of friendship and cooperation which would not yield substantive results. "Wishful thinking does not promote *détente*, rather does it jeopardize, it; a strong defense capability is and will continue to be the foundation from which steps of *détente* appear to be most promising. Without adequate provisions to safeguard our external security there can be no *détente*."[215]

The 1979 *White Paper* adds that the basis for an effective *détente* is the principle of the renunciation of force - and even the threat of force - as embodied in the agreements and arrangements entered into by the Federal Republic during recent years with the Soviet Union, Poland, Czechoslovakia, and the GDR, together with the Quadripartite Agreement on Berlin and the Final Act of the CSCE. Such accomplishments constitute particular proof that concrete agreements can be reached with regard to practical problems, even if questions of principle would have to remain open. The *White Paper* cites the Federal Republic's own insistence on refusing to compromise on the German Question, "in keeping with the mandate given by the Basic Law", as a case in point.[216]

An initial picture emerges, therefore, of a Germany whose outlook is essentially rational, peaceful, and supranational - yet simultaneously committed to a strong defense against the threat posed by the Warsaw Pact. As will be seen, this picture tended to be borne out by the way in which the Federal Republic reacted to the neutron bomb episode as it came to focus on that country.

Published indications are that, if the NATO governments knew before mid-1977 of the plans for deploying the neutron bomb in Europe, they attached no

---

[215] White Paper 1975/1976, page #68.

[216] White Paper 1979, pages #42-43.

special importance to them, assuming the measure to be a minor, continuing modification in NATO weaponry rather than a major ethical issue. A White House aide later said that, when the West Germans had been briefed on the ER weapons in 1976, they were "not tremendously enthusiastic" about them.[217] I assume that if there had been unusual interest devoted to the neutron bomb prior to its becoming an issue in the United States, then President Carter's attention would have been focused upon it some time before he "read about it in the papers".

The first indication to Germany that the neutron bomb was going to be a major issue probably came in early July 1977, when NATO Headquarters in Brussels was being sought out by neutron bomb proponents for encouraging comments that could be relayed to the United States Senate, which was then moving toward a funding decision (resolved on July 13 in favor of the bomb). General Haig was publicly quoted as saying that the NATO allies had given the neutron weapons "enthusiastic support".[218] Not so, said the West German Embassy in Washington, where a spokesman commented: "I could not agree as far as the German side is concerned. Public discussion only now is picking up steam, and there is no clear-cut opinion yet."[219]

A few days later came the first feedback from Germany on the U.S. Senate decision to approve funding. On July 17 Egon Bahr, former chief strategist for former Chancellor Willy Brandt, Minister for Development Aid for Chancellor Helmut Schmidt, and now executive secretary of Schmidt's ruling Social Democratic Party,

---

[217] Pincus, Walter, "Kissinger Reportedly Unaware of Neutron Weapons Decision" in the *Washington Post*, July 19, 1977, page #A-2.

[218] *Ibid.*

[219] *Ibid.*

was quoted in the current edition of the weekly party newspaper *Vorwärts* as describing the neutron bomb as "a symbol of the perversion of human thinking". "Is this supposed to be the latest progress?" fumed Bahr. "Is mankind going crazy?" The neutron weapon, he continued, had "turned the scales of values upside down. The aim now is to take care of materials. Man has become second class."

Bahr's comments, the first by a major political official within the ruling Bonn coalition to comment on the proposed deployment, could have been a trial balloon sent up by Schmidt to signal his government's "moral repugnance" to a weapons system which could have elicited the, same adverse reaction among Germany's anti-nuclear groups as it was apparently doing in the United States. The spontaneity of Bahr's outburst is all the more difficult to credit in view of the German government's prior knowledge of the bomb's impending development.

Chancellor Schmidt himself had said nothing publicly about the weapon, but after Bahr's remark he stated that it was as yet too early for the German government to take. an official stand on the matter, but that it would raise "significant psychological and strategic questions" about West Germany's relationship with NATO and the Warsaw Pact.

Other senior officials of the Bonn government echoed Schmidt's no-comment position. Defense Minister Georg Leber again denied Haig's report of German military officials' support, and General Wolf Graf Baudissin added that he doubted whether the new warhead would actually serve to increase security. The German news magazine *Der Spiegel* commented that the weapon "is by far not as harmless as some of the planners for atomic war are suggesting". [220]

An aide of Schmidt's said on July 17 that he did not know if the Chancellor and President Carter, who had just met in Washington for talks, had discussed the neutron bomb at all. In view of the growing furor in Washington about a nuclear weapon destined for NATO, it is reasonable to suppose that the subject did come up, in which case Schmidt seems to have reached the decision that public comment by him would have been premature. In answer to reporters' probing, government sources would admit only to "a certain uneasiness" among those party officials who first learned about the bomb when the story broke in the American press. "A number of them are somewhat astonished," one official observed. [221]

One explanation for the German government's hesitant response was suggested on August 8th by *Business Week*. Though Schmidt himself privately favored the bomb, said the magazine, he would now benefit from a low profile on the issue since the high-radiation bomb had touched off heated debate in Germany. *Business Week* speculated that he might also hope to get more support from moderates for a dramatic increase in Germany's own expenditures for conventional defense weapons if he could persuade the United States to keep the bomb out of Germany. [222]

The next news from Germany came a month later, on the eve of the September 28 debate in the House of Representatives of the controversial "Weiss Amendment" to kill funds for the neutron bomb. After weeks of discussions in the Bundestag, the unofficial consensus

---

[220] *New York Times*, July 24, 1977, page #8.

[221] *Washington Post*, July 18, 1977, page #A-1.

[222] *Business Week*, August 8, 1977, page #42.

was apparently that West Germany would not prevent introduction of the new weapon if President Carter gave the go-ahead. "We don't want to give an answer before it is decided by the President to produce the weapons," said one of Helmut Schmidt's principal aides, while another added, "We are not going to invite deployment before your President has even made that decision and make political fools of ourselves." The Bundestag did not endorse the bomb, but, as one of Schmidt's assistants commented, "at least no major obstacle was put in its path."

Conrad Ahlers, a member of the Bundestag Defense Committee and of Schmidt's ruling Social Democrat Party, made a speech which was generally taken to reflect the coalition government's current stance. "In my opinion," said Ahlers, "we will have to learn to live with the neutron bomb and to include it in our defense concept."

Defense Minister Leber also dismissed as too emotional the earlier comments of Egon Bahr. While he avoided an unequivocal answer to the deployment question, he remarked that the neutron bomb was neither more nor less humane than other atomic weapons. During a speech in the Bundestag Leber gave his opinion that the neutron bomb would not lower the nuclear threshold and that the guidelines for use of nuclear weapons would not be changed by its deployment. Leber's attitude was taken by one Bonn newspaper to mean that "indications are that a basic decision has been taken in favor of the neutron bomb."

The *Frankfurter Allgemeine Zeitung* newspaper said, nevertheless, that there was widespread dismay at the Carter Administration for allowing the entire subject of the bomb to become a matter for public discussion. Yet the newspaper betrayed something of the Germans' own confusion by suggesting that the United States had blundered by not being more open and informative with its allies and the public.

Adding to the Germans' dissatisfaction was a new U.S. NATO strategy assessment, portions of which had been revealed in the press at the same time that the neutron bomb had become known to the public. The assessment suggested that the United States might give up one-third of West German territory in the face of an initial Soviet attack.

Questioned on this subject, Carter Administration officials answered that the official status of the assessment had been misrepresented - that it was just one of many options which the government had elected to study on a routine basis. Most probably that was in fact the case - and the concept should not have come as a thoroughly unrealistic surprise to the Germans. [223] It was only a short time later, for instance, that in the December issue of Strategic Review Manfred Worner, Chairman of the Armed Services Committee of the Bundestag, elected to lobby for the neutron bomb on the grounds that there would be a three-month delay in getting additional U.S. forces to Germany in the event of a Warsaw Pact invasion. [224]

If there were a certain amount of confusion in Washington, there appears to have been some equally confused thinking in Bonn. On one hand the German leaders were unhappy that the Carter Administration had let the cat out of the bag at all - they may have been unfamiliar with the Congressional review procedures that in effect took the decision out of Carter's hands - while on the other hand they were embarrassed at being "caught helping to conceal the secret" from the German citizenry, and therefore criticized the U.S. for "not being more open

[223] *Washington Post*, September 27, 1977, page #A-15.

[224] *New York Times*, December 2, 1977, page #2.

and informative". The statement by the unnamed official that Germany would not invite deployment until Carter had made a unilateral decision on the matter is particularly ironic, because of course that is not what happened. It was a few days after the German endorsement of deployment that Carter decided to defer production and deployment.

The comments are all the more intriguing because they came only a short time after the secret September 20, 1977 meeting of the NATO Nuclear Planning Group in Brussels, during which the European NATO governments were asked to endorse by October both production and deployment of the neutron weapon. [See Chapter Six.]

On January 24, as will be treated in greater detail in Chapter Eight, Soviet General Secretary Brezhnev sent letters to the various NATO government heads, warning them in what one source described as a "rude manner" against acceptance of the neutron bomb.[225] The West Germans responded a week later with a rejection, but it was not worded in such a way as to commit the Bonn government to an endorsement either.[226] Options were still being kept open.

Then on February 23, the day after British Prime Minister Callaghan spoke out in the House of Commons on behalf of the neutron bomb[227], FRG government spokesman Klaus Bölling agreed in a public statement that "matters of introducing modernized weapons into the defense potential of the North Atlantic Alliance are a matter for consultations within the Alliance. During such consultations the Alliance's security requirements and

---

[225] *New York Times*, January 24, 1978, page #3.

[226] *New York Times*, January 30, 1978, page #10.

[227] *Times of London*, February 22, 1978, page #1.

possibilities of progress in negotiations on armaments control are examined."

Production decisions concerning the neutron bomb were "exclusively within the competence" of the United States, continued Bölling, and alliances of so-called non-nuclear-weapons countries, including the Federal Republic of Germany, do not participate in such decisions about production. Bölling concluded with an appeal for progress in arms control and disarmament "before developments actually reach a state of stationing neutron weapons in Europe".[228]

It is difficult to imagine a more non-provocative proclamation, but the Soviet Union didn't see it that way. The following week *Tass* lashed out at Callaghan, German Foreign Minister Hans-Dietrich Genscher, and NATO Secretary General Joseph Luns for their support of the bomb. [Callaghan, at least, was named the chief culprit.][229]

A sampling of editorial opinion in the German press at about this point in time indicates some of the considerations that were being raised by the public and the media:

The *General-Anzeiger*, pointing to the Soviet Union's 20,000 tanks in Central Europe and deployed intermediate-range ballistic missiles with a destructive potential 2,000 times greater than that of the neutron bomb, called Soviet policy "two-faced" and suggested that the U.S.S.R. would lose no time in deploying its own neutron bomb once it had developed one. As for the debate in the West, said the paper, the crucial consideration should be to keep anti-American attitudes

---

[228] Teletype #1098E/0-2302: Security Policy from the German government to the German Information Center, New York City, ca. February 24, 1978.

[229] *Times of London*, March 1, 1978, page #1.

out of it, since an atmosphere of distrust would only serve the interests of the East Bloc. "Europeans ought not to lack confidence in themselves to such an extent that they shift the entire responsibility to the U.S. President."[230]

In Dortmund the *Westfälische Rundschau* said that deploying the neutron bomb under present conditions would be foolish. It could be better used as a contingency move - a "warning" of alternatives should current East-West negotiations fail to make progress toward slowing down the "insane" armament competition.[231]

"There can be no doubt whatever," countered the *Stuttgarter Nachrichten*, "that it is in our interest to integrate the neutron bomb into NATO's defense armory." But again the possibility of renouncing deployment in exchange for a comparable Soviet disarmament gesture was raised, though the paper called such chances remote.[232]

The *Frankfurter Allgemeine Zeitung* suggested that the importance of the neutron bomb to NATO lay not in its usefulness in waging war, but rather in its value as a deterrent to war. It also summed up the current postures of the major German political parties: "The CDU/CSU has taken a strong stand in advocating its deployment. The FDP is not straightforwardly in favor, true enough, but neither is the FDP opposed; it wants to gain time. The Social Democrats, on their part, are preparing for an orderly retreat by shifting the decision to Carter."[233]

----

[230] *General-Anzeiger* (regional Wuppertal daily), February 22, 1978.

[231] *Westfälische Rundschau* (regional Dortmund daily), February 22, 1978.

[232] *Stuttgarter Nachrichten* (regional Stuttgart daily), February 22, 1978.

[233] *Frankfurter Allgemeine Zeitung* (national Frankfurt daily), February 23, 1978.

In Essen the *NRZ* called Bölling's statement that not only was a decision on the neutron bomb up to the United States, but that Bonn should refrain from seeking to exert any influence "a declaration of absolute political irresponsibility". In a situation where European security is at stake, said the paper, there is no reason why Germany and the other European NATO members should not take a forthright stand one way or the other.[234]

The *Mannheimer Morgen* tended to agree. The current confusion in Europe over the issue, it said, was standing in the way of a decision on the bomb, and Bonn's attitude was particularly important. Nor, in the long run, could the responsibility be described as exclusively an American one.[235]

In a major story on March 3, 1978, the influential *Die Zeit* called Foreign Minister Hans-Dietrich Genscher's recent persuasion of the Free Democratic Party to approve a resolution backing the neutron bomb a "tactical move" that, under the circumstances, was inadequate. By this he had hoped both to reassure the United States and to put pressure on the Social Democratic Party, senior partners in the ruling coalition in the Bonn government, to endorse the bomb. Genscher overestimated his chances, however, because the final resolution passed by the FDP was scaled down to a conditional approval of deployment of the bomb in Germany and a recommendation to consider including it on the arms limitation agenda.

Genscher, said *Die Zeit*, had not appreciated the fact that the rank and file of the FDP did not draw a clear-cut distinction between opposition to nuclear power and opposition to nuclear weapons systems. At the same time

---

[234] *NRZ* (regional Essen daily), February 23, 1978.

[235] *Mannheimer Morgen* (regional Mannheim daily), February 24, 1978.

the SPD leadership was anxious to avoid "unpredictable outbursts of party opinion" such as had occurred the previous November at the party's conference in Hamburg.

The Christian Democratic opposition, noted *Die Zeit*, remained "unanimously and unconditionally in favor of equipping NATO with the bomb. This testifies to cohesion within CDU/CSU ranks on security, but it exaggerates differences between government and opposition on the issue."[236]

Also on March 3, speaking before the Far East Society of Hamburg, Helmut Schmidt gave his own version of the official position of the government. "Thank God," he said, "the emotions - or the emotionalism - unleashed by this topic have receded somewhat. Better information about the crucial elements of the story appears to have penetrated to the public, and a somewhat more objective discussion is emerging." After some additional remarks on the general repugnance of nuclear weapons, the Chancellor made his point:

> The Federal Republic of Germany is not a nuclear state. In common with many other countries, it has foregone production and possession of nuclear weapons. It follows that we can make no relevant production decisions. This position could serve as a guideline for other countries too, so as to lessen the danger of nuclear weapons proliferation or to limit the power of employing such weapons. In other words, we take no part in decisions about production, nor do we intend to do so in the future.

---

[236] *Die Zeit*, March 3, 1978.

Our country is a member of NATO, an alliance designed for collective defense only. Our own armed forces have been integrated into this alliance. Thanks to them we contribute appreciably to overall military capacity. In view of the nuclear threat we all face, we rely on the U.S., as the leading nuclear power of the alliance, for necessary protection and for the appropriate manufacturing decisions.

Questions that pertain to the introduction of new weapons into the defense resources of the alliance are subject to regular consultations within it. In this context, security requirements of the alliance, as well as the possibility of progress in armament control negotiations, are the subject of regular joint examination. [237]

Schmidt's hands-off attitude was not acceptable to Washington. Carter canceled a NATO negotiations session on the bomb scheduled for Brussels on March 20 and ordered Deputy Secretary of State Warren Christopher to go to Bonn to tell Schmidt that Carter would cancel the neutron project if the allies continued to refuse to participate in the production decision.

Before Christopher's March 30 arrival in Bonn, however, the instructions were changed. Now he was to tell Schmidt that Carter's "strong inclination" was to cancel the neutron weapons.

Schmidt, said Walter Pincus:

... was amazed at Carter's change of mind. He was said to have asked the American diplomat

---

[237] Schmidt, Helmut, Address to the Far East Society (Ostasiatischer Verein) of Hamburg, March 3, 1978. Transcript provided by the German Information Center, New York City.

to recheck with Carter, who at the time was traveling in Latin America. When Christopher resumed his meeting with Schmidt on March 31, the West German leader made it clear he was now prepared to support Carter if the production decision was to be made. He also asked that, if Carter decided against going ahead with the neutron weapons, he announce the decision was his own and not because the NATO governments did not support him. [238]

Foreign Minister Genscher was promptly dispatched to Washington on April 4th to give the appearance of telling President Carter that the Federal Republic formally supported production. [239] The *Washington Post* said that Carter bad already made his deferment decision, but that plans to announce the cancellation of the neutron weapons were postponed until after Genscher left Washington so that the Germans would be able to save face. [240] The *New York Times* agreed, noting that there was a sudden fear in Germany and particularly in the SPD that Carter was about to blame the deferment - and the debacle - on the FRG's reluctance to endorse the bomb. At the same time there was confusion in Bonn because, as one Schmidt aide put it, high Carter Administration officials including Zbigniew Brzezinski had been emphasizing the weapon's importance for months and seeking West German support for it. [241]
Genscher was back in Bonn on April 5th, and Bölling called a press conference to issue an official statement on

---

[238] *Washington Post*, April 5, 1978, page #A-1.

[239] *New York Times*, April 4, 1978, page #4.

[240] *Washington Post*, April 5, 1978, page #A-1.

[241] *New York Times*, April 5, 1978, page #1.

the trip. If the purpose of Genscher's visit had been to make a show of FRG support of the neutron bomb, however, Bölling's words did not convey that impression. Rather they were simply one more reaffirmation of Germany's neutrality on the matter:

> The question of producing the neutron bomb has always been an autonomous or ... sovereign decision of the U.S. political leadership. In this respect nothing has changed. That is the view of the U.S. Administration which we have always shared.
>
> No decision on the issue has been made so far, as the White House confirmed yesterday (April 4). Within NATO, consultations are being continued.
>
> As is generally known, this is a matter that affects the alliance as a whole. It is not, as has been contended incorrectly on occasion, a German-American matter.
>
> The Chairmen of the political parties and of their Bundestag delegations will be kept abreast of the status of the discussions about this topic. The Federal Chancellor, I might add, talked with Dr. Kohl a few days ago and provided him with certain items of information. He will shortly take up the matter with the leader of the opposition once more, and of course also with SPD Chairman Willy Brandt, as well as with Messrs. Wehner and Mischnick, the Chairmen of their Bundestag delegations.[242]

---

[242] Bölling, Klaus, press conference, Bonn, April 5, 1978.

But behind this facade of consensus the German political atmosphere was somewhat less than serene. The left wing of the SPD strongly opposed the neutron weapon and could be expected to resent any last-minute pro-bomb moves by Schmidt[243]; the CDU and other neutron bomb supporters were seen by some observers as gearing up to charge the Chancellor with being an appeaser of the Soviet Union.[244] At that time Schmidt's center-left coalition government could command only a small majority in the Bundestag, so even minor realignments in political support could have had serious consequences for the administration.

Under the circumstances it was difficult for Schmidt to know just what approach to take. A defense spokesman for the junior party in the coalition, the Free Democrats, said in a newspaper interview that "the leading politicians of all three parties have realized that we need the neutron weapon ... to balance the superiority of the Warsaw Pact in conventional weapons."[245] It was unclear, however, what his comment was expected to accomplish.

In the meantime the German news media were rushing to judgment. "Washington's impatience was understandable," *Die Welt* editorialized. "The European allies, who years ago were demanding just such a weapon for the battlefield, have been behaving like cats on hot bricks." The independent *Frankfurter Allgemeine Zeitung*'s defense correspondent added: "Militarily the West surrenders a weapon able to smash Soviet tanks. Politically it abandons an attempt to restore the arms balance on the central front. Strategically it surrenders a convincing element of deterrence. In the psychological

---

[243] *Washington Post*, April 6, 1978, page #A-1.

[244] *New York Times*, April 6, 1978, page #8.

[245] *Washington Post*, April 6, 1978, page #A-1.

barrage from the East and from some Western leftists, NATO is preparing for partial capitulation."[246]

On April 7, when Jimmy Carter announced his deferment decision in Washington, FRG State Secretary Klaus Bölling issued a concurrent statement in Bonn:

1. In conjunction with the decision of U.S. President Jimmy Carter to postpone production of neutron weapons, Chancellor Helmut Schmidt, together with Vice Chancellor and Foreign Minister Hans-Dietrich Genscher and Minister of Defense Hans Apel, are to report to the members of the Foreign Affairs Committee and the Defense Committee of the German Bundestag in a joint committee session.

2. The government of the Federal Republic of Germany reaffirms the view it has steadfastly upheld in agreement with the U.S.: The decision on production of a nuclear weapon is exclusively a sovereign decision of the nuclear-weapon-producing country concerned - in this case the U.S. The German federal government welcomed the opportunity for the NATO consultation that took place this afternoon, and during which the consequences of the U.S. President's decision on neutron weapons were discussed.

3. The German federal government takes note of the President's decision to postpone production of neutron weapons, and to take the ultimate decision in the light of the Soviet Union's conduct - with the resultant requirements in regard to defense policy and

---

[246] *Ibid.*

the resultant possibilities for the alliance in regard to armament-control policy. This government emphasizes the U.S. President's statement about the significance of Soviet conventional and nuclear weapons programs and its distribution of military forces - factors that affect the security of North America and western Europe.

4. This government shares the American President's conviction that the technological possibilities of the West must be maintained, and in compensating for existing disparities must be used to maximum advantage.

5. This government continues as before to attach major significance to the utilization of the possibilities, inherent in the fact of the neutron weapons, of deriving and pursuing armaments-control policies, this not least in order to do away with disparities in the power relationship - especially in regard to medium-range potentials and armor. Accordingly the planned alliance consultations on utilization of possibilities in regard to armament-control policies have particular weight for this government. Therefore, too, the government will continue to play an intensive participating role in these consultations.

6. The German federal government's contribution to the alliance consultations will continue to be determined by the Federal Republic of Germany's vital interests and its co-responsibility for safeguarding security and peace. This aspect has been explicated in the government policy statement of February 23. Points of orientation in the NATO consultations are the security requirements of

the alliance and the major significance the alliance attaches to progress in disarmament and weapons control.

7. We welcome and share the U.S. President's determination with regard to modernizing the NATO weapons system and to strengthening the joint forward defense.[247]

Reaction in Germany was highly mixed. The CDU opposition said that Carter's decision was in part a consequence of the SPD's inability to control its own left wing, forcing Schmidt to compromise German security and behave as a "kind of secret Soviet ally". Observers speculated that the incident could offset benefits to the government of recent economic gains and weaken FDP loyalty in the coalition.[248]

Possibly this somewhat negative atmosphere prompted Schmidt to make a more determined effort to portray his government's responsibility and security consciousness. When he reported to the 83rd Session of the Bundestag on April 13, in any event, he emphasized his willingness to have the neutron bomb stationed in Germany - if Germany were not the only NATO country to host the warheads. Schmidt made an attempt to appeal to both his own coalition and the conservative opposition alike. From the periodic SPD/FDP applause and the lack of retorts from the CDU/CSU - as occurred during the discussion of other subjects later on in Schmidt's address, for example - it would appear that he succeeded. [Schmidt's Bundestag statement concerning the neutron

---

[247] Teletype #1036E/1-0804: Neutron Weapons (Infofunkübersetzung) from the German government to the German Information Center, New York City, ca. April 7, 1978.

[248] *New York Times*, April 9, 1978, page #IV-4.

bomb is reproduced verbatim as an Appendix to this chapter.]

Evidently the Carter Administration, far from seeking to make Helmut Schmidt the scapegoat for the deferment, was attempting to bolster his position - particularly since he had in the final analysis come out in support of the weapon. In Bonn the day after Schmidt's Bundestag speech, Harold Brown stated that the decision to delay the bomb would not affect either United States or NATO military strength - an intriguing statement from an official who had argued so strongly for the bomb only a short time previously. West German Defense Minister Hans Apel replied to Brown with a West German offer to consider sharing the Airborne Warning and Control System (AWACS) with the United States.[249]

It will be recalled that one of the factors making 1977-78 a comparatively inconvenient time for West Germany to be confronted with the neutron bomb was the scheduled visit of Leonid Brezhnev to that country in May of 1978 for talks on disarmament, *détente*, and trade.[250] Brezhnev arrived as scheduled on May 5 and stayed for four days, but on the whole the visit did not turn out to be particularly productive. At the formal dinner on the eve of his arrival the Soviet leader called for

[249] *New York Times*, April 14, 1978, page #6.

[250] See William G. Hyland, "The Soviet Union and Germany" in Wolfram Hanrieder (Ed.), *West German Foreign Policy 1949-1979* (Boulder: Westview Press, 1979). On pages 124-5 Hyland states: "To counter the Soviet military threat in Europe, the Federal Republic has always been the area for emplacing weapons systems intended to strengthen the alliance. Each step in this direction, whatever the particular weapon, not only risks a further deepening of the country's division, but also emphasizes Germany's vulnerability to Soviet counterpressures ... Thus even Helmut Schmidt wavered on the neutron bomb and was driven by domestic politics to urge Moscow towards new initiatives in MBFR."

a ban of the neutron bomb[251]; during the following days he refused to reduce Soviet troop strength in east Europe as a reciprocal measure. Brezhnev's press spokesman, Leonid Zamyatin, said at the end of the visit that the Soviet Union had no intention of negotiating over the weapon but instead planned to seek a ban on it at the forthcoming special United Nations session on disarmament.

The Brezhnev visit fell short of expectations in other ways as well: West German officials conducting trade negotiations with the Soviets expressed misgivings about the long-term economic cooperative agreement that was signed on May 6, and no progress was made in talks on the issue of the Federal Republic's expansion of ties with West Berlin.[252]

Appearing on CBS-TV's *Face the Nation* on May 28, however, Schmidt displayed no regret that he - and Carter - had not taken a tougher stand. Rather he praised Carter's neutron bomb decision as a positive gesture and one which he still hoped would be reciprocated by the Soviets.[253]

But a somewhat harsher assessment of German-American relations over the bomb was given the next month in a June 29 news article from Bonn by Rowland Evans and Robert Novak, two *Washington Post* correspondents. In January of 1978, they said, the top-level West German Security Council, encouraged by the Carter Administration, had secretly agreed to support U.S. construction of the neutron warhead. Carter had been personally informed of the Council's decision, which was the result of six months of negotiations on the

[251] *New York Times*, May 5, 1978, page #1.

[252] *New York Times*, May 6, 1978, page #3.

[253] *New York Times*, May 29, 1978, page #1.

weapon's military, political, and strategic implications.
There had been no disagreement, said Evans and Novak,
between Bonn and Washington.

Schmidt's explicit understanding had been that the
weapon would go into production as scheduled. For the
following two years the Soviet Union would be asked to
reciprocate for non-deployment of the warhead by
removing its SS-20 mobile missiles from Europe or
reducing its huge tank force. If no agreement could be
reached, the neutron warheads would be deployed.
Commented the reporters:

> To carry this issue against his muscular
> left wing, Schmidt fought a bitter and
> debilitating rear-guard action from the summer
> of 1977 to the day in March that Deputy
> Secretary of State Warren Christopher flew to
> the Chancellor's home in Hamburg to tell him
> Jimmy Carter had changed his mind. [Stunned,
> Schmidt asked in effect: Are you speaking with
> your master's voice? His and mine, said
> Christopher.] "Carter made Schmidt look like a
> jackass," one Western diplomat told us.[254]

---

[254] *Washington Post*, June 29, 1978, page #A-27.

Appendix to Chapter Seven:
Delivery of a declaration of the government concerning the results of the NATO Council meeting of April 7, 1978 in Brussels and the meeting of the European Assembly in Copenhagen on April 7-8

Deutscher Bundestag - 8. Wahlperiode - 83. Sitzung. Bonn, Donnerstag, den 13 April 1978, pages #6501-6503.

Note: Portions of the transcript omitted in the later Press and Information Office Bulletin are in Italics.

Schmidt, German Chancellor: The consultation in the NATO Council, if I may insert this here, has been characterized for some time by our and our allies' growing anxiety about certain shifts in the military balance of power in Europe in favor of the Warsaw Pact. As long as we are not successful in guaranteeing the necessary equilibrium through arms-control measures - if at all possible at a lower level than before - the alliance must find recourse in military efforts in the conventional and also in the nuclear field to guarantee its safety. Only in this manner can the governments of the member states of the alliance fulfill the responsibility they have for protecting their people.

This judgment in no way frivolously overlooks the terror that every weapon which would be necessary, which is available by political and military necessity, carries with it. We do this with the purpose of hindering unfriendly developments which might lead to a situation in which these weapons for mutual defense would actually have to be engaged.

For fifteen years it has been the general view of all members of the alliance that tactical. nuclear weapons and their modernizing are a means which cannot be renounced in order to compensate for the otherwise [greatly] superior military potential [opposed to us] of the Warsaw Pact. The discussions on the so-called neutron bomb belong in this context.

The President of the U.S.A. on the 7th of April made known his decision "to postpone the production of weapons with enhanced radiation". The final decision on the introduction of elements with enhanced radiation into tactical nuclear weapons currently available in Europe should only cane later.

The decision of America, which must follow later, will be influenced by the restraint to be shown by the Soviet Union in its conventional and nuclear weapons programs and peacetime troop deployment, insofar as they concern the security of the U.S.A. and the security of western Europe,.

President Carter at the same time instructed the American Defense Secretary to proceed with modernization of the Lance and of the 203-mm weapons system. Lance is a relatively short-range rocket. The 203-mm weapons system is an artillery cannon of the armed forces.

For some months the East has carried on a great public campaign against the production of the neutron bomb and against its possible peacetime deployment in Europe. At the same time the Warsaw Pact on its part has introduced new long-range nuclear weapons systems.

On the subject of the so-called ER weapons or neutron bombs, consultations have been going on since autumn of last year, in the NATO Council but also bilaterally. In this from the beginning the German government considered the relationship between the ER weapons and the balance of power, which was imperiled in Europe by the increasing disparity in conventional weapons and in intermediate-range nuclear weapons.

Therefore the German government made the proposal at an early date of using the option of neutron weapons as a political tool for arms limitation.

The pertinent elements of our position were and are:

First: In the time of Chancellor Adenauer the German government had already formally renounced the use of atomic weapons. This we confirmed by our ratification of the Non-Proliferation Treaty. Participation in the decision of a nuclear-weaponed state on the production of nuclear weapons, for example the neutron bomb, would be contrary to all previous practice of the Federal Republic, which is not a nuclear-weaponed state. Therefore there had to be, and therefore any eventual decision to go into production must remain a sovereign decision of the U.S.

Dr. Mertes (Gerolstein) (CDU/CSU): Formally, yes.

Schmidt: It was, after all, never otherwise. There are some persons I know who would like to have it otherwise. I would not like to be one of them; I would also not like to give this impression to our western friends and allies.

- Applause by SPD and FDP -

Secondly: After a possible decision by the U.S.A. to go into production, the possibilities which presented themselves to progress in the arms limitation negotiations, especially to the, extent of the actual deployment of the neutron bomb, should be examined and such possibilities should then actually be used in negotiation.

Thirdly: The German government in the consultations has declared its readiness to permit the storage of ER weapons on the territory of the Federal Republic of Germany if, within two years of the American decision for production, the Western side does not abstain from deployment because meanwhile corresponding results are at hand in the negotiations on armament limitation. Here this government proceeded expressly from the assumption that, in such an event, a joint decision would be taken by NATO. The German federal government at the same time made the point that the deployment of ER weapons could not be carried out on German territory alone.

These three points, which I have just briefly placed before you, the German government formulated as established policy many months previously, and they have been maintained until today. For me there is no apparent reason to change this position. I might emphasize that the German government let its position on the subjects of arms limitations political usefulness and ER weapons deployment be guided by the consideration that the political decisions of the entire alliance were represented.

In consultations we-have met intensively not only bilaterally with the Americans and the English, but also multilaterally with the governing bodies of the alliance. Our NATO ambassador has carried out specific instructions as made plain by the other high officials of this state including the Foreign Minister and the Chancellor.

Before the continuing alliance consultations about the neutron bomb came to a definitive conclusion, the American President indicated that he wished to reexamine the decision on its production. In a statement in Hamburg on March 31st I myself have expressed our unchanged position to our American friends, and on the 4th of April in Washington Federal Minister Genscher also explained it as previously reported. So much for the past.

Now a word of appraisal: The decision of the American President on April 7 puts the production, introduction, and deployment of neutron bombs in suspension. It keeps the possibility of the arms-control use of neutron weapons consciously and intentionally open. Independently of this it includes further modernizing of existing nuclear weapons here. The Federal government greets this contribution of the American President to the politics of world arms limitations.

- Applause by SPD and FDP -

Chapter Eight:
The Soviet Union's Reaction

As may well be imagined, the Soviet Union was not at all pleased with the idea that the neutron bomb might be added to the NATO arsenal. Having devoted a good deal of time, effort, and resources to the strengthening of the Warsaw Pact's ground-attack capabilities, the Soviets were now faced with the possibility that their new, threatening leverage over Western Europe might be undermined by the psychology, if not the fact of a "clean/ surgical" NATO nuclear weapon. [255]

The result was a massive Soviet propaganda effort to portray the bomb as a barbaric, inhumane weapon. Formal threats to build a Soviet neutron bomb, or to retaliate militarily in some way (such as expanding the Warsaw Pact's existing arsenal of nuclear weapons), were kept to a minimum - presumably so that Western nations and popular opinion would not be frightened or antagonized into rallying behind the neutron bomb as a "get-tough" measure. Retrospectively it would seem that the Soviet Union handled the situation masterfully, achieving its political goals - at least on the surface.

Reaction from the Soviet Union to the initial publicity regarding the neutron bomb in June of 1977 was not long in coming. A few days after the first *Washington*

---

[255] For a discussion of Soviet European theater posture at the time of the neutron bomb episode, see Chapter Four. See also Thomas Wolfe, "Military Power and Soviet Policy" in William E. Griffith (Ed.), *The Soviet Empire: Expansion and Détente* (Lexington: Lexington Books, 1976), pages #179-195. See also Coit Dennis Blacker, "The Soviet Perception of European Security" in Derek Leebaert (Ed.), *European Security: Prospects for the 1980s* (Lexington: Lexington Books, 1979), pages #137-161. See also Richard G. Head, "Technology and the Military Balance" in Wolfram Hanrieder (Ed.), *Arms Control and Security: Current Issues* (Boulder: Westview Press, 1979).

Post publicity, *Pravda* commentator Yevgeny Grigoryev accused the United States of preparing for a new "dangerous spiral" in the arms race under the pretext of protecting the West and safeguarding human rights. Specifically cited were the B-1 bomber, the 12-A missile warhead, the Trident submarine, research into neutron-based bombs, and new-generation nuclear artillery shells. In addition to his comments regarding an American "step up" of the arms race, Grigoryev accused the Carter Administration of failing to meet the American public's expectations with regard to progress on SALT-II.[256]

Grigoryev's article was followed in early July with another *Pravda* attack by Yuri Kornilov, who denounced the neutron bomb as inconsistent with Carter's human rights campaign. Kornilov also suggested that the program would jeopardize SALT-II and might stimulate an "extremely dangerous" new round of the arms race. In the same issue commentator Tomas Kolesnichenko discounted Carter's decision against production of the B-1 bomber, saying that the B-1 was merely shelved in favor of newer and more effective strategic weapons.[257] And also in early July Soviet television began to discuss and denounce the neutron bomb's development to the general populace.[258]

On July 21 the neutron bomb was criticized by Warsaw Pact representatives in the ongoing NATO-Warsaw Pact troop reduction negotiations, and a two-month recess in the meetings was abruptly called. Each side accused the other of holding up progress; for the previous four years of negotiations, however, no

---

[256] *New York Times*, June 20, 1977, page #10.

[257] *New York Times*, July 10, 1977, page #1.

[258] *New York Times*, July 13, 1977, page #11.

agreements of any consequence had been reached.[259] Ten days later the Soviet new agency *Tass* rejected Carter's description of the neutron bomb as a tactical weapon[260] and remarked that the bomb's development "can only bring the world closer to a nuclear holocaust".[261]

The first major statement was published in *Pravda* at the beginning of August. Georgi A. Arbatov, the Soviet Union's most prominent specialist on United States affairs, said that the U.S.S.R.'s critical attitude was sincere, not propagandistic as accused by President Carter. Responsibility for the current "chill" in *détente*, argued Arbatov, was Carter's for his insistence upon meddling in the internal affairs of other countries through his human rights campaign. The neutron bomb came in for a share of heavy criticism, and Arbatov concluded by expressing concern that the atmosphere of cooperation worked out by Nixon and Brezhnev was now being undermined by the Carter Administration.[262]

Arbatov's assault was followed by another statement from *Tass* accusing Carter of "yielding to the Pentagon" in approving the neutron bomb by his signing of the Public Works bill that included the ERDA financing for the bomb's development. The United States, said *Tass*, would bear full responsibility for the consequences of "this dangerous step".[263] Simultaneously the government newspaper *Izvestia* published a petition by 28 communist parties in North America and Europe to ban the bomb.[264]

---

[259] *New York Times*, July 22, 1977, page #6.

[260] Carter, Jimmy, press conference, July 12, 1977.

[261] *New York Times*, July 31, 1977, page #7.

[262] *New York Times*, August 4, 1977, page #10.

[263] *New York Times*, August 10, 1977, page #5.

[264] *Ibid.*

The first statement on the neutron bomb by Leonid Brezhnev himself was included in a speech on August 17 welcoming Yugoslavia's Tito to the U.S.S.R. on a state visit. SALT talks, said Brezhnev, had been slowed down by the "hostile propaganda campaign" on the civil rights issue; he also criticized the neutron bomb funding.[265]

Such initial Soviet reactions to the bomb were predictably condemnatory, but they also seemed to be somewhat perfunctory and rhetorical. One explanation for this may be that the Soviets were sensitive to the danger of creating Western enthusiasm for the bomb by seeming overly worried about it; another might be that they were simply undecided as to its real significance and wanted to register disapproval without making a major issue out of it, which could have jeopardized progress that the U.S.S.R. wished to make at the ongoing SALT-II talks.

On November 2 Leonid Brezhnev delivered a Report at a Joint Meeting of the CPSU Central Committee. Every new type of weapon, he said, "represents an equation having several unknown quantities in terms of political as well as military-technical or strategic consequences. Rushing from one type of arms to another - apparently with the naïve hope of retaining a monopoly on them - only accelerates the arms race, heightens mutual distrust, and hampers disarmament measures." The Soviet Union would continue to ensure its defensive capabilities, he added, but it would not seek military superiority over the other side. He characterized the existing relation of forces as being in a rough equilibrium and insisted that neither

---

[265] New York Times, August 17, 1977, page #1.

the U.S.A. nor the U.S.S.R. should attempt to upset that balance. [266]

By December of 1977 the Soviets apparently decided that they had a firm enough grasp on the trend of world public opinion to venture a stronger stand. The first sign of a more active approach came in the form of a message sent by the U.S.S.R. Parliamentary Group to the Parliamentary Groups of the United States, Canada, and the nations of West Europe on December 16. Once more the principal theme of the communiqué was the threat of a renewed arms race should the United States proceed with the manufacture of the neutron bomb and its deployment in Europe:

> Referring to the resolution of the 64th Inter-Parliamentary Conference on "The role of Parliaments in furthering relaxation of international tensions and progress in the field of nuclear disarmament, including nuclear weapons and new weapons of mass destruction", the U.S.S.R. Parliamentary Group urges the Parliamentary Groups and all Parliamentarians of the West European countries, the United States of America, and Canada to use their high prestige and influence to prevent the production of the neutron bomb, a new weapon of mass destruction, and its deployment in Europe. In keeping with this resolution, the Parliamentarians should without delay express themselves resolutely on this question so that détente becomes irreversible and so that they prevent a return to

---

[266] Brezhnev, Leonid, Report at a Joint Meeting of the CPSU Central Committee the Supreme Soviet of the USSR and the Supreme Soviet of the RSFSR: "The Great October Revolution and Mankind's Progress", November 2, 1977.

the cold war and the breaking out of a nuclear conflict.[267]

Simultaneously at the MBFR negotiations in Vienna, Soviet delegate Nikolai Tarasov rejected the possibility of any tradeoff between Warsaw Pact troop levels and the deployment of either the cruise missile or the neutron bomb. NATO negotiators denied that they had even suggested such a tradeoff.[268]

A few days later Leonid Brezhnev made the Soviet position somewhat more explicit in an interview which appeared on the front page of the December 24th issue of *Pravda*. After calling for substantive steps towards world disarmament and accusing NATO of undermining any such efforts by a revival of the arms race, he turned to specifies:

> Take, for instance, the neutron bomb. This inhumane weapon, especially dangerous because it is presented as a "tactical", almost "innocent" one, is now being persistently foisted upon the world. In this way an attempt is being made to erase the distinction between conventional and nuclear arms, to make transition to a nuclear war outwardly unnoticeable, as it were, for the peoples. This is a downright fraud, a deception of the peoples.
>
> The neutron bomb is being insistently recommended for deployment in Western Europe. Well, this may be an easy and simple matter for those who live far from Europe. But

---

[267] Appeal of the U.S.S.R. Parliamentary Group to the Parliamentary Groups of the West European Countries, the United States of America and Canada, December 16, 1977.

[268] *New York Times*, December 16, 1977, page #7.

the Europeans, who live, figuratively speaking, under one roof, are presumably of a different opinion. They will hardly care to have an additional dangerous load placed on this common roof of theirs, which is sagging as it is under the enormous weight of weaponry.

The Soviet Union is strongly opposed to the development of the neutron bomb. We understand and wholly support the millions of people throughout the world who are protesting against it. But if such a bomb were developed in the West - developed against us, a fact which nobody even tries to conceal - it should be clearly understood that the U.S.S.R. will not remain a passive onlooker. We shall be confronted with the need to answer this challenge in order to ensure the security of the Soviet people, its allies and friends. In the final analysis, all this would raise the arms race to an even more dangerous level ...

We do not want this to happen, and that is why we propose reaching agreement on the mutual renunciation of the neutron bomb so as to save the world from the advent of this new mass annihilation weapon. This is our sincere desire; this is our proposal to the Western powers.[269]

Soviet Major General Rair Simonyan, writing in *Pravda*, added that the Soviet Union was justified in raising the question of forward-based forces - including the neutron bomb - in Europe as germane to SALT-II because of the ability of those forces to strike the U.S.S.R.

---

[269] Brezhnev, Leonid, Interview in *Pravda*, December 24, 1977, page #1. See also *New York Times*, December 24, 1977, page #7.

directly. Deployment of the neutron bomb or sale of the cruise missile to other NATO countries, said Simonyan, would further complicate any future SALT-II negotiations.[270]

Referring to Carter's visit to Poland shortly thereafter, Tass noted that the American President "bypassed in silence" the entire question of nuclear disarmament and condemned him again for his support of neutron bomb production.[271] Senior Polish officials, calling the neutron bomb the "single major outstanding issue" between the United States and Poland, acknowledged that they were conducting a campaign against its European deployment and rejected any possibility that the bomb could be discussed as a possible tradeoff against the U.S.S.R.'s SS-20 missile.[272]

Also on January 5, 1978 Brezhnev sent a personal letter to President Carter on the subject of the neutron bomb. The contents of this letter were not disclosed by either the United States or the Soviet Union, and the Soviet Embassy in Washington will not elaborate upon it, characterizing it as a confidential communication between Brezhnev and Carter. The U.S. Department of State has verified the existence of the letter but has said that the text and content cannot be disclosed. "We are authorized to say publicly," said Mark Parris of the Office of Soviet Affairs in October 1979, "only that the contents of the letter are substantially the same as previously announced Soviet-released statements." He then referred specifically to the December 24th *Pravda* article

---

[270] *New York Times*, December 28, 1977, page #7.

[271] *New York Times*, January 2, 1978, page #4.

[272] *New York Times*, January 15, 1978, page #5.

containing the interview with Leonid Brezhnev.[273] Parris said that President Carter did not reply to the letter.

Extracts from the letter made their first public appearance in a column by Jack Anderson entitled "Arms Race" printed on February 23, 1981. Brezhnev said to Carter:

> It is no secret that the decision whether to start production and deployment of neutron weapons depends now above all upon the U.S. Government, upon you personally, Mr. President ... The seriousness of the subject demands that talk be candid.

Brezhnev said that the Soviet Union's position on deployment of the neutron weapon in Western Europe was "sharply negative". The deployment would not be responsive:

> ... to the spirit of the times, to the interest of strengthening peace and détente, to peoples' aspirations. By their nature and their destructive characteristics, neutron weapons can strike not only people wearing military uniforms, but also huge masses of the population. These are inhuman weapons of mass destruction; they are directed against people. Their appearance will not diminish the likelihood of nuclear conflict but enhance it. The reality is that if neutron weapons are ever used, a devastating scythe will sweep across the territories of entire countries, probably not leaving a single inch untouched.

---

[273] Interview with Mark Parris, Office of Soviet Affairs, U.S. Department of State, Washington, D.C., October 19, 1979.

The Soviet leader made it clear that the U.S.S.R. would not regard the neutron bomb as a purely tactical device which would enable the U.S. to avoid the danger of nuclear escalation:

> Perhaps some entertain the hope to stay on the sidelines if and when the point is reached that neutron weapons are killing Europeans. This calculation is illusory in substance. Today neutron weapons are thought of in connection with one means of delivery, but tomorrow or the day after they may be attached to other vehicles of a completely different range - not of hundreds but of thousands of kilometers.

The immediate threat in the letter, indicated Anderson, was Brezhnev's warning that the U.S.S.R. might cancel the SALT-II negotiations if the neutron bomb appeared on the scene. Brezhnev said:

> In what light would the negotiations currently underway ... appear if simultaneously the deployment of neutron weapons was forced? Not much would be left of people's trust in solving the problem of disarmament, and in the success of ongoing negotiations. Moreover the negotiations themselves, at least in some cases, would face the threat of being broken off ... If the choice of the United States is in favor of the weapon, this will put the Soviet Union before the necessity to meet the challenge, that is to act in the same way as we

were forced to act when atomic weapons came into being.[274]

On January 24th Brezhnev sent anti-neutron bomb letters "written in a rude manner" to the heads of state of other NATO countries, but the texts of these, have also been treated as confidential.[275] The recipients indicated that they would reply individually to the letters.[276]

The January 25th *Pravda* contained another major editorial on the neutron bomb. In a moralizing tone reminiscent of the Chinese at their most Maoistic, Pravda described the bomb as "barbarous" and claimed that it constituted an attempt to prepare for a war in which the nuclear threshold would be lowered and the distinction between conventional and nuclear weapons erased. "Reports come in daily from various countries," it said, "of the mounting wave of wrathful protests against the militarists' inhuman plans." Mass demonstrations were occurring in Washington, Paris, Bonn, London, The Hague, Oslo and other cities, "led by the world's progressive forces [and] encouraged by the Joint Appeal of 28 Communist and Workers' Parties of Europe and North America to ban this new horrible weapon of mass destruction and prevent its deployment." Highlights included an "International Week of Protest Against the Neutron Bomb" climaxing with an "International Day of

---

[274] Brezhnev, Leonid, quoted in Anderson, Jack, "Brezhnev Sent Tough Note", *Santa Barbara News-Press*, February 23, 1981. See also Anderson's abbreviated account in "Arms Race"/"Merry-Go-Round" appearing the same date in the *Washington Post* and other major newspapers.

[275] *Strategic Survey 1978*. London: International Institute for Strategic Studies, 1979, page #107. See also *New York Times*, January 24, 1978, page #3.

[276] *New York Times*, January 28, 1978, page #48.

Action for Stopping the Arms Race and for Disarmament", backed by the World Conference Against Atomic and Hydrogen Bombs in Hiroshima, the congress of the Women's International League for Peace and Freedom, most participants in a meeting of the Socialist International Bureau held in Madrid, and the International Peace Bureau.

Pravda's sermon then rose to new heights of indignation and self-admiration:

> The struggle against death and destruction caused by neutron weapons is rapidly gaining momentum. The Soviet people and the peoples of the fraternal socialist countries wrathfully condemn the criminal designs of the U.S. and NATO militarists. There are various groups and organizations in Western Europe, the U.S.A., and Canada which provide leadership for the movement of the broad masses against the Pentagon's plans, which present a deadly threat to mankind.
>
> In a small country like the Netherlands, nearly 700 thousand people have signed a petition against the neutron weapon. Signatures for similar petitions are also being collected on a large scale in other countries, including those of Asia and Africa.
>
> Peaceloving nations throughout the world have hailed the recent Soviet proposal calling on the Western countries to reach agreement to renounce on a mutual basis the production of the neutron bomb. This initiative and other concrete proposals of the Soviet Union aimed at ending the dangerous arms race and achieving disarmament meet the cherished dreams of all people of good will, all people

who want a stable peace and condemn actions that increase the threat of another world war. [277]

Two days later, no doubt to emphasize its dedication to peace and disarmament, the Soviet Union deployed over three hundred of its new SS-20 medium-range mobile missiles near the Polish border. [278]

As is implied by the *Pravda* article, the international Soviet-aligned communist community had been marshaled to support of the Soviet position. From the time when news of the existence of the neutron bomb was first released, sentiments not unlike Brezhnev's had been appearing from a variety of sources - some obviously communist interest groups, but others of an independent pacifist or news media orientation. To the extent that their messages fueled world public opinion, they encouraged the Soviet Union to continue its hard line against the neutron bomb.

The tone and content of these messages emphasize, in varying degrees and with varying propagandistic clichés, the following themes: (a) The neutron bomb will jeopardize *détente* and refuel the arms race. (b) Deployment of the bomb will make actual nuclear war in Europe all the more probable. (c) The neutron bomb is an inhumane weapon. (d) The neutron bomb is not a purely "defensive" weapon, since its first use would lead to world nuclear war. A list of some of the more interesting sources of such statements can be found in the bibliography to this paper; to quote all of them would be redundant and not particularly illuminating. A few examples may be given:

---

[277] "'No!' to the Neutron Bomb" in *Pravda*, January 25, 1978.

[278] *Strategic Survey 1978*, page #130.

In an open letter to President Carter, the Members of the U.S.S.R. Academy of Sciences opened with a denial that the neutron bomb could be considered a defensive weapon and continued with a reminder that the first use of nuclear weapons, even those of very small yield, could lead to a world war. Should the United States produce the neutron bomb, added the. Academy, its monopoly over it would be "very short-lived".[279]

From Dr. F. Barnaby, Director of SIPRI, Stockholm came an appeal based upon the presumed contribution of the neutron bomb to increased possibilities for nuclear war. He identified 10,000 units of tactical nuclear weapons as deployed in Europe, of which about 6,000 were American, 3,500 Soviet, and a few hundred British and French and remarked that detonation of even a small portion of them would result in the complete annihilation of the continent. Barnaby's misgivings concerning the bomb hinged upon the notion that its use would be more tolerable than the use of existing tactical nuclear weapons:

> The idea that tactical nuclear war can be made "acceptable" by choosing the right type of weapon is very dangerous. Moreover it is absurd. Nuclear weapons, however limited the sphere of their use might be, cannot be passed off as conventional; and the hope that the use of nuclear weapons would not entail the employment of all the available types of nuclear weapons, including strategic ones, is unrealistic. Practice shows that the mutually hostile countries would hardly surrender

---

[279] A.P. Aleksandrov et al., "An Open Letter to U.S. President Jimmy Carter from Members of the U.S.S.R. Academy of Sciences". Reprint provided by the Soviet Embassy, Washington, D.C.

before bringing into play every type of weapon available to them.

A decision to deploy the new generation of nuclear weapons in Europe, Barnaby concluded, would be "tantamount to a catastrophe".[280]

An editorial in *l'Unita* of Italy in September of 1977 took issue with the neutron bomb proponents' reported claim that the weapon would be a stabilizing factor in Europe. The notion that an inequality of forces existed between NATO and the Warsaw Pact to begin with, said *l'Unita*, was at odds with the most recent annual report of the International Institute for Strategic Studies in London, which showed the strength of the two military groupings on the continent to be about equal. Moreover U.S. Defense Secretary Harold Brown, appearing on Rome television in October, had admitted that a balance of forces did exist. It followed that the neutron bomb would be "a factor upsetting the existing balance".

l'Unita registered its concern over the probable lowering of the nuclear threshold and denied that the neutron bomb could be considered as a purely defensive device. "As General Nino Pasti, former Air Force Commander of NATO's South Zone, has said: 'It is only the purpose for which this or that weapon is used that imparts to it either an offensive or a defensive character.'"

However, concluded the paper, the military technicalities of the neutron bomb were secondary to the political effect it was having on the international situation. It was a "complete contradiction" of efforts toward *détente*, the nuclear non-proliferation effort,

---

[280] Barnaby, Dr. F., "Europe on the Threshold of a 'New Generation' of the Nuclear Weapons" in *Blätter für Deutsche und Internationale Politik*, No. 8, 1977.

MBFR, and SALT-II and should be rejected on those grounds. [281]

The Canadian *Globe and Mail* reminded its readers of the "simpler" days of World War II when it was an easy task to tell friend from foe:

> Perhaps the time has come for a similar nostalgic look at the simple, decent attitudes of the good old Cold War. Remember the struggle for "men's hearts and minds"? Western democracy, we believed, would win in the end if its ideals were more noble, its heart more compassionate, its values more humane.
>
> Those dear, simple, idealistic days ended close to a decade ago when Henry Kissinger ushered in the age of early 18th century realism, the what's-in-it-for-us school of diplomacy, and détente, interpreted as the prolongation of the Cold War by means that, when discovered, had best be disowned.
>
> We don't have to talk about values any more; we have the neutron bomb to speak for us: It kills people and other living things but leaves property intact, unscratched, the lustre untouched on the burnished brass and buffed rosewood of a first-class coffin.

Harold Brown and Zbigniew Brzezinski had spent many of the closing months of 1977 lobbying for the bomb in Europe, said the Globe and Mail, and they had achieved some limited success in NATO in general and in Britain, West Germany, and Belgium in particular. The deterrence arguments given for the neutron bomb could,

---

[281] Editorial, "Plans That Contradict the Spirit of *Détente*" in *l'Unita*, Italy. Reprint provided by the Soviet Embassy, Washington, D.C.

said the paper, be characterized by C. Wright Mills' term "crackpot realism"; the "message of the gut" was that any measure that would make the use of nuclear weapons "more thinkable" would increase, not decrease the probability of an eventual nuclear holocaust.[282]

In such statements as these, one can see the general unfamiliarity of the public and even presumably better-informed political, military, and scientific commentators with the actual characteristics of the neutron warheads, the specific ways in which they were planned for incorporation in the overall strategic picture, and the probable effects such weapons - assuming they were as clean/surgical as they were portrayed as being - would have on the Warsaw Pact's own tactical and strategic contingency plans.

What was being argued about, in other words, was not the reality of the neutron bomb; it was the propaganda image of that weapon - an image for which Leonid Brezhnev could not claim sole responsibility, since most of his arguments had already been raised in the context of the U.S. legislative debates on the issue.

Also significant is the fact that nuclear weapons were once more held up as a subject on which the whole world felt entitled to pontificate. The U.S. President's decision was not "his" decision, or even NATO's, but rather something to be determined on the basis of international opinion and consensus. Since these are generally on the side of reduced war danger and reduced nuclear weapons "presence", the Soviet Union and its allies lobbied hard to identify that point of view with the non-introduction of neutron weapons into the NATO arsenal.

---

[282] Editorial, "Nostalgia and Neutrons" in *Globe and Mail*, Canada. Reprint provided by the Soviet Embassy, Washington, D.C.

By contrast, the opposing point of view - that such an introduction would reduce the risk of actual nuclear war - received little attention except in the cursory way that the above commentaries evidence. If a case were to be made for the peace-value of neutron bomb deployment, it would have to be found in the strategic and political-military publications of the United States and West Europe [for example, Air Vice-Marshal Stewart's article in *Strategic Review* (see Chapter Four)].

The thrust of a pro-neutron bomb argument, had one been aggressively put forward, might have been along the following lines:

The most effective way of preventing nuclear war is to deploy weapons so horrifying in their effect that the other side would not dare to initiate a situation in which they might be called into play. This is, of course, deterrence. If the use of those same weapons once hostilities began seemed all the more likely because of their "clean/surgical" characteristics, then the Warsaw Pact would be all the more unlikely to risk an attack on the grounds that NATO would not be willing to use the nuclear weapons at its disposal. Deterrence again.

Hence the presumed suitability of the neutron bomb for actual use is exactly that characteristic which makes it viable as a war deterrent. Why should the Soviets be deterred from starting a war in the face of old-style nuclear weapons which it would be increasingly likely that NATO dare not use because of their side-effects against densely-populated West Europe?

Immediately the question comes to mind: Why was not this argument presented more forcefully and with greater effect - either in the United States, in NATO, or before world public opinion? The answer appears to be simply that no one thought to emphasize it; pro-neutron bomb forces were arguing their case on a more narrowly-phrased "get tough with the Soviets" basis, which did not carry the rationale through to its deterrence implications. In making a case for military strength, therefore, neutron bomb advocates lost sight of the rationale for peace through deterrence that would have justified that military strength. They were concerned only with showing Moscow that the NATO/United States tiger had a new, sharper set of teeth.

By early 1978, as is detailed in Chapter Six, the United States had begun to think less of proceeding full-tilt with manufacture/deployment plans and more of trying to use the neutron bomb as a lever for negotiation with the Soviets. Another interpretation of such proposals was that they were merely a cover; by making "impossible" demands of the Soviets - which they would reject - the United States could introduce the neutron weapon into Europe more righteously, saying that it was doing so only because of Soviet intransigence.

The Soviets would have none of it, apparently convinced that they could achieve their goals without sacrificing any of their existing advantages. On February 14, 1980 *Tass* grumbled that the Soviet Union would develop its own neutron bomb if the United States persisted in the manufacture and deployment of the weapon.[283]   Two weeks later the news agency assailed German Foreign Minister Genscher, NATO Secretary-General Luns, the *London Times*, and British Prime Minister Callaghan for their part in supporting the bomb.[284]   Then on March 10 the Soviet Union and its allies submitted a proposal to the Geneva Disarmament Conference calling for an outlawing of the neutron bomb as, in the words of Soviet representative Viktor I. Likhatchev, a "cruel and barbaric" weapon. United States

---

[283] *New York Times*, February 14, 1978, page #10.

[284] *Times of London*, March 1, 1978, page #1.

representative Adrian S. Fisher refused to consider the motion.[285]

The next day *Tass* reiterated the call for a universal ban on the neutron bomb, calling United States efforts to link non-deployment of the bomb to "unrelated issues" (Soviet troop strength and/or the SS-20) a mere "subterfuge". *Tass* added that the Soviet government would be ready to begin talks on a mutual renunciation of the bomb at any time and would be prepared to "conclude the appropriate international agreement".[286]

Notable in the *Tass* statement is the Soviet effort to preserve its interpretation of the actual significance of the neutron bomb - not to accept an interpretation of the bomb in any other context. Having proclaimed the neutron bomb a "mass-murder" weapon [implying that it is "criminal" in effect, unlike existing conventional and nuclear weapons, which presumably are "legitimate"], the Soviet Union avoided raising the specific possibility of matching the United States by developing neutron weapons of its own, instead warning less specifically of "a new stage in the arms race".

Various U.S. Government sources have said that it is unlikely that the Soviet Union has a neutron weapon-building capability at this time.[287] Soviet Embassy Research Assistant Igor S. Neverov maintains, however, that the Soviet Union does in fact have a neutron

---

[285] *New York Times*, March 10, 1978, page #4.

[286] Statement by *Tass*, March 11, 1978. Reprint provided by the Soviet Embassy, Washington, D.C.

[287] Interviews with U.S. government officials, executive and legislative branches, Washington, D.C., October 1979.

weapon-producing capability and that it first tested neutron weapon systems in the 1950s.[288]

The Soviets' strong fixation on outlawing the neutron bomb outright rather than seeking any solution which would allow their partial production and/or deployment also suggests this, as does the extraordinary vehemence of their propaganda campaign against what many U.S. leaders originally thought to be a "minor modification" in NATO's arsenal.

Another interpretation of the Soviets' antipathy toward the neutron bomb is simply that they feared it would be an effective weapon against the Warsaw Pact; hence its deployment would be both an effective practical deterrent to invasion and an effective psychological force within the NATO countries, enabling them to overcome their existing fear of the Warsaw Pact. Preservation of that fear is all the more necessary to Soviet policy if in fact the U.S.S.R. is pursuing an effort towards "Finlandization" in lieu of outright invasion of West Europe.

Brezhnev's proposal to the United States and NATO governments that an agreement be reached for all parties not to produce neutron bombs seems eminently fair and rational on the surface. If possession of the neutron bomb would in fact give the United States and NATO advantages over a neutron bomb-armed Warsaw Pact, however, then the case is somewhat different. And this latter supposition seems to be the correct one.

First there is the aforementioned technology question. If the U.S.S.R. does not now have the technology, presumably it would not take it long to develop it, since the Soviets have mastered the necessary basics of fission and fusion bomb design. But it would be

---

[288] Interview with Igor S. Neverov, Research Assistant, Soviet Embassy, Washington, D.C., October 23, 1979.

one more military/scientific drain on an economy that is already heavily strained in that area.

It seems reasonable to assume that the Soviets would rather keep their military efforts oriented in directions where they feel themselves to have the advantage, i.e. large-scale production of advanced conventional weapons systems and tactical and strategic missiles with old-style nuclear warheads. It is noteworthy that the neutron warhead's theoretical advantages in "surgical/clean" usage are useless unless the delivery system is highly accurate, and there is considerable skepticism in the West about the accuracy of Warsaw Pact nuclear systems. Their danger is ensured by proportionately more powerful warheads.

Besides the technology question there is the matter of the actual usage of neutron weapons by both sides. As was noted in Chapter Three, neutron-heavy explosions are very effective against personnel and vehicles in the open but are far less effective against concrete and earth barriers. It is not difficult to see that the Warsaw Pact would have to move west to invade Europe, and that only NATO would be in a position in such circumstances to use concrete- and earth-fortified positions. NATO would therefore have usable neutron weapons, while any possessed by the Warsaw Pact would be useless in front-line combat except possibly in defense against NATO counterattack.

There remains the Soviet argument that use of neutron weapons by NATO would trigger Warsaw Pact use of whatever tactical and/or strategic nuclear weapons it had, thereby igniting a thermonuclear world war. Again this argument has merit at face value, if one assumes that the Soviet Union would not initiate the use of tactical nuclear weapons without NATO doing so first, and if one assumes that NATO in a desperate defense would not use whatever tactical nuclear weapons it had, neutron or not.

The first assumption is contrary to Soviet combat doctrine [see Chapter Four], and the second is contrary to all unclassified information that is available concerning NATO war plans. The point here is not that neutron weapons would make escalation into nuclear combat any less probable; the point is rather that, should war break out in Europe, there is every reason to believe it would quickly become nuclear anyway.

The rationale behind the Soviet argument therefore falls apart. If there is a legitimate question concerning the wisdom of deploying the neutron bomb, it is rather whether the device in its present state of development is in fact predictable and controllable in its effects, because misuse of such a weapon by field commanders ignorant of unknown or unannounced characteristics of neutron-heavy explosions could result in tragedy [see Chapter Three].

Close upon the heels of the *Tass* statement came an editorial article by Melor Sturua in *Izvestia*. It is interesting because it did not hinge its argument on the same precepts as the Brezhnev or *Tass* statements; rather it commented on the September 30, 1977 U.S. Congressional decision not to approve the Weiss Amendment to delete neutron bomb production funds. In the same article Sturua let it be known that Soviet intelligence was conducting some background investigations of its own into the political/industrial forces behind the new weapon's production and deployment. As details of the production process of nuclear weapons by the United States tend to be classified and difficult to verify, the *Izvestia* account must stand on its own merit:

> Which are the firms that are directly involved in the development and manufacture of the neutron bomb?

The bomb was "hatched" in Livermore, California, in a laboratory which is formally under the University of California in Berkeley. But actually it sells its ideas to the military monopolies and exists on their dollars.

The idea of developing the U-70 neutron bomb, Model 3, for the Lance missile originated in Sunday Corporation, a subsidiary of Western Electric. The blueprints coming off its drawing boards are delivered to three military-industrial giants: Rockwell International in Los Angeles, which makes strategic bombers, including the temporarily "frozen" B-1, jet fighters, and missiles - in short, weapons of mass destruction; the Monsanto nuclear-chemical trust in St. Louis; and Bendix, which makes aerospace-electronic equipment, with headquarters in New York.

Rockwell International, Bendix, and Monsanto manufacture various components of bombs and warheads which are then assembled at government-owned plants near Amarillo in Texas.

Rockwell International and Bendix have their super-bosses, so to speak, which are the powerful Du Pont, Mellon, and Morgan financial groups. Monsanto, too, is backed by Morgan money and power.

So much for the formidable "midwife" of the neutron bomb. Small wonder, then, that its lobby managed so effectively to silence the lawmakers in the Capitol and force them to rubber-stamp the "birth certificate" of the neutron bomb, a newborn with a huge layette:

a silver spoon in its mouth worth many millions of dollars.

It was noted at a recent National Security Council Meeting chaired by Zbigniew Brzezinski, continued *Izvestia*, that since September of 1977 not a single West European government had officially endorsed a production decision. [289]

Toward the conclusion of a cross-country trip in which his attention had been focused on Soviet-Chinese border issues, Leonid Brezhnev addressed the matter of the neutron bomb in a speech given on board the Soviet cruiser *Admiral Senyavin* on April 7th, a short time before President Carter's deferment announcement was given in Washington that same date. Saying that the Soviet Union's series of concrete proposals for disarmament and for relaxation of European tension was well-known, Brezhnev then turned his attention to the neutron bomb:

> This is a new type of mass destruction weapon. Any talk about such weapons being "defensive" in character does not correspond to reality. These are nuclear offensive weapons, weapons designed chiefly to destroy people.
>
> This weapon increases the risks of a nuclear war.
>
> Faced with a mass protest movement against the plans to develop and deploy these weapons in Europe, the U.S.A. and some other NATO countries are trying to mislead the peoples by pretending that they are ready to hold talks with the Soviet Union on this

---

[289] Melor Sturua, "The Neutron Shadow" in *Izvestia*, U.S.S.R. Reprint provided by the Soviet Embassy, Washington, D.C.

question while in fact they are trying to make it the subject of bargaining and tying this weapon to unrelated issues. Concealed behind all this is only a desire to evade considering the clear-cut and concrete proposal for mutual commitment not to manufacture neutron weapons.

Such maneuvering, of course, does not testify to any serious intention to achieve disarmament. Nor does it facilitate progress toward this goal.[290]

In this speech the actual tactical role of neutron warheads is reversed; now Brezhnev calls them "offensive" weapons. One cannot imagine him being privately convinced of this, all the more so since any sort of eastward attack by NATO is virtually impossible because of its force structure and logistical design. As for "destroying people", all weapons - neutron, nuclear, and conventional - are guilty of this depressing characteristic. The distinction that Brezhnev fails to make is that neutron weapons are theoretically able to destroy large masses of soldiers without destroying other categories of people who may happen to be nearby.

The *Admiral Senyavin* speech, therefore, marks a deliberate step into pure propaganda without some basis for Soviet misunderstanding or ignorance of the actual situation. It is the speech of someone who is not on the defensive, but feels that he has already won his main point and is now seeking to see how much farther he can go. Whether Brezhnev expected specific results from that speech is something that cannot be determined, however, because Carter's almost simultaneous deferment

---

[290] Brezhnev, Leonid, Speech on board the Cruiser *Admiral Senyavin*, April 7, 1978. See also *New York Times*, April 8, 1978, page #1.

announcement changed the entire situation for the Soviets.

As will be recalled, NATO leaders followed the deferment announcement with a statement calling upon the Soviet Union to make some sort of reciprocal gesture [See Chapter Six]. The next day *Tass* dismissed President Carter's announcement as an "insignificant tactic", accusing Carter of trying to create a favorable public opinion for the future deployment of the bomb in West Europe, and saying that he "made no mention of the Soviet Union's clear-cut proposal to agree on a reciprocal basis not to produce, stockpile, or deploy neutron weapons anywhere". The statement concluded:

> The President, clearly seeking to get from the Soviet Union concessions on other unrelated matters, tried to connect the ultimate decision on renunciation of production of neutron weapons in the U.S. with measures for consolidation of the Soviet Union's defense potential that have nothing to do with neutron weapons.[291]

In its coverage of the deferment decision, *Pravda* echoed *Tass*, calling the deferment decision simply a "maneuver" to allow continued development of the weapon.[292] The following week *Pravda* added that the Soviet Union was unwilling to link the issue of arms-control talks with the neutron bomb, as had been proposed by Carter.[293] The comment was probably in

---

[291] *Washington Post*, April 9, 1978, page #A-30. See also *New York Times*, April 9, 1978, page #19.

[292] *New York Times*, April 10, 1978, page #5.

[293] *New York Times*, April 17, 1978, page #4.

anticipation of the arrival of Secretary of State Cyrus Vance in Moscow on April 19 for talks on strategic arms limitations.

Brezhnev reported on the outcome of Vance's visit in a speech given to the 18th Congress of the All-Union Leninist Young Communist League on April 25:

> Along with other peace forces in the world, the Soviet Union is taking active steps to prevent the development of the neutron weapon, which is a new and particularly inhuman weapon of mass annihilation.
>
> Our stand on this issue is absolutely clear and radical: that the countries concerned should, before it is too late, conclude an agreement reciprocally renouncing manufacture of this weapon. And may mankind be delivered from it once and for all.
>
> Unfortunately the United States, which is poised to develop the neutron bomb, has not yet agreed to our proposal. But President Carter has recently declared that he has postponed a final decision on starting the manufacture of the neutron weapon. This of course does not settle the matter and is at best a half-measure.
>
> However, I can say that we. have taken the President's statement into account and that we too will not start production of neutron weapons so long as the United States does not do so. Further developments will depend on Washington ... [294]

---

[294] Brezhnev, Leonid, Speech at the 18th Congress of the All-Union Leninist Young Communist League, April 25, 1978. See also *New York Times*, April 26, 1978, page #3.

At a news conference the same day, Jimmy Carter once more rejected Brezhnev's proposal for a joint ban on the bomb, stating that the Soviets were well aware that it was designed for use against Soviet tank forces in Europe and that the Soviets themselves would have no need for such a weapon. The United States remained interested in negotiating over the neutron bomb, he continued, but such negotiations would have to focus on Soviet military forces that appeared to threaten NATO. [295]

Brezhnev's May 5-9 trip to Bonn is discussed in Chapter Seven. There was some speculation that the evident coolness of that trip would be reflected in the Soviet attitude at the United Nations special General Assembly session on disarmament on May 27th, but the speech of U.S.S.R. Foreign Minister Andrei Gromyko on that occasion was comparatively mild. His government, he said, would be prepared to negotiate substantial cuts in the level of missiles and bombers upon completion of the SALT-II negotiations, and he portrayed the current international political climate as being favorable to serious arms limitation efforts. He made only passing mention of the neutron bomb as "adding a new dimension to the arms race". [296]

Thereafter the Soviet Union's preoccupation with the neutron bomb seemed to taper off. There would be a periodic snarl from *Tass* when some Western leader would speak favorably about the weapon - on September 26th it denounced NATO Secretary-General Luns as a "neutron maniac" [297] - but on the whole the urgency of the issue had passed.

---

[295] *New York Times*, April 26, 1978, page #3.

[296] *New York Times*, May 27, 1978, page #1.

[297] *New York Times*, September 26, 1978, page #69.

Even after Carter ordered production of neutron warhead components on October 19, the, Soviet reaction was not as negative as it could have been. Returning from Moscow on October 25 after discussing SALT-II and the neutron bomb, Secretary of State Vance described the talks as "useful and constructive", while *Tass* responded that "both sides were brought closer together on some issues".[298]

And finally on November 18 Brezhnev, hosting a visit of twelve United States Senators to the Kremlin, said that the U.S.S.R. did not want to cause a nuclear war "because we are not crazy" and claimed that the Soviet Union had tested a neutron weapon many years previously but had never produced it on a mass scale.[299]

In April of 1979 the Soviet Union commenced deployment of its new nuclear-armed SS-21 short-range missile in the Warsaw Pact - the first new nuclear missile to be deployed in eastern Europe in over a decade.[300] No subsequent announcement concerning the possible deployment of the neutron warhead was made by the Carter Administration; it was only during the opening months of the Reagan Administration that the issue would resurface.

---

[298] *New York Times*, October 25, 1978, page #48.

[299] *New York Times*, November 18, 1978, page #1. Note also the statement of Igor Neverov in this regard; see Note #285.

[300] *New York Times*, April 24, 1978, page #1.

Chapter Nine:
Neutrons for the 1980s?

Rumors of French experimentation with the neutron bomb were finally confirmed in June of 1980, when the party of French President Valery Giscard d'Estaing strongly endorsed the weapon in a white paper on defense policy. There was immediate opposition, both from the Gaullists (who felt that the neutron bomb was not as convincing a deterrent as France's normal tactical nuclear weapons) and from the Communists (who echoed the 1978 Soviet line). French General Pierre Gallois, principal strategist of French nuclear planning under de Gaulle, objected to the neutron bomb on grounds of its theoretical utility:

> The neutron bomb is a form of Maginot Line. It is a typical idea of generals who want to fight the 1940 war over again in 1980. But why should the Soviets give up the idea of surprise they would get from a strike with their SS-20 missiles against Western Europe? If they massed 100 tank divisions, that would give NATO time to react.
> Besides, nobody stops to think that since the second world war, West Europeans have unconsciously built a real Maginot Line 400 miles long and more than 50 miles wide - the continuous urban strip that stretches from Holland to Switzerland. Can you imagine the Soviets engaging their tanks in trying to conquer that non-stop city in house-to-house warfare?

If we build the neutron bomb, it would be just another case of copying what the Americans do - or, in this case, don't do.[301]

Gaullist Party leader Jacques Chirac argued that a national defense strategy based on the use of neutron warheads would create the impression of a French move towards the U.S./NATO doctrine of "flexible response". Existing plans, which the Gaullists support, call for a tactical nuclear strike against invading forces, followed by a "massive retaliation" strategic nuclear attack on the principal cities of European Russia.[302]

Two weeks after the appearance of the white paper, the French President confirmed in an interview that France had developed and tested a neutron bomb prototype. Research concerning the weapon, he added, had commenced in 1976.[303]

French Socialists were quick to add their criticism to that of the Gaullists; Socialist leader Francois Mitterrand, who in May 1981 would defeat Giscard for the French Presidency, accused Giscard of "lacking, the character to push the button" for a massive retaliation nuclear strike; hence Giscard's quest for a less-drastic nuclear option. The Socialists and the Gaullists went on record as favoring neutron technology development but as opposing its deployment in lieu of existing French nuclear weapons.[304]

---

[301] Koven, Ronald, "France Moves Toward Making Neutron Bombs", Washington Post, June 7, 1980, page #A-1.

[302] *Ibid.*

[303] *New York Times/Paris*, "France Tells of Neutron Weapons Test", *San Francisco Chronicle*, June 27, 1980, page #1.

[304] Koven, Ronald, "Giscard Reveals Successful Test of Neutron Bomb", *Washington Post*, June 27, 1980, page #A-1.

Giscard denied that he was backing down on France's tough national defense posture, saying, "Any nuclear attack against French soil will automatically elicit a strategic nuclear response." He did not, he continued, advocate any single nuclear weapons system. He compared such an approach as similar to that of French reliance on the Maginot Line. A nation's defense, he said, involves the "soul of the people" rather than weaponry alone.[305]

The White House, asked to comment on the French neutron bomb developments, said that there would be "no change" in the President Carter's 1978 deferment decision. Of Giscard's statement a Presidential aide remarked: "That was the decision we expected him to make."[306]

The French Communist Party newspaper *l'Humanite* demanded that France renounce deployment of neutron weapons. Finally Giscard, perhaps following the example of Carter, announced that he would defer any decision on neutron bomb deployment until after the next French election. Since Mitterrand won that election, it seems doubtful that neutron weaponry will replace France's existing nuclear deterrent.[307]

The news from France may have encouraged U.S. Presidential aspirant Ronald Reagan to include Jimmy Carter's handling of the 1977-78 neutron bomb issue in his criticisms of the Democratic incumbent.[308]

---

[305] *Ibid.*

[306] Pincus, Walter, "Carter Decision Unchanged on Neutron Arms Production", *Washington Post*, June 28, 1980, page #A-15.

[307] Koven, Ronald, "French Communists Denounce Neutron Arms", *Washington Post*, July 3, 1980, page #A-22.

[308] *Ibid.*

Nevertheless Reagan made no definitive statements as to whether he would reverse or modify Carter's decision.

The neutron bomb regained the headlines within weeks after Reagan's inauguration, however, when. the new Secretary of Defense, Casper W. Weinberger, announced in his first press conference that he favored production and deployment of the warhead.[309]

International response was prompt. In Bonn Kurt Becker, speaking for the West German government, stated that the Federal Republic was no longer willing to permit the neutron bomb to be deployed on its territory per the terms it had specified in 1978.[310] From Moscow *Tass* warned that any such deployment would "worsen Western relations with the Soviet bloc and start a dangerous new round of the arms race".[311] Former White House Press Secretary Jody Powell, appearing on NBC's *Today* show, challenged the Reagan Administration to show that the Federal Republic had agreed to any deployment provisions. Powell also disputed the new Defense Secretary's assertion that Carter's deferment decision had caused significant consternation in the Federal Republic and elsewhere.[312]

In what may have been a foreshadowing of later rivalry with Weinberger, Secretary of State Alexander Haig officially advised the U.S.' NATO allies to disregard the Defense Secretary's comments because they did not reflect Administration policy. Haig approved a message to all NATO members saying that the Administration had made no decision on the neutron bomb and in any case would consult with NATO before taking any new steps.

---

[309] *New York Times*, February 4, 1981.

[310] *New York Times*, February 5, 1981.

[311] *Ibid.*

[312] *Ibid.*

Weinberger, who can hardly have appreciated Haig's approach, confirmed that his views were his own but added that they were certainly consistent with the Republican Party's platform. [313]

In a *Washington Post* interview on February 10, 1981, Weinberger said that he favors deployment of neutron warheads in Europe, because they "could do quite a lot" to offset the Soviet tank advantage. He said:

> The American government made a policy determination some time ago that it was good and necessary and a helpful addition to the strength of theater nuclear forces. When you look at the number of Russian tanks and the other items, the enhanced radiation warhead could do quite a lot to restore some kind of balance there. And I believe that's one of the reasons the Russians are reacting so strongly to this slight suggestion.

After remarking that he felt that the neutron warhead could contribute to deterrence, Weinberger made reference to the other NATO countries:

> It's nothing that we are going to force on them. It's nothing about which we are going to say, "All right, it's here. You've got to take it or leave it." It's got to be after a process of consultation and agreement. Some areas seem to be against it; some areas seem to be strongly for it. [314]

---

[313] *New York Times*, February 6, 1981.

[314] Wilson, George C., "Weinberger Pushes Neutrons for NATO", *Washington Post*, February 11, 1981, page #A-1.

West German legislator Peter Corterier responded a few days later with a general criticism of Weinberger's position and a complaint concerning the Reagan Administration's "lack of interest" in pressing for strategic arms control talks with the Soviet Union. Corterier's remarks were notable for being the first open criticism of the new U.S. administration by an associate of Helmut Schmidt.[315]

Then on February 15 the House of Representatives' Foreign Affairs Committee released extracts from an updated version of the Arms Control Impact Statement on the ER warhead. While containing no assessment of the warhead's consequence that was not included in the ACIS described and quoted in Chapter Five of this study, the extracts were presumably intended to stress the danger that neutron deployment might increase Soviet disposition to use their own nuclear weapons in the event of war, as well as the questionable advantage of neutron weapons in the area of damage limitation.[316]

On March 24 Dutch Defense Minister Pieter B.R. de Geus informed Weinberger that the Netherlands opposes any deployment of neutron weapons on its soil.[317]

A sampling of comments from the world press indicates much the same sort of sentiment that had surfaced in 1978:

Threats to press the arms race by introducing new weapons such as the neutron

---

[315] *New York Times*, February 13, 1981.

[316] *New York Times*, February 15, 1981.

[317] *New York Times*, March 24, 1981.

bomb are the wrong way to handle the U.S.S.R. - England.[318]

[Weinberger's] hint that the U.S. would produce the neutron bomb hits the Europeans at an unfavorable moment. - Germany.[319]

Objections aired two years ago against the neutron weapon are still valid. - the Netherlands.[320]

With its aim of killing people while saving buildings and equipment, the neutron bomb illuminates the madness and immorality of modern nuclear warfare. - Sweden.[321]

This is the clearest indication so far that the Reagan Administration is intent on liquidating the inhibitions on U.S. military policy in the wake of Vietnam. - India.[322]

The policy of easing international tension is rapidly becoming a dead letter. - Japan.[323]

And in the *Progressive* Samuel H. Day Jr. took Weinberger to task for supposing that neutronization of NATO had not been proceeding on schedule. The Secretary's remarks, said Day, had caused "considerable puzzlement among those who for the last two years have

---

[318] Calvocoressi, Peter, *Sunday Times*, London, England, February 8, 1981.

[319] *Süddeutsche Zeitung*, Munich, Germany, February 6, 1981.

[320] *De Volkskrant*, Amsterdam, the Netherlands, February 6, 1981.

[321] *Dagens Nyheter*, Stockholm, Sweden, February 5, 1981.

[322] *The Hindu*, Madras, India, February 6, 1981.

[323] *Asahi Shimbun*, Tokyo, Japan, February 5, 1981.

been busily manufacturing the neutron warhead" for the Department of Energy.[324]

The next Soviet reaction came in the pages of *Red Star*, the official newspaper of the Soviet defense establishment, during March 1981. A feature article warned that "if the U.S. manufactures the neutron bomb and deploys it in Europe, the U.S.S.R. will most certainly take the necessary defensive steps". It continued: "Deploying the neutron bomb in West Europe would turn Europe into a hostage of the United States, and it certainly guarantees U.S. influence over Europe." *Red Star* concluded with a policy statement that the U.S.S.R. opposes the manufacture of such "barbaric weapons".[325]

Confirmation of the Reagan Administration's actual production plans was forthcoming in June 1981, when representatives of the Department of Energy testified to the House Armed Services Committee that production of the neutron warhead components for the Lance missile had begun and that the necessary tritium had been allocated. The committee was also informed that initial production of the 8-inch neutron artillery shell would begin in July.[326] Congressman Ted Weiss again moved to halt component production, but his amendment was defeated on June 11 by a vote of 293 to 88.[327]

Finally, in September of 1981, the Soviet news agency *Tass* responded at length to the Reagan

---

[324] Day, Samuel H., "Neutrons for NATO", *The Progressive*, April 1981, page #9.

[325] *Red Star*, March 1981.

[326] "U.S. Beginning Work on Neutron Arms", *Washington Post*, June 6, 1981.

[327] "House Supports Neutron Warheads", *Washington Post*, June 12, 1981.

Administration's neutron policies with a restatement of the Soviet position during the Carter Administration:

> Dangerous madness has seized the ruling circles of the United States. Only thus can one assess President Reagan's decision on neutron weapons production and the reasons behind it.
>
> The main rationale is a no-proof assertion that the neutron warhead is a defensive weapon designed to prevent war. Nothing could be further from the truth, because the weapon lowers the threshold of nuclear conflict and thereby makes it more likely, and because in combat qualities it undoubtedly is one of the most sophisticated types of offensive thermonuclear arms.
>
> Even at a distance of three-quarters of a mile from the epicenter of the explosion of a neutron bomb only one kiloton in yield, which means a destruction of 1-3/4 square miles, a field of absolutely lethal radiation will be formed. On an area of close to six square miles, people will receive doses that will cause the development of malignant tumors later and genetic disruptions in their descendants.

The Reagan Administration, concluded *Tass*, "is turning down Soviet peace initiatives, urging on the arms race instead and now embarking on neutron weapon production, which its predecessor did not dare to do".[328]

It would appear, then, that little new thought was given to the image or consequence of the neutron bomb after the initial 1977-78 crisis. Despite the increasing Soviet threat and the change in U.S. administrations, the

---

[328] Shishkin, Gennadi (Foreign Editor) in *Tass*, September 16, 1981.

bomb came to the forefront of news not as a systematically developing political and military option, but rather as a sensationalist topic along the lines of the original debate.

As of mid-1982 the future of the weapon remains as uncertain as it was when President Carter announced his deferment of production. But certain implications of both the bomb and the political atmosphere surrounding it remain, and it is now appropriate to examine them.

Chapter Ten:
Conclusions

The 1977-1978 neutron bomb episode may not be especially helpful in substantiating any particular model of the United States decision-making process, but it does serve to illustrate intranational, supranational, and international linkages which can occur in such a situation. The previous chapters have discussed out the major actors and their various efforts to influence the development of events; now it is possible to review the entire episode in search of comprehensive principles.

Key actors with decision-making power were the President, the Congress, NATO (specifically the NPG), and the West German government. Key actors with influence short of decision-making power were the press, the Soviet government, and possibly the British government (in its role as a NATO leader). Non-actors who could have been actors had the situation developed differently included the U.S. scientific community, the Pentagon, non-governmental interest groups, and non-NATO countries other than the U.S.S.R.

There is some room for debate in this set of assignments, particularly with regard to the non-actor category. Certainly there was some effort made by each of the non-actors cited. On balance, however, that effort does not seem to have been significantly influential. The British government could also be said to be a non-actor, but it is assigned an influential role because of its trend-setting power in NATO. By taking a stand for the neutron bomb, in other words, it could have broken the ice for other European NATO members to do the same. And by not taking a stand (save for some pro-deployment remarks), the British government almost certainly contributed to foot-shuffling in the rest of the European NATO membership.

A glance at the sequence of events shows that, while no mandatory decision-making process was followed, resolution of the problem tended to follow a logically-justified procedure. There seemed to be no point at which responsibility for the decision was misrouted. A summary of what took place might look like this:

1. President requests budgetary authority.
2. Congress debates and grants authority.
3. President requests deployment sanction from NATO.
4. NATO makes no collective objection to deployment but refers question to sovereign governments.
5. A *de facto* decision not to deploy is made by the European NATO members.
6. President defers production pending positive Soviet response.
7. After no adequate Soviet response, President orders building of components but no deployment.

... with the press interpreting events from #2 through #7 and with the Soviet Union attempting to influence events from approximately #3 through #6. The result was an orderly resolution of the problem. Contrast this orderly resolution, for instance, to the way in which the 1962 Cuban Missile Crisis was dealt with, allowing, of course, for time and stress differences in the two situations:

When the missiles in Cuba were discovered, Congress was not consulted, nor did the President assume immediate and personal responsibility for a decision. Rather an ad hoc "Executive Committee" was formed in a somewhat haphazard manner, and only the vaguest of guidelines were given to it as to acceptable courses of action. Although the situation could have been considered NATO-relevant (since NATO-member America was threatened), NATO did not assume any role of importance in the crisis. Cuba was not dealt with directly. And finally communications with the Soviet Union were highly imprecise and indirect, keeping both the U.S. and the U.S.S.R. in some degree of ignorance about the other's real intentions. One result was that the crisis brought the two countries very close to deliberate or accidental nuclear war; another was that the Soviet Union was frightened into embarking upon a crash military buildup program which is just now beginning to frighten the United States in return.[329]

At no stage in the neutron bomb episode, however, could the situation be described as "out of control" in the way that the 1962 crisis was at some moments; various delays in neutron bomb decisions were quite possibly irritating to certain parties but were not irregular or unjustified in themselves. Rather they were part of a reasoned, rational decision-making process.

The result of the neutron bomb episode was a consensus of sorts between all actors involved. Even the Soviets, who had emphatically denounced the idea of the neutron bomb during the 1977-1978 debate, seemed

---

[329] For a general account of the Cuban Missile Crisis, see James Daniel and John Hubbel, *Strike in the West: The Complete Story of the Cuban Crisis* (New York: Holt, Rinehart & Winston, 1963) and also Henry Pachter, *Collision Course: The Cuban Missile Crisis and Coexistence* (New York: Frederick Praeger, 1963). For an account of the functioning of the "Ex Com", see Robert Kennedy, *Thirteen Days: A Memoir of the Cuban Missile Crisis* (New York: W.W. Norton Company, 1971). For critical analyses of the way that the crisis was handled, see Graham T. Allison, "Conceptual Models and the Cuban Missile Crisis" in the *American Political Science Review*, September 1969 and also Irving L. Janis, *Victims of Groupthink: A Psychological Study of Foreign Policy Decisions and Fiascos* (Boston: Houghton Mifflin, 1972).

generally complacent about the result, though it did fall far short of the complete ban on the weapon they had originally sought. One reason is that the Soviet Union may be conducting further research toward neutron weapons of its own; historically it has never left a technological gap of a military nature unfilled. Another reason, not necessarily exclusive of the first, is that the U.S.S.R. felt that it had done all that it could to influence the situation and that further pressure could prove counterproductive by irritating the West into taking a tougher stand.

The final consensus deserves praise for being the product of international consideration and deliberative process, then, but it can be criticized on at least two general grounds:

First there is the question of the technological and safety factors that were seemingly omitted from or ignored in the discussion, resulting in a final decision based upon emotional judgments rather than upon actual facts about the characteristics of the bomb. This point has been discussed in detail in Chapters Three and Five.

The technological problems of neutron warfare will probably be corrected sooner or later when and if deployment of the bomb takes place, since the Defense Department insists on high standards of reliability and control for weapons systems that it deploys. Field testing procedures and the necessary familiarity of great numbers of individuals and Defense Department agencies with new systems make it virtually impossible to conceal serious tactical defects, even in weapons with high security classifications. The problem is emphasized in this paper rather because it was not adequately realized, considered, or resolved during the formal decision-making process.

The second problem is perhaps not as "dangerous" but is in some ways more fundamental: As one looks at the deliberative process that took place, one begins to feel a certain doubt that the eventual production of the bomb could have been stopped at all. Technically, of course, it could have been halted by either a Presidential decision or a Congressional vote. But there seems to have been what I can best describe as an "undercurrent of inevitability" about the weapon - an assumption that, once available as an option, it would be manufactured one way or another. This is evident in a certain lack of urgency by the bomb's proponents when pleading their case, as well as in the readiness of the White House to follow through with a budget request from the Ford Administration with which it was not familiar.

Indeed the principal governmental opponent of the bomb, Senator Mark Hatfield, doesn't seem to adjudge his efforts very positively if the comments of his foreign policy advisor Jack Robertson are indicative. When asked in 1979 whether he felt that the 1977 Congressional neutron bomb debate had actually accomplished anything substantive, Robertson's response was discouraged and pessimistic. The Hatfield effort had forced the Congress and the American public to think about certain ethical aspects of the matter, he reflected, but that was the most that could be said. Asked how he felt about the ongoing production of the bomb's components today, Robertson answered, "Ambivalent." No continuing effort was being made to examine or slow the process, he added, because of lack of success in the 1977 effort and also because of time and resources needed for other, more current problems.[330]

Robertson's cynicism was echoed a few blocks away at the Soviet Embassy, where Research Assistant Igor Neverov observed that the construction of the neutron

---

[330] Interview with Jack Robertson, Washington, D.C., October 26, 1979.

bomb is proceeding as though the much-publicized Congressional and NATO consultations never happened. While somewhat tolerant of the overemotional Soviet propaganda fielded against the bomb, Neverov felt that the *Izvestia* image of the U.S. government as being subject to the manipulation of a few relatively powerful individuals and financial groups has not been disproved.[331]

In the absence of precise cost-comparisons (which are either classified or otherwise do not seem to be available), it is difficult to identify a particular profit motive which might have lent emphasis and "inevitability" to the neutron bomb. It can be said that the same contractors who are working on neutron warhead components would probably be equally capable of producing second-generation "conventional" nuclear warheads for the Lance and 8-inch artillery. And in fact this is taking place simultaneous with the neutron component production. So while the profit motive may be granted, the exclusive fixation of that motive upon the neutron bomb does not necessarily follow. This is an area of inquiry in which adequate information to resolve the question is not yet accessible, however. When and if such information does become available, the subject might prove worthy of further investigation.

The financial aspects of the neutron bomb raise another question: Could Soviet antipathy towards the weapon have anything to do with their already-strained defense budget and a consequent reluctance to undertake an expensive neutron bomb catch-up program of their own? It would be tempting to answer affirmatively, but the recent history of Soviet arms decisions argues against it.

---

[331] Interview with Igor Neverov, Soviet Embassy, Washington, D.C., October 23, 1979.

Consider, for example, the case of the Anti-Ballistic Missile (ABM) dialogue and resultant provisions in SALT-I. In that instance the Soviet Union effectively signed away its inferior ABM technology in return for the United States' signing away its more advanced technology (the Safeguard system). Since that time Soviet ABM research has continued, with SA-5 surface-to-air missiles - among the 12,000 SAMs deployed throughout the Soviet Union - being tested in an ABM mode in conjunction with long-range acquisition and tracking radar systems.[332] This research and testing program continues despite U.S. assumptions that it is not necessary due to the Mutually-Assured Destruction (MAD) doctrine, and despite its additional strain on the Soviets' sizable defense budget.[333] If the ABM situation is any indication, then, it is improbable that the U.S.S.R. would refrain from neutron bomb research merely because the United States agreed not to assemble its neutron warheads for the time being.

The neutron bomb episode is instructive for the look that it provides at the image-interpretive power of the press. This can be analyzed as a two-part phenomenon:

First there is the power of the press to set the context for a debate on a given problem by singling out certain aspects of that problem for emphasis in news stories and editorials. In the case of the neutron bomb, emphasis was accorded the ethics of the weapon and not its deterrent or technological capabilities. To some extent this inclined governmental and popular debate to that

---

[332] Coalition for Peace Through Strength, *An Analysis of SALT-II.* Washington, D.C.: American Security Council, 1979, page #14.

[333] Approximately 11-15% of Soviet GNP is devoted to defense, with annual increases in defense spending of approximately 5% each year for the past 15 years. See *Time*, October 29, 1979, page #26.

same emphasis. Secondly the press records and offers judgment concerning the outcome.

There is a chicken-and-egg dilemma here, to be sure; it is always difficult to establish to what extent the press is leading an argument as opposed to monitoring it. Suffice it to say that press treatment of the neutron bomb issue did not devote much time to areas other than those of fairly simple ethical considerations.

In Leonid Brezhnev's statements and responses on the neutron bomb, we can see an evident effort to play to the power of the media in Western societies rather than to governments *per se*, since his arguments were almost invariably keyed to the sort of oversimplified, sensationalistic, ethical questions being stressed by newspaper editorials and articles.

If the Soviet government indeed felt that the bomb would finally be produced because of capitalist profit motives, then one may interpret Brezhnev's polemics more as an effort to disrupt NATO political cohesion and encourage disaffection for the Carter Administration in the United States than as a serious attempt to stop the bomb. This interpretation is also substantiated to some degree by the relatively mild response of the Soviets to the component-production decision when it did occur, and by the general disinterest of Western governments in even the more threatening comments from Moscow.

German statements concerning the neutron bomb, as antiseptic as they are, are curiously unconvincing, coming as they do from a country with a long and harsh education in the realities of international conflict. Assuming that it is in fact politically expedient for the Schmidt government to speak with a soft voice in order to preserve its underlying coalition, can more pragmatic realities lie beneath the surface?

Ideally the Germans would like to have enough say in NATO nuclear weapons policy to deter any U.S.

decisions to reduce its nuclear presence in Europe; this accounts for their support of the MLF proposal in 1963.[334]   At the same time they want to minimize the image of their involvement with nuclear weapons for political reasons, both internal (coalition building) and external (*Ostpolitik*).

The United States' recent NATO-strengthening efforts seem to have enabled the Germans to maintain their low nuclear profile, but it is worth noting that the country is by no means unprepared to discuss nuclear issues more authoritatively than it did in this instance. The Bonn government has spent over DM 17 billion in nuclear research[335] , and in terms of peaceful uses of atomic energy West Germany ranks fourth in the world (after the United States, Japan, and France). By 1984 it is expected to rise to second place.[336]   The German armed forces have shown a strong interest in obtaining access to nuclear weapons[337] , and proposals for a nuclear-armed European Defense Force have found significant support in the Bundestag.[338]

In the 1977-1978 situation Germany was caught off-balance, and attempted to solve the problem by procrastination. The result was interpreted by many

---

[334] Richardson, James L., *Germany and the Atlantic Alliance: The Interaction of Strategy and Politics*. Cambridge: Harvard University Press, 1966, page #70.

[335] *Der Spiegel*, March 15, 1976.

[336] Rogers, Barbara and Cervenka, Zdenek, *The Nuclear Axis: Secret Collaboration Between West Germany and South Africa*. New York: New York Times Books, 1978, page #49.

[337] See West German Government Bulletin #155/S.1527 of August 20, 1960, entitled *Nuclear Weapons for the Defense Forces (The Shield)*.

[338] Kiep, Walther Leisler, *A New Challenge for Western Europe: A View from Bonn*. New York: Mason & Lipscomb Publishers, 1974, pages #178-179.

observers to be a humiliation for Germany, teaching the Schmidt government that it is somewhat risky to place blind trust in the nuclear weapons policies of the United States. "It's not a question of the tail wishing to wag the dog," comments a Schmidt advisor. "But when the dog ignores the tail, then the tail has to wag itself."[339]   The result may well be an increasingly more assertive role for Germany in the future. And this too may have been on Brezhnev's mind when he avoided direct criticism of German support of the neutron bomb during his 1978 visit to the country.

In general, foreign reactions to the neutron Bomb episode tended to focus on the ethical aspects of the question and avoid technological or tactical considerations. Of notable interest may be the opinion of the People's Republic of China, although it was not officially consulted by any party to the decision:

China's reaction to the President's deferment decision was communicated by two New China News Agency dispatches on April 8 and April 11, 1978.

In the first dispatch the picture given was of Carter opting for restraint despite strong support for the weapon among his advisors, in order to encourage reciprocal gestures by Moscow.

The April 11 dispatch noted that Carter's gesture had "obviously failed to satisfy Moscow's appetite", and that in fact the Soviet Union had been encouraged to apply more pressure for further U.S. concessions as a consequence.

Before the deferment announcement the Chinese had consistently indicated their approval of Carter's supposed

---

[339] *Newsweek*, March 12, 1979, page #44.

intent to proceed with the manufacture and deployment of the bomb despite Soviet propaganda and pressure. [340]

On the subject of the bomb's actual usefulness as a battlefield weapon, we return to the oft-discussed question of whether it is better to build less-destructive weapons whose use is more acceptable and therefore probable, or whether it is preferable to build more highly-destructive weapons which are thus less likely to be used.

Here there is a conflict with deterrence rationale, because deterrence is a function of the threat of use of a weapon and not of its destructive power *per se*.

The more the West wishes to emphasize deterrence, it would seem, the more it would favor producing and deploying "usable" weapons. The neutron bomb, in the view of deterrence-oriented proponents and destruction-fearing critics alike, was the first nuclear weapon that could be interpreted as "usable".

And the problem was further complicated by the "nuclear threshold" question: If the neutron bomb itself could be considered usable, mightn't its use trigger the use of other tactical nuclear weapons which, in the absence of that trigger, might be shunned as "unusable"?

---

[340] Personal interview with General Wang Qiming, Assistant Military Attaché, Embassy of the People's Republic of China, Washington, D.C., October 25, 1979.

See also reports of and commentary concerning the President's decision in:

Politika (Belgrade, Yugoslavia), April 8, 1978.

Mlada Fronta (Prague, Czechoslovakia), April 8, 1978.

Trybuna Ludu & *Zycie Warsawy* (Warsaw, Poland), April 8 & 11, 1978.

Le Monde, Le Figaro, L'Aurore (France), April 8-10, 1978.

Corriere Della Sera & *La Stampa* (Italy), April 8 & 9, 1978.

Cumhuriyet (Turkey), April 10, 1978.

Aftenposten (Oslo, Norway), April 8, 1978.

Rizospastis (Athens, Greece - communist party KKE paper), April 8, 1978.

Soviet doctrine draws no line at the use of nuclear weapons on the battlefield, and the Soviets' commitment to preemptive warfare also argues for an early resort to nuclear weapons by the Warsaw Pact in the event of a westward invasion. Once more there is a grey area, however, because NATO analysts cannot be certain whether the Soviets would adhere rigidly to such doctrine if they had reason to think that NATO would hesitate to use its own nuclear weapons if the invaders did not do so first. In other words, doctrinal principles aside, the Warsaw Pact might observe a nuclear threshold due to its conviction that NATO would do so unless provoked. The Pact could choose this option if in fact it felt capable of seizing objectives in West Europe by conventional might alone, and if it came to the conclusion that NATO would allow it to do so rather than initiate a nuclear exchange.

Realizing this, NATO has voiced its intention to resort to a first use of nuclear weapons if necessary. But, as with Soviet doctrine, neither NATO nor the Warsaw Pact can be quite certain whether such statements are more factual or propagandistic. Part of deterrence involves keeping the other side guessing, with the hope that it will fear the worst.

By not introducing the neutron bomb to NATO, the United States has opted for less danger of crossing the nuclear threshold, but one might also say that it has thus opted for less deterrence as well. The subsequently approved introduction of second-generation "conventional" nuclear warheads into the NATO arsenal is an obvious effort by the alliance to have its cake and eat it too, and to some extent the effort may succeed if the Soviets believe the new warheads to be more usable. But the "dirty" and blast-emphatic nature of those warheads - i.e. the features which distinguish them from their neutronic brethren - make them less usable in the event of an invasion, hence less of a deterrent, etc., *ad infinitum*.

And so a critical examination of the 1977-1978 neutron bomb episode yields the conclusion that it was essentially a non-resolvable problem. As it was finally dealt with, it minimized certain complications that could have followed a more or less belligerent choice, but political commentators, depending upon their point of view, will be free to focus on either the deterrent or the usable features of the bomb and view the compromise with corresponding alarm. "According to my knowledge of post-World War II history," observed Franz Josef Strauss the day after Carter's deferment announcement, "this is the first time that an American President frankly and obviously has done what be was told by a Russian Czar."[341]

There is no immediate way to answer such objections to the *status quo*, since the merit of the decision cannot be determined by an examination of the European situation as it is; any arms policy relevant to NATO can only be judged in a "negative" manner if invasion does not take place, and in a "positive" manner if invasion occurs and is thwarted because of the policy. In this context the neutron bomb policy resulting from the 1977-1978 debate may be judged "negatively" successful.

---

[341] *Die Welt*, April 8, 1978.

Bibliography

"Miss Clagthorpe, please direct this group of students to 'Weapons, Nuclear (Neutron), Top Secret, Declassified'."

- Oliphant, *The Washington Star*

Academy of Sciences, U.S.S.R., "An Open Letter to U.S. President Jimmy Carter from Members of the U.S.S.R. Academy of Sciences" [concerning the neutron bomb], undated.

American University, *Area Handbook for the Federal Republic of Germany*. Washington, D.C.: U.S. Government Printing Office, 1978.

American University, *East Germany: A Country Study*. Washington, D.C.: U.S. Government Printing Office, 1978.

Appeal of the U.S.S.R. Parliamentary Group to the Parliamentary Groups of the West European Countries, the United States of America and Canada. Moscow: December 16, 1977.

Army, Department of the, "Chapter #10 - Tactical Nuclear Operations" in *FM #100-5: Operations.* Washing ton D.C., 1978.

Atlanta Constitution. [See individual chapter footnotes for specific articles.]

Atlas. [See individual chapter footnotes for specific articles.]

Barnaby, Dr. F. (Director of the International Peace Research Institute SIPRI, Stockholm), "Europe on the Threshold of a 'New Generation' of the Nuclear Weapons" in *Blätter für Deutsche und Internationale Politik*, Number #8, 1977.

Becker, Kurt, "Neutron Bomb: Bonn Keeps Safety Catch on its Opinions" in *Die Zeit*, March 3, 1978.

Becker, Kurt, "Schmidt Strives to Mend U.S. Relations" in *Die Zeit*, March 31, 1978.

Beer, Francis A. (Ed.), *Alliances: Latent War Communities in the Contemporary World.* New York: Holt, Rinehart and Winston, Inc., 1970.

Bennett, W.S.; Sandoval, R.R.; and Shreffler, R.G., "A Credible Nuclear-Emphasis Defense for NATO" in *Orbis*, 1977.

Black, Brigadier General Edwin, "The Realities of the Neutron Bomb" in *Washington Report* #77-8. Boston, Virginia: American Security Council, 1977.

Bölling, Klaus, Press Conference, Bonn, Germany, April 5, 1978.

Braunschweiger Zeitung. Brunswick, Germany, April 6, 1978.

Brezhnev, Leonid I., Interview in *Pravda*, December 24, 1977.

Brezhnev, Leonid I., Speech at the 18th Congress of the All-Union Leninist Young Communist League", April 25, 1978.

Brezhnev, Leonid I., Speech on Board the Cruiser *Admiral Senyavin*, April 7, 1978.

Brown, Harold; Perry, William J.; and Jones, David, [Documentation on] "American Defense Policy" in *Survival*, Volume XXI, Number 3. London: International Institute for Strategic Studies, May/June 1979.

Burt, Richard, *New Weapons Technologies: Debate and Directions* (Adelphi Paper #126). London: International Institute for Strategic Studies, 1976.

Business Week. [See individual chapter footnotes for specific articles.]

Canby, Steven, *The Alliance and Europe: Part IV: Military Doctrine and Technology* (Adelphi Paper #109). London: International Institute for Strategic Studies, 1975.

Cane, John W., "The Technology of Modern Weapons for Limited Military Use" in *Orbis*, Volume #22, Number 1. University of Pennsylvania: Foreign Policy Research Institute, Spring 1978.

Carter, Jimmy, "Informal Question-and-Answer Session with Reporters, Winston-Salem, North Carolina, March 17, 1978", *Administration of Jimmy Carter, 1978*.

Carter, Jimmy, "Remarks and a Question-and-Answer Session at a Town Meeting, Spokane, Washington, May 5, 1978", *Administration of Jimmy Carter, 1978*.

Carter, Jimmy, "Remarks and a Question-and-Answer Session with Reporters Following a. Meeting with Chancellor Helmut Schmidt, Bonn, Federal Republic of Germany, July 14, 1978", *Administration of Jimmy Carter, 1978*.

Carter, Jimmy, "Statement by the President: Enhanced Radiation Weapons, April 7, 1978", *Administration of Jimmy Carter, 1978*.

Chace, James and Ravenal, Earl C. (Eds.), *Atlantis Lost: U.S.-European Relations After the Cold War.* New York: New York University Press, 1976.

Chicago Tribune. [See individual chapter footnotes for specific articles.]

Christian Science Monitor. [See individual chapter footnotes for specific articles.]

Cohen, Samuel T., "Neutron Bomb: Pro and Con" in *Washington Report* #77-8. Boston, Virginia: American Security Council, 1977.

Congressional Budget Office, *Planning U.S. Strategic Nuclear Forces for the 1980s.* Washington, D.C.: U.S. Government Printing Office, June 1978.

Conrad, Bernt, "Neutron Bomb Hovers Over Genscher and Christopher" in *Die Welt,* March 31, 1978.

Coffey, J.I., "Arms Control, Tactical Nuclear Forces and European Security." University of Pittsburgh: Center for Arms Control and International Security Studies, undated.

Committee on Armed Services, United States Senate, "Statement of General Alexander Meigs Haig, Jr., USA-Ret." in *Military Implications of SALT-II Treaty* - 79-128. Washington, D.C.: Stenographic Transcript of Hearings, Thursday, July 26, 1979, 2:30 P.M.

Committee on Foreign Relations, United States Senate, *Briefings on SALT Negotiations.* Washington, D.C.: U.S. Government Printing Office, 1978.

Committee on Foreign Relations, United States Senate, *Fiscal-Year 1980 Arms Control Impact Statements.* Washington, D.C.: U.S. Government Printing Office, 1979.

Congressional Record, 95th Congress, 1st Session, Volume 123, No. 115, July 1, 1977.

Daedalus, Winter 1979. Richmond, Virginia: American Academy of Arts and Sciences, 1979.

Daedalus, Spring 1979. Richmond, Virginia: American Academy of Arts and Sciences, 1979.

David, Colonel Rene, "The Neutron Bomb: Myth or Reality?" in *Revue de Defense Nationale*, Paris, France, July 1972.

Davis, Lynn Etheridge, "Limited Nuclear Options: Deterrence and the New American Doctrine" in *Adelphi Papers*, #121. London: International Institute for Strategic Studies, 1976.

Davis, Paul C., "A European Nuclear Force: Utility and Prospects" in *Orbis* #17. University of Pennsylvania: Foreign Policy Research Institute, Spring 19173.

de Borchgrave, Arnaud, "Nightmare for NATO" in *Newsweek*, February 7, 1977.

Dettke, Dieter, *Allianz im Wandel: Amerikanisch-europäische Sicherheitsbeziehungen im Zeichen des Bilaterismus der Supermächte*. Frankfurt, Germany: Alfred Metzner Verlag, 1976.

Deutscher Bundestag - 8. Wahlperiode - 83. Sitzung. Bonn: April 13, 1978.

Die Welt. Bonn, Germany, March 30, 1978.

Die Welt. Bonn, Germany, April 5, 1978.

Digby, James, "New Technology and Super-Power Actions in Remote Contingencies" in *Survival*, Volume XXI, Number 2, March-April 1979.

Digby, James, "Precision-Guided Weapons" in *Adelphi Papers* #118. London: International Institute for Strategic Studies, 1975.

dpa German Press Agency, Interview with Chancellor Helmut Schmidt, April 12, 1978.

Edmonton Journal. [See individual chapter footnotes for specific articles.]

Ermath, Fritz W., "Contrasts in American and Soviet Strategic Thought" in *International Security*, Volume #3, Number 2. Cambridge: MIT Press, Fall 1978.

Even-Tov, Ori, "The NATO Conventional Defense: Back to Reality" in *Orbis*, Volume, #23, Number 1. University of Pennsylvania: Foreign Policy Research Institute, Spring 1979.

Fair, Stanley D., *Precision Weaponry in the Defense of Europe*, Military Issues Research Memorandum. Carlisle Barracks, Pennsylvania: Strategic Studies Institute, U.S. Army War College, 1974.

Facer, Roger, *The Alliance and Europe: Part III: Weapons Procurement in Europe Capabilities and Choices* (Adelphi Paper #108). London: International Institute for Strategic Studies, 1974.

Financial Times. [See individual chapter footnotes for specific articles.]

Frank, Lewis Allen, *Soviet Nuclear Planning: A Point of View on SALT*. Washington, D.C.: American Enterprise Institute for Public Policy Research, 1977.

Frankfurter Allgemeine Zeitung. Frankfurt, Germany, February 23, 1978.

Frankfurter Allgemeine Zeitung. Frankfurt, Germany, April 6, 1978.

Galen, Justin, "NATO's Theater Nuclear Dilemma: A New Set of Crucial Choices" in *Armed Forces Journal International*. Washington, D.C.: Army and Navy Journal, Inc., January 1979.

Galen, Justin, "Restoring the NATO-Warsaw Pact Balance: 'The Art of the Impossible'" in *Armed Forces Journal International*. Washington, D.C.: Army and Navy Journal, Inc., September 1978.

General-Anzeiger. Wuppertal, Germany, February 22, 1978.

Glass, George A., "The United States and West Germany: Cracks in the Security Foundation?" in *Orbis*, Volume 23, Number 3, Fall 1979. University of Pennsylvania: Foreign Policy Research Institute, 1979.

Gompert, David C.; Mandelbaum, Michael; Garwin, Richard L.; and Barton, John, *Nuclear Weapons and World Politics: Alternatives for the Future.* New York: McGraw-Hill, 1977.

Goodman, Elliot R., *The Fate of the Atlantic Community.* New York: Praeger Publishers, 1975.

Griffith, William E. (Ed.), *The Soviet Empire: Expansion and Détente.* Lexington: Lexington Books, 1976.

Hackett, General Sir John et al., *The Third World War.* New York: Macmillan Publishing Company Inc., 1978.

Halperin, Morton H., *Bureaucratic Politics and Foreign Policy.* Washington, D.C.: The Brookings Institution, 1974.

Hanrieder, Wolfram F. (Ed.), *Arms Control and Security: Current Issues.* Boulder, Colorado: Westview Press, 1979.

Hanrieder, Wolfram F. (Ed.), *West German Foreign Policy 1949-1979.* Boulder, Colorado: Westview Press, 1979.

Hanrieder, Wolfram F. and Auton, Graeme P., *The Foreign Policies of West Germany, France, and Britain.* Englewood Cliffs, N.J.: Prentice-Hall, Inc., 1980.

Hatfield, Senator Mark O., "Arguments Against the Neutron Bomb". Washington, D.C.: Office of Senator Hatfield, 1977.

Hess, Stephen, *Organizing the Presidency.* Washington, D.C.: Brookings Institution, 1976.

Holst, Johan J. and Nerlich, Uwe (Ed.), *Beyond Nuclear Deterrence: New Aims, New Arms.* New York: Crane, Russak & Co., Inc., 1977.

Horton, Frank B.; Rogerson, Anthony C.; and Warner, Edward L. (Ed.), *Comparative Defense Policy.* Baltimore: Johns Hopkins University Press, 1974.

Houston Chronicle. [See individual chapter footnotes for specific articles.]

Hunt, Kenneth, "New Technology and the European Theater" in Kemp, Geoffrey; Pfaltzgraff, Robert L. Jr.; and Ra'anan, Uri, (Eds.), *The Other Arms Race.* Lexington, Massachusetts: D.C. Heath and Company, 1975.

Hunter, Robert, *Security in Europe.* Bloomington: Indiana University Press, 1969.

International Security, Winter 1978/1979. Cambridge, Massachusetts: MIT Press, 1979.

International Security, Spring 1979. Cambridge, Massachusetts: MIT Press, 1979.

Izvestia. [See individual chapter footnotes for specific articles.]

Jervis, Robert, *The Logic of Images in International Relations.* Princeton: Princeton University Press, 1970.

Johnson, David T. and Schneider, Barry R., *Current Issues in U.S. Defense Policy.* New York: Praeger Publishers, 1976.

Kahan, Jerome H., *Security in the Nuclear Age: Developing U.S. Strategic Arms Policy.* Washington, D.C.: The Brookings Institution, 1975.

Kahn, Herman, *On Thermonuclear War.* Princeton: Princeton University Press, 1960.

Kelleher, Catherine McArdle, *Germany and the Politics of Nuclear Weapons.* New York: Columbia University Press, 1975.

Kelman, Herbert C., *International Behavior: A Social-Psychological Analysis.* New York: Holt, Rinehart and Winston, 1965.

Kennan, George F., *Russia and the West.* New York: The New American Library, Mentor Book, 1961.

Kennedy, Edward M., "Senator Edward M. Kennedy Opposes Funds for the Neutron Bomb". Washington, D.C.: Office of Senator Kennedy, 1977.

Kennedy, Robert, *Precision ATGMs and NATO Defense*, Military Issues Research Memorandum. Carlisle Barracks, Pennsylvania: Strategic Studies Institute, U.S. Army War College, 1978.

Kiep, Walther Leisler, *A New Challenge for Western Europe: A View from Bonn*. New York: Mason and Lipscomb 1974.

Kissinger, Henry A., *Nuclear Weapons and Foreign Policy*. New York: Harper and Brothers, 1957.

Kissinger, Henry A., *The Troubled Partnership*. New York: McGraw-Hill, 1965.

Lawrence, Richard D. and Record, Jeffrey, *U.S. Force Structure in NATO*. Washington, D.C.: Brookings Institution, 1974.

Leebaert, Derek (Ed.), *European Security: Prospects for the 1980s*. Lexington: Lexington Books, 1979.

Link, Werner and Feld, Werner J. (Eds.), *The New Nationalism: Implications for Transatlantic Relations*. New York: Pergamon Press, 1979.

Los Angeles Times. [See individual chapter footnotes for specific articles.]

Ludz, Peter; Dreyer, H. Peter; Pentland, Charles; and Ruehl, Lothar, *Dilemmas of the Atlantic Alliance*. New York: Praeger Publishers, 1975.

Manchester Guardian. [See individual chapter footnotes for specific articles.]

Mannheimer Morgen. Mannheim, Germany, February 24, 1978.

Markov, Moisei, "Mankind Must Safeguard Itself". Moscow: Soviet Pugwash Committee, undated.

Marcum, Philip C. and Montgomery, Kingsley V., *Foreign Area Officer Trip Report: Bundeswehr*. Washington, D.C.: Department of the Army, 1979.

Mehnert, Klaus, *Der deutsche Standort*. Stuttgart: Deutsche Verlags-Anstalt, 1967.

Menaul, Air Vice-Marshal Stewart W.B., "The Shifting Theater Nuclear Balance in Europe" in *Strategic Review*, Fall 1978. Washington, D.C.: United States Strategic Institute, 1978.

Merkl, Peter H., *German Foreign Policies, West and East*. Santa Barbara: ABC-Clio Press, 1974.

Morland, Howard, "The H-Bomb Secret: How We Got It; Why We're Telling It" in *The Progressive*, Volume #43, Number #11. Madison, Wisconsin: The Progressive, Inc., 1979.

Moynihan, Daniel P., "The President and the Press" in Tugwell, Rexford G. and Cronin, Thomas E. (Eds.), *The Presidency Reappraised*. New York: Praeger Publishers, 1974.

Nash, Henry T., *Nuclear Weapons and International Behavior*. Leyden, The Netherlands: A.W. Sijthoff International Publishing Company, 1975.

NATO Facts and Figures. Brussels: NATO Information Service, 1976.

NATO Texts of Final Communiqués 1977. Brussels: NATO Information Service, 1977.

Neustadt, Richard E., *Alliance Politics*. New York: Columbia University Press, 1970.

New Conventional Weapons and East-West Security (Part II) (Adelphi Paper #145). London: International Institute for Strategic Studies, 1978.

"New Stage in Soviet-U.S. Nuclear Arms Race", *Beijing Review*, No. 22, June 1, 1979.

New York Times. [See individual chapter footnotes for specific articles.)

NRZ. Essen, Germany, February 23, 1978.

NRZ. Essen, Germany, April 4, 1978.

Osgood, Robert Endicott, *NATO: The Entangling Alliance*. Chicago: University of Chicago Press, 1962.

Pfaltzgraff, Robert L. Jr., *The Atlantic Community: A Complex Imbalance*. New York: Van Nostrand Reinhold Company, 1969.

Pranger, Robert J. and Labrie, Roger P. (Eds.), *Nuclear Strategy and National Security: Points of View*. Washington, D.C.: American Enterprise Institute for Public Policy Research, 1977.

Precision ATGMs and NATO Defense. Carlisle Barracks: U.S. Army War College, September 11, 1978.

Press and Information Office, Federal Republic of Germany, *Abrüstung und Rüstungskontrolle Dokumentation*. Bonn: Köllen Druck & Verlag, 1978.

Press and Information Office, Federal Republic of Germany, *Bulletin Nr. 32/S.293: Zur Entscheidung von Präsident Carter über die Neutronenwaffe*. Bonn: April 11, 1978.

Press and Information Office, Federal Republic of Germany, *Jahresbericht der Bundesregierung 1977*. Bonn, 1978.

Press and Information Office, Federal Republic of Germany, *White Paper 1975/1976: The Security of the Federal Republic and the Development of the Federal Armed Forces*. Bonn, 1976.

Press and Information Office, Federal Republic of Germany, *White Paper 1979: The Security of the Federal Republic of Germany and the Development of the Federal Armed Forces*. Bonn, 1979.

Record, Jeffrey, *U.S. Nuclear Weapons in Europe: Issues and Alternatives*. Washington, D.C.: Brookings Institution, 1974.

Richardson, James L., *Germany and the Atlantic Alliance: The Interaction of Strategy and Politics*. Cambridge: Harvard University Press, 1966.

Richardson, R.C., "Can NATO Fashion a New Strategy?" in *Orbis*. University of Pennsylvania: Foreign Policy Research Institute, 1977.

Rogers, Barbara and Cervenka, Zdenek, *The Nuclear Axis: The Secret Collaboration between West Germany and South Africa*. New York: New York Times Books, 1978.

Rogers, Patrick F., "The Neutron Bomb" in *Army*, Volume #27, Number 9. Washington, D.C.: Association of the United States Army, September 1977.

San Francisco Chronicle. [See individual chapter footnotes for specific articles.]

Schlesinger, James R., *Annual Defense Department Report, FY 1975*. Washington, D.C.: U.S. Government Printing Office, 1974.

Schmidt, Helmut, Address to the Far East Society (Ostasiatischer Verein). Hamburg, Germany, March 3, 1978.

Schmidt, Helmut, *Defense or Retaliation: A German View*. New York: Frederick A. Praeger, 1962.

Schmidt, Helmut, *The Balance of Power: Germany's Peace Policy and the Super Powers*. London: William Kimber, 1969.

Schutzhi, Horst, "Quo Vadis, FRG?" in *G.D.R. Review*, September 1979. Berlin: Verlag Zeit im Bild, DDR, 1979.

Spanier, John, *Games Nations Play*. New York: Holt, Rinehart and Winston, 1972.

Speed, Roger, *Strategic Deterrence in the 1980s*. Stanford: Hoover Institute Press, 1979.

Spielmann, Karl F., *Analyzing Soviet Strategic Arms Decisions*. Boulder, Colorado: Westview Press, 1978.

Statements on the Neutron Bomb by:

    All-Union Central Council of Trade Unions, Moscow, August 1977.

    Anderlini, Senator Luigi, interview published in *Paese Sera*, Italy.

Bartsch, Professor Hans-Werner, Doctor of Theology, Frankfurt University, Federal Republic of Germany.

Bechert, Professor Karl, Department of Theoretical Physics, University of Mainz, Federal Republic of Germany.

Burhop, Professor Eric, President, World Federation of Scientific Workers, Britain.

El'Azzawi, Mundhir Fahmi Hussein, Chairman of the Iraqi Association of Lawyers, Iraq.

Executive of the Netherlands Labour Party.

Fuchs, Georg, President, International Institute for Peace, Austria.

General Secretariat of the International Organization of Journalists.

Gomes, Professor Ruy, Vice-Chancellor, University of Oporto, Portugal.

Hangaard, Sven, Parliamentary Leader of the Radical Liberals.

Holtz, Professor Hans Heinz, Doctor of Philosophy, Marburg University, Federal Republic of Germany.

Joint Appeal of 28 Communist and Workers' Parties of Europe and North America.

Kekkonen, Urho, President of Finland.

Pasti, Nino, Italian Senator and former assistant to the Supreme Allied Commander - Europe, NATO. *Unita*, September 13, 1977.

Pauling, Professor Linus, Winner of the Nobel Peace Prize and of the Nobel Prize in Chemistry.

Pimen, Patriarch of Moscow and All Russia.

Prokhorov, Alexander, Lenin and Nobel Prize Winner, U.S.S.R.

Pugwash Conference, Declaration in Munich, August 1977.

Ramzayev, P., D.Sc., Member of the II Committee of the International Radiation Association.

Semeiko, Lev, Executive Secretary, Disarmament Commission, Soviet Peace Committee.

Semyonov, Nikolai, Lenin and Nobel Prize Winner, U.S.S.R.

Social-Democratic Party of Switzerland, Resolution.

Söder, Karin, Foreign Minister of Sweden.

Sorsa, Kalevi, President of the Social-Democratic Party, Finland.

Standing Committee on Disarmament of the World Federation of Scientific Workers.

Twente University of Technology, Holland: Report on the Neutron Bomb.

Vermeylen, Pierre, Minister of State, Member of the Bureau of the Socialist Party of Belgium, Vice-President of the International Liaison Form of Peace Forces.

Von Baudissin, Wolf, Director of the Hamburg Institute of World Affairs and former Bundeswehr General.

Von Ehrenstein, Professor Dieter, Doctor of Physics, Bremen University, Federal Republic of Germany.

Women's International Democratic Federation, December 22, 1977.

World Federation of Democratic Youth.

World Federation of Trade Unions.

World Peace Council, Berlin, September 9-12, 1977.

Strategic Survey 1978. London: International Institute for Strategic Studies, 1978.

Stuttgarter Nachrichten. Stuttgart, Germany, February 22, 1978.

Suddeutsche Zeitung. Munich, Germany, March 3, 1978.

Suddeutsche Zeitung. Munich, Germany, March 31, 1978.

Times of London. [See individual chapter footnotes for specific articles.]

Text of the telegram on the neutron bomb sent to President Carter by 26 U.S. Representatives and 5 U.S. Senators on August 24, 1977.

Thomson, Jeffrey R., *U.S./U.S.S.R. Strategic Forces - Asymmetrical Developments: A Net American Assessment.* D.C.: University Press of America, 1977.

Toronto Star. [See individual chapter footnotes for specific articles.]

U.S. Arms Control and Disarmament Agency, "The Effects of Nuclear War". Washington, D.C., 1979.

U.S. News and World Report. [See individual chapter footnotes for specific articles.]

Wall Street Journal. [See individual chapter footnotes for specific articles.]

Washington Post. [See individual chapter footnotes for specific articles.]

Westfälische Rundschau. Dortmund, Germany, February 22, 1978.

Wolff, Jürgen, *Armed Forces for Defence: The Bundeswehr's Role in NATO.* Bad Godesberg: Inter Nationes, 1977.

About the Author

Michael A. Aquino is a Lt. Colonel, Psychological Operations, U.S. Army (Ret.). He is a graduate of the Industrial College of the Armed Forces, National Defense University; Defense Intelligence College, Defense Intelligence Agency; Foreign Service Institute, Department of State; U.S. Army Special Warfare Center (Special Forces ("Green Beret")/Psychological Operations/Civil Affairs/Foreign Area Officer); U.S. Army Command & General Staff College; U.S. Army Intelligence School, and U.S. Army Space Institute. Decorations include the Bronze Star, Meritorious Service Medal, Air Medal, Army Commendation Medal (3 awards), Special Forces Tab, Parachutist Badge, USAF

Space & Missile Badge, and the Republic of Vietnam Gallantry Cross, Psychological Warfare Medal (First Class), & Air Service Medal (Honor Grade).

Academic credentials include the B.A., M.A., and Ph.D. in Political Science from the University of California, Santa Barbara; and the M.P.A. in Public Administration from George Washington University. He has taught as Adjunct Professor of Political Science, Golden Gate University.

He is an initiate of the Priesthood of Set.

In 2006, following his retirement as a U.S. government officer, he was recognized by Scotland's Lord Lyon King of Arms as the 13th Baron of Rachane, Argyllshire. He is a member of Clan Campbell. He, his wife Lilith, and cats live in San Francisco, California.